The Agile Librarian's Guide to Thriving in Any Institution

The Agile Librarian's Guide to Thriving in Any Institution

Michelynn McKnight

LIBRARIES UNLIMITED

An Imprint of ABC-CLIO, LLC

A B C  C L I O

Santa Barbara, California • Denver, Colorado • Oxford, Eng

Library of Congress Cataloging-in-Publication Data

McKnight, Michelynn.
  The agile librarian's guide to thriving in any institution / Michelynn McKnight.
      p. cm.
  Includes bibliographical references and index.
  ISBN 978-1-59158-668-5 (acid-free paper)
  1. Library science—Vocational guidance. 2. Librarians—Professional relationships. 3. Librarians—Professional ethics. 4. Career development. I. Title.
  Z682.35.V62M37 2010
  020.23--dc22   2009041908

14 13 12 11 10   1 2 3 4 5

This book is also available on the World Wide Web as an eBook.
Visit www.abc-clio.com for details.

ABC-CLIO, LLC
130 Cremona Drive, P.O. Box 1911
Santa Barbara, California 93116-1911

This book is printed on acid-free paper ∞
Manufactured in the United States of America

Contents

Preface

Agile Librarians are professionals who love their work and are appreciated for it. They enjoy the rewards of high respect not only from the people they serve, but also from the administrators in their organizations who direct organizational goals and budgets. Agile Librarians have expertise in their profession and in the business of gaining and maintaining influence, as well as in marketing and public relations. Agile Librarians not only know what they do best, but they demonstrate it and constantly proclaim its value, knowing that is also part of the profession.

Librarians are providers of tailored information creation, organization, storage, and retrieval services. Nardi and O'Day (1999) call them "a keystone species in the information ecology" (p. 79–81). The stereotype of the shy but bright and helpful person who is a caretaker/guardian for a warehouse of print materials has nothing to do with the information services the personable, creative, expert real librarians of today provide their clients.

Corporations, school boards, university administrations, hospitals, and city councils all require fiscal accountability and evidence of return on investment (ROI) from their libraries. In each of these games, there are plenty of other players who do not understand what librarians really can do and who believe that they can do it better. If the librarians do not understand politics and marketing, these other players will get more staff and support at the expense of the library. In the practice of librarianship, quality, marketing, and politics are essential and not optional.

Thoughtful use of professional expertise and political skills, supplemented by image development, good marketing, research, and evaluation practices can ensure that non-librarian decision makers (boards, clients, committees, executives, managers, patrons, politicians, principals, tax payers, teachers, trustees, users, and other stakeholders) fully appreciate the value and utility of library and information services.

What you have in your hand is a collection of practices that will make a difference. You do not need to read through the book sequentially to find something immediately useful. This is not a comprehensive text on marketing, management, evaluation, professional image, or advocacy, but it will point you to further reading in areas you choose to pursue. (Once set on a course of discovery, there's no stopping a good librarian!) A practicing librarian, teacher, or graduate student in library and information science can read this book straight through or consult sections on individual techniques as needed.

A group may use it as a discussion stimulant. It may be used as a text, a reference, a professional reader's advisory, or a just a source of encouragement and motivation.

My own practice was mostly in a hospital library, but I have also worked in school, academic, and public libraries. I now teach graduate LIS students who will go into many different kinds of information services. Even within the same type of library, librarians work in different organizational cultures and institutions with differing goals and values. Although some institutions may seem to value and respect library services more than others do, that respect can *never* be taken for granted.

Here is your guidebook to what you can do today, this week, or this month to make a difference. Here are positive, active methods to get your library and information service the attention and support they deserve.

For 10 years, I taught the continuing education class "Proving Your Worth: Professional Business, Marketing, and Political Tools to Convince Non-Librarian Decision Makers of the Value of Your Essential Services" for practicing librarians. Some of the material in this book came from my search for relevant professional research to support my own practice of evidence-based librarianship, and some of the material originated from my personal experience. Much of it stemmed from the observations and shared wisdom of more than a thousand participants in the "Proving Your Worth" classes sponsored by 30 different library associations, councils, and consortia. I took notes and I kept up with many of the participants by e-mail, finding out what worked for them and what did not. I have kept and reread all of the evaluations from all of the class participants, and this book includes some of their favorite real-life stories and suggestions for further reading. Some former participants read chapters as I wrote them.

The excellent professional practice of librarians with good business and political skills will not be hidden, ignored, or judged as worthless. It will be recognized as a great value to the government, company, or institution wise enough to have such an information service. We are Agile Librarians—doing better what we have always done well!

References

Nardi, Bonnie A. and Vicki O'Day. 1999. *Information Ecologies: Using Technology with Heart.* Cambridge, MA: MIT Press.

Acknowledgments

I offer profuse thanks to Blanche Woolls for her tireless guidance and support in the development of this book. She and others at Libraries Unlimited are a joy to work with. I am grateful to Carol Rain Hagy, my graduate assistant at Louisiana State University, for her excellent proofreading.

Molly Harrington deserves my thanks for coining the phrase "Proving Your Worth" and for inviting me to make the first presentation in Des Moines that led to the class. And, most of all, I want to thank all of the Agile Librarians who participated in the classes. I learned so much from you!

Chapter 1

Knowing Your Value to the Organization

No library or information service exists for its own sake. Each is part of a larger organization and its community. The librarians within the institution, school, university, government agency, public library, corporation, or nonprofit organization create and provide excellent information services in many forms using many methods. Their services include obtaining information directly for clients, organizing information sources for access, guiding clients in their own information seeking, and teaching information literacy skills. Not every institution has a librarian, but for those that do, librarians provide information to the organization as a whole, to specific divisions and groups of people within the organization, and to individuals.

Many librarians do not report to librarians; those who do report to librarians know that the library director reports to someone who is not a librarian. The administrators who make decisions about funding and policies for libraries and information services may not understand what professional librarians contribute to the success of the organization. Some may even think that librarians, albeit intelligent, helpful, and good with details, are only technical or clerical staff rather than professionals. Traditionally, people have thought of librarians as being intelligent and helpful, but that is not enough! The Agile Librarian's responsibility is not only to know the practice of the profession, but also to demonstrate it and to proclaim it.

Professional librarians have specialized expertise needed by every school, company, government, institution, or agency. Because not every such organization has a librarian, each librarian must not only know, but also communicate clearly, the value of a librarian to the organization. Furthermore, every librarian has an ethical professional responsibility to provide that value to the organization and to promote it to society at large.

This book assumes that librarians have the specialized expertise developed through education in a school of library and information science, in continuing education, and in professional practice. It does not teach the basic science and skills necessary for that expertise. Some readers may have practiced the profession for so long that they are tempted to take that expertise for granted; some who are newer to practice will have a different perspective. All must not only know precisely the librarian's value to

1

the organization, but also constantly communicate that value fluently, convincingly, and with conviction.

The proclamation of this value is not optional! Agile Librarians know that if they cannot or do not describe that value to leadership, no one else will. Administrators are not born with a "librarian appreciation gene." It's a respect that must be earned and an attitude that must be learned. The price of hiding that value from leadership can be the loss of positions, the closure of libraries, and the deprivation of needed information services. Even in institutions such as universities and public schools, which must have librarians for accreditation, the professional role may be misunderstood or underestimated by top administration. Information services that faculty and students need may be funded for other, less-qualified staff to provide. To keep this from happening, librarians must constantly ensure understanding of their value.

Librarians can, and indeed must, continuously carry on three activities that can dispel the dangerous mists of misunderstanding. Simply put, they must *know* and continually explore their own professionalism and how it directly contributes to the success of the organization. They must *show* that professionalism by constantly demonstrating the needed expertise in direct service to the organization. And they must *tell* administrators, clients, and other stakeholders about the value of their services to the organization.

To raise librarians' awareness of their value in organizations, this chapter begins with a review and emphasis of librarians' major areas of expertise and professionalism. Then it progresses through three sections that provide an overview of how to ensure that others understand what librarians really do best. To repeat, the three strategies to promote awareness of librarian importance are "know," "show," and "tell": know how the institution needs that expertise, show that expertise through the provision of services, and tell non-librarians what librarians do and how valuable it is. All three are absolutely necessary.

Librarians' Specialized Expertise

Librarians' practice is diverse, but it always includes a knowledge of clients' information needs, knowledge of sources of information, and making connections between the two in many systems and media. The professional librarian is the bridge between what people need to know and the sources of that information.

Determining Information Needs and Desires

Librarians create collections and guides to information sources that support information services to particular constituent populations. They are experts at discovering the information and resource needs of the organization, of groups of people within the organization, and of individuals. The Agile Librarian thoroughly understands the mission of the larger institution and the details of how it functions. Some services grow out of existing expectations of information services, but Agile Librarians can develop useful services beyond such expectations.

It is not enough for librarians to know the universe of information sources; they also must know exactly what information their current and potential clients need and seek. Making that connection requires skill and expertise in analyzing the information needs of a single individual, a small group of library users, a large population of potential library users, and various combinations thereof. This process includes, but is by no means limited to, observing behavior and asking people what they want or believe they need. The Agile Librarian learns and uses marketing research techniques developed in other industries to discover unexplored information needs.

Strictly speaking, true information needs are not observable, and library services are based on both the expressed information needs or desires and the observable information behaviors of library users. An illustration of the difference between "needs" and "desires" and the observable information behaviors of users is found in Beitz, Fey, and O'Brien's study of hospital nurses. The researchers gave nurses two well-designed surveys about the prevention and care of decubitus ulcers (pressure ulcers of the skin, or "bed sores"). One researcher asked the nurses what they thought their information needs were on the subject, and the other tested them on their actual knowledge. Most nurses who indicated that they had little or no information needs on the subject did poorly on the test of their knowledge. Conversely, the nurses who expressed a "need" for more information were the ones who already knew more and did well on the test (Beitz, Fey, and O'Brien, 1998)!

This nursing study was conducted from the perspective of nurse educators. Nurse educators and other professional teachers often teach material for which the student has expressed no desire or interest. Librarians, on the other hand, regularly use the term "information need" for any expressed information desire or observable, information-seeking behavior. With the exception of teaching information literacy, they do not set the client's learning goals. Educators begin with a curriculum of information that students may not know, but that they need to know. Librarians must start with what the client wants to know, even if neither the librarian nor the client knows exactly what the client *needs* to know at the beginning of a search. Query identification and development is an expertise the Agile Librarian knows, shows, and tells.

Ultimately, information services are for individuals. Many individuals will use library information systems in any medium without direct contact with librarians, and librarians skillfully purchase and construct useful information retrieval systems for these individuals. Other times the librarian's role is to help the individual discover information needs and to provide value-added information service, which the user may not have expected or realized would be useful.

Individual service is quite obvious in reference service when the librarian refers a person who wants certain information to a reliable source of that information. It is a personalized professional library service, a one-to-one interaction between a librarian and a client, known as the "reference interview." This synchronous personal and interactive interview is the librarian's primary means of discovering what information an individual desires at any given time. It may take place face-to-face in a library, on the telephone, online in live "chat," or in some other medium. A client may submit a request through an asynchronous medium such as e-mail, voicemail, or a written message, but the librarian often must follow up on such messages to clarify the client's goal and provide the best service.

Some reference interviews are initiated by the librarian, not the client. In the real world, not all reference interviews will occur at the reference desk, through virtual reference, or through other formal communication channels. Questions may come up in an elevator, in the hall, over lunch, or in a setting completely unrelated to the institution. The Agile Librarian can use the interview to help the client clarify goals, a very crucial stage in providing successful information service. After the question is clear, the search for information begins, the information is retrieved, and the librarian checks again to see whether the information need has been met. Finally, the client is invited to return with any additional requests.

Librarians are skilled at making this complex interaction look like a casual conversation, and library service users may believe that the librarian is just an innately helpful, nice person who happens to work in a library. The Agile Librarian incorporates phrases into the interview that imply that this interest in the question is a professional service. For instance, instead of replying "No problem!" to a question that Agile Librarians can answer quickly based on their education and experience, they will say "I know how to find that for you" or "I can research that for you." Agile Librarians won't say, "No problem!" because that can imply that any idiot could find this answer and that the client should have been able to find it without any help.

Knowledge of Information Sources

Library service users may expect librarians to be knowledgeable in some areas, for instance, public library fiction collections, but not in specialized sources. Scholars may not expect university librarians to be capable of using important sources in their particular disciplines, and physicians may not expect hospital librarians to understand how to retrieve information from medical databases, even though that is exactly the kind of expertise such librarians have. A responsible professional, the librarian constantly and carefully studies resources considered for purchase, resources that have been purchased, and other accessible information sources. With a few key words, a well-constructed thesaurus of controlled vocabulary subject headings, and expert knowledge of database structure and searching options, the Agile Librarian can perform searches of esoteric bibliographic databases with far greater efficiency and effectiveness than most specialists in that field, even if the librarian has only a rudimentary knowledge of the subject.

Librarians are experts in evaluating information sources in terms of reliability, authority, currency, appropriate scope, accessibility, and ease of use. The Agile Librarian's continuing curiosity and education extends beyond the sources learned in library school to newly available resources, especially those important to the needs of the parent institution. Agile Librarians read reviews and attend conferences to learn more. Sometimes information about new sources comes directly from users! Teachers and other clients often discover new sources at their professional conferences. Experts in a discipline may be familiar with esoteric sources. Agile Librarians seek opportunities to learn from clients as well as from their own professional activities.

Connecting Needs and Sources

The Agile Librarian's greatest value to the institution is in bridging the gap between information needs and information sources. No one else in the organization has a higher level of skill in searching many information storage and retrieval systems. Some will have expertise with a few systems, but no one but a professional librarian can have such broad, agile expertise.

Information services range on a spectrum from completely mediated expert searching on one end, through joint professional-client searching with varying degrees of in-context instruction, all the way to complete client "do-it-yourself" searching. A professional librarian practices at many different points on this spectrum. The development of user-friendly search systems for the non-information professional has had the effect of raising the complexity of searches professionals do for their clients because the clients are more likely to do the "quick-and-dirty" searches themselves. Sometimes the quest must be owned by the librarian, sometimes it is shared by the librarian and the client, sometimes it is taught by the librarian, and sometimes it is witnessed by the librarian (Atlas, 2000). Other library quests may be completely invisible to the librarian. In any case, it is the professional librarian who makes it all possible for the entire organization.

Librarianship as a Profession

Sociologists such as Andrew Abbott (1988, 1998) have researched and described the nature of occupations and professions, and occupations that evolve into professions, including librarianship. One official definition of "profession" from the Oxford English Dictionary is "An occupation in which a professional knowledge of some subject, field, or science is applied; a vocation or career, especially one that involves prolonged training and a formal qualification." (*Oxford English Dictionary,* 2007).

Are there professional traits that librarianship shares with the traditional professional practices of law, health care, education, and religious ministry? Michael Winter, in *The Professionalization of Librarianship* (1983, p. 10), identifies a minimum of six common traits: professional association, formal education, a theoretical and practical body of knowledge, ethics codes for professional practice, service orientation, and community recognition. These will be discussed individually.

Common Traits

The first of Winter's "common traits" is the professional association. One definition of "professional association" is "[A] representative occupational association concerned with general standards of professional activity (Winter, 1983, p. 10). Professional associations can be described both formally and informally. Professionals have formal, structured organizations made up of practicing members of the profession, and they associate frequently with other practitioners on an informal basis.

Professional associations have mission statements, bylaws, officers, committees, meetings, and publications, and they sponsor a variety of programs that support the profession. The American Medical Association (AMA) and the American Bar

Association (ABA) are good examples of professional associations. They create and maintain standards and guidelines for the medical and legal professions, provide networking opportunities for their members, and advocate on behalf of their professions to policy makers and the general public.

Librarians also have many formal associations at the local, state or province, national, and international levels. The American Library Association (ALA, http://www.ala.org/), the largest and oldest association, is influential in its independent actions. The ALA also has divisions, for instance, the American Association of School Librarians (AASL, http://www.ala.org/ala/aasl), the Association of College and Research Libraries (ACRL, http://www.ala.org/ala/acrl), and the Reference and User Services Association (RUSA, http://www.ala.org/RUSA) within and governed by ALA. The Black Caucus of ALA and REFORMA are affiliated with ALA. State associations such as the California Library Association and the Texas Library Association send representatives to ALA's Council, whereas individual state school library associations such as the California School Library Association and the Pennsylvania School Librarians Association send representatives to the AASL Affiliate Assembly.

Other large national and international librarians' associations based in the United States include the Special Libraries Association (SLA, http://www.sla.org/), the Medical Library Association (MLA, http://www.mlanet.org/), and the American Association of Law Libraries (AALL, http://www.aallnet.org/). Librarians also participate in the American Society for Information Science and Technology (ASIS&T, http://www.asis.org/), the Society of American Archivists (SAA, http://www.archivists.org/), and many others.

Formal associations have mentoring and professional acculturation programs. They accredit educational programs, help match employers with qualified job seekers, and provide a variety of award and grant programs to their members. Other membership benefits include vendor discounts and reduced prices for association meetings and publications.

Some associations have peer credentialing programs. Note that licensing is legal and administered by a government agency, whereas credentialing is the recognition of expertise by one's professional peers. In that sense, a school librarian's state certificate is a license to practice in that state's schools. Many medical specialty associations have formal boards for the certification of specialists in that field. The Medical Library Association's credentialing program, The Academy of Health Information Professionals (AHIP, http://mlanet.org/academy/), is very successful. Members may use the initialism "AHIP" after their names and usually frame and hang their certificates on the walls of their offices, just as do lawyers and physicians. Tenure is a peer credentialing of professionals within an academic institution. Presently no national licensing or credentialing programs exist for all librarians in the United States.

Most professionals are active in their associations and have learned to participate in them in a spirit of give and take. The few who are unhappy with their associations tend to be "over-givers" or "over-takers." The former see themselves as exalted leaders who do not need to take time to learn from their colleagues. They fret and fuss that they are the only ones who can do anything well and tend to berate others for not doing enough for the association. The takers are readily recognized by their complaints about what the association does not do for them and their unwillingness to serve on the committees or task forces that could bring about the very changes in the organization that they desire.

The librarian's non-librarian administrator often is not familiar with the librarian's professional associations. It is the Agile Librarian's responsibility to know such associations, to show their importance by participating in them, and to tell the administrator about these activities. Some employers will fund librarians' association dues or meeting expenses; some will not. In any case, the Agile Librarian will think outside the job and participate whether or not the employer supports it financially. Indeed, many professional activities simply don't show up in the institution's job description. Professional activity and a professional identity are much bigger than the job description.

On an informal level, professionals frequently consult with each other in a spirit of respect and cooperation. They often share enough interests to socialize outside of work. They serve as mentors for each other, and often the mentoring relationship is bidirectional. Janet Cowen, a one person librarian (OPL) in the Maine Medical Center Library, Portland, Maine, explains:

> Over the years, people have asked me how I found time, as an OPL . . . to participate in the national, regional and local professional associations. My response has always been that it's because of that participation that I have survived, and even thrived. We talk about "serving'" as an officer or committee chair or committee member, and while there is the aspect of service, we also take as much from the network of friends and colleagues as being in service permits us. It's very much a two-way street, and I'd have to say that I've received much more than I've given." (Cowen, 2000).

A common model of mentoring relationships is that of an older, more experienced practitioner guiding a less experienced one. Yet in the most successful mentoring relationships, the sharing and teaching flows both ways; each can learn from the other. Whereas the more experienced practitioner can give the novice the benefit of that experience, the novice may have fresh insights from having been in library school more recently. Or it may be simply a matter of concentrating on different interests. No one is an expert in everything; everyone has something to share. This professional practice is evident in law firms, in which the newest member of the firm is recruited because of the need to fill a void of expertise in a specific area. Although the junior partner learns from the senior partners, in that particular area of expertise the learning flows in the opposite direction.

Winter's second common professional trait is formal education. A profession requires "[T]he establishment of formal educational programs affiliated with a university (Winter, 1983, p. 10). The American Bar Association accredits Juris Doctor degree programs, the American Medical Association accredits medical education programs, and the American Library Association accredits university programs for the master of library and information science degree (MLIS). These are all professional postgraduate degrees that are significantly different from academic master's degrees, which generally involve another year or two of studies begun as an undergraduate student. Although some students may pursue undergraduate pre-law or pre-medicine programs, such programs are in no way a requirement for admission to law or medical schools. Likewise, candidates for admission to an MLIS program must have an undergraduate degree, but it does not matter what their major subject was.

In 1886, the first formal library education program associated with a university opened at Columbia University. Although the Association of American Library Schools (AALS, now the Association for Library and Information Science Education, ALISE) became official in 1915, library school faculty from library schools had been meeting informally for some time before that (Davis, 2005). Currently, there are 57 university affiliated MLIS programs in the United States and Canada that are accredited by the American Library Association (American Library Association, 2007).

Professional education only begins with the postgraduate degree. Professional librarians continue their educations throughout their careers. Library associations, library schools, and individual libraries provide continuing education courses for practicing librarians. Professional librarians supplement their learning from these courses with independent reading, conferences with colleagues, and other educational activities. AHIP and other certification programs require documentation of continuing education.

Winter's third trait of professions is a theoretical and practical body of knowledge. Professionals see to "the creation and maintenance of a body of theoretical and practical knowledge—the mastery of which is a precondition of admission to professional status—along with the presence of a core of scholars who regularly contribute to this body of knowledge" (Winter, 1983, p. 10). Librarians' knowledge and expertise in connecting people with information is not an inborn personality trait, although some personality strengths are helpful. They learn this expertise through education and experience. It is knowledge that the general public does not have and should not be expected to have. According to McKinney (2006), Library and Information Science (LIS) master's degree programs accredited by the ALA emphasize expertise in the following areas:

professional ethics
resource building
knowledge organization
technological knowledge
knowledge dissemination
service
knowledge accumulation
education and lifelong learning
knowledge inquiry
research
institution management

These could be summarized as expertise in managing information resources, in managing information services, in managing information organizations, and in applying information tools and technologies to human information needs.

Of course, when librarians explain their profession to a non-librarian administrator in terms of information services, the administrator's eyes may glaze over because so many different professions and occupations use that phrase to describe their activities. The Agile Librarian must use other appropriate terms, such as "knowledge based information," "reliable published knowledge," or "current authoritative sources," especially when trying to differentiate between the management of information *content* and the management of the information *conduit* (the realm of corporate information technology departments) (Cowen and Edson, 2002).

Scholars and practitioners alike research the principles and practice of the professional librarianship and publish their work in respected, peer-reviewed journals and books. LIS research is published by Libraries Unlimited, Academic Press, Information Today, Neal-Schuman, Scarecrow Press, Oxford Press, and others. Databases that track the literature of the discipline include *Library Literature and Information Science, Library and Information Science Abstracts, Library and Information Science Technology Abstracts, Web of Knowledge (Social Sciences Index), Education Resources Information Center (ERIC),* and others.

Codes of ethics for professional practice is the fourth of Winter's common traits. All professions have standards of ethical service in the practice of the profession, and librarianship is no exception. Winter includes in his common traits of professions "the development of ethics codes regulating the conduct of professional workers" (Winter, 1983, p. 10). All those who provide information services require not only knowledge and expertise, but also respect for the profession, the clients, and society. That respect is expressed in the ethical use of knowledge and expertise. ALA, MLA, SAA, and ASIS&T each have formally written codes of ethics or guidelines for ethical practice. They vary because their constituencies practice in different kinds of institutions. ALA's code emphasizes practice in public libraries, whereas ASIS&T's is more appropriate for practice in corporate libraries that don't involve public service as part of their mission. SLA refers to ASIS&T guidelines as appropriate for special librarians.

Much like doctors, lawyers, and clergy, librarians' ethics require respect for clients' privacy and the preservation of confidentiality for client conversations and requests. Professional service ethics also demand (1) provision of the best possible information excluding personal opinion, (2) promotion of equity of information access while respecting intellectual property rights and the institutional mission, (3) professional development of the self and others, and (4) advocacy for library services and information access in society at large.

Some conflicts between librarians and non-librarian administrators or boards arise because the administrators are unaware of these professional service values. The administrators may interpret librarians' actions as personal stubbornness or as power games. The Agile Librarian will have communicated

Web Sites for Association Codes of Ethics

American Association of Law Libraries: http://www.aallnet
.org/about/policy_ethics.asp

American Library Association: http://www.ala.org/ala/
aboutala/offices/oif/statementspols/codeofethics/codeethics
.cfm

American Society for Information Science and Technology:
http://www.asis.org/AboutASIS/professional-guidelines
.html

Medical Library Association: http://www.mlanet.org/about/
ethics.html

Society of American Archivists: http://www.archivists.org/
governance/handbook/app_ethics.asp

Tips for Today

A simple and easy way to "tell" is to frame it and hang it on the wall.

Have you ever noticed when you visit your doctor that no matter what examining room they put you in, there's always some framed credential hanging on the wall? Often an original looking version of the same credential is on the wall of several different examining rooms. It's there to give you confidence in the professional.

(1) If you have a credential (perhaps AHIP) or certification for a particular state or country, frame it (or an attractive copy if you fear damaging or losing the original) and hang it on your office wall. Use the credential initials after your name where appropriate on business cards, e-mail signatures, or the like.

(2) Pick a formal association code of ethics that is most applicable to your practice. Print it attractively, frame it, and hang it on the wall. The next time someone asks you to do something that is unethical you can point out the appropriate section of the code. This not only gives credibility to your profession, but also emphasizes that your policies are not just personal whims or petty power games. Include a copy of the code in library brochures and on the library Web site. You may even include part or all of it in your social networking site or as a tagline to your e-mail.

(3) Frame your Library and Information Science diploma and hang it on the wall. Use the appropriate degree letters (for instance, MLIS) after your name on your social networking site, on business cards, and in e-mail signatures. You earned it!

these principles as positive professional values long before any such conflicts arise.

The fifth trait of a profession, service orientation, is "the cultivation of an orientation of service to a specified group of persons" (Winter, 1983, p. 10). Abbott asserts, "The tasks of professions are human problems amenable to expert service. They may be problems for individuals . . . or for groups." (1988, p. 35). The practice of any profession, Abbott continues, includes some type of diagnosis, treatment, inference, and academic knowledge (Abbott, 1988, p. 40–58). In librarianship these practices would include information needs analysis as diagnosis, collection development, information organization, information retrieval as treatment, the process of information service as inference, and professional education as academic knowledge. Doctors, lawyers, religious professionals, and librarians give certain kinds of advice in the practice of their professions; that advice is a very important part of their service.

The Agile Librarian remembers that the collection and systems exist only to support the service, not the other way around. In the title of the first chapter of *The Visible Librarian*, Judith Siess proclaims "The Primacy of Customer Service" (Siess, 2003). It may be impossible to overestimate the importance of excellent client service to professional librarianship, yet the temptation remains for the librarian to become so focused on and mired in library management tasks that this "primacy" is out of sight and out of mind.

Indeed, career counselors who do not understand the intense and constant interaction librarians have with people may mistakenly recommend the profession to people who are intelligent, task oriented, and uncomfortable in social situations. Based on the common stereotype of librarians, such people may be drawn to the profession only to find themselves absolutely miserable with the life, especially the daily interpersonal relations of a practicing librarian. The medical doctor who doesn't like interacting with patients and the lawyer who dislikes conversation with clients will suffer similarly. Such poor professionals may see their clients as interruptions that bother them and take them away from other pursuits they prefer. These doctors, lawyers, and librarians would be happier and more effective in indirect service roles such as pathology, legal research, and technical services in a very large library. Daniel Goleman, in *Working with Emotional Intelligence,* describes truly service-oriented professionals as knowing how to "understand customers' needs and match them to services or products, seek ways to increase customers' satisfaction and loyalty, gladly offer appropriate assistance [and] grasp a customer's perspective, acting as a trusted advisor" (Goleman, 1998, p. 151). The Agile Librarian confidently and sincerely enjoys helping people with all aspects of their information behavior and constantly monitors information services in the lives of clients.

The last of Winter's common traits is community recognition, "the social recognition of professional status from some significant segment of the surrounding community" (Winter, 1983, p. 10). A significant segment of employers of librarians clearly recognizes librarians' professional status. Employers regularly include the ALA-accredited professional degree as a requirement in job descriptions. Many agencies that accredit particular institutions or programs require that librarians in those institutions or serving such programs have that ALA-accredited degree. Librarians are described as professionals in many state and federal laws and regulations; for example, the U.S. *Code of Federal Regulations* refers to immigrant librarians as practicing professionals (United States, 2006).

As librarians and their associations, most notably recently, the Special Libraries Association, discuss and consider alternate names for information professionals, the accepted definition of a librarian as a "specialist in the care and management of a library" (*Merriam-Webster's Collegiate Dictionary*, 2003) is understood by the general public. What is not so generally known is the formal education, professional ethics (especially regarding confidentiality), and service orientation of the profession. For instance, *The Online Dictionary of Librarian and Information Science* expands the definition of "librarian" to include services for library users and not just management of the collection. It defines a librarian as "A professionally trained person responsible for the care of a library and its contents, including the selection, processing, and organization of materials and the delivery of information, instruction, and loan services to meet the needs of its users . . ."(Reitz, 2004). A more comprehensive definition would include professional librarians who provide information services beyond, or even in the absence of, traditional libraries. One example is that of the many librarians who have provided information services during and after major community-wide disasters even though their libraries were destroyed or unavailable.

Although most practicing librarians are fulfilled by their profession and believe that their work is valued by society, many observe that their salaries reflect a low level of community recognition of the profession (Orwig, 1991). In this sixth trait of a profession, there may be more room for improvement than in the other five. Delighted clients may say to the Agile Librarian, "*You* don't act like a *librarian!*" Typically, the librarian isn't sure what to do with this kind of personal compliment that insults the profession. This Agile Librarian may be the only one this client has seen in action. In any case, at this moment the Agile Librarian is the embodiment of the profession, and the best response is "*This is* what a real librarian does."

Acting the Role of Librarian in the Institution

Librarians not only must have a thorough knowledge of professional practice, but also must clearly demonstrate the profession's most valuable features and effectively communicate its value. To put it simply, librarians must "know," "show," and "tell." To do all three well, the Agile Librarian has to develop a proactive habit of efficient professional self-management that goes beyond the job description or institutional requirements. Real professionals think outside the job.

Know How the Institution Needs This Profession

So far this chapter has emphasized the expertise professional librarians must have to provide particular services. But does the institution really need these services? Current use of librarians' services may not be an accurate gauge of need, especially if the potential users don't know how useful librarians can be. Sometimes library services are eliminated because the librarians were working with a mental model of an idealized or outdated library service that really didn't fit the current institution. Agile Librarians must adapt their approach to the institution in which they work. For example, the librarians cannot successfully provide services on an academic model in a non-academic organization. Information literacy teaching methods used in a high school library, where there can be formal classes, are very different from effective in-context methods for researchers using a chemical company's library services. Hospital libraries and medical school libraries may have similar collections, but very different services. Collections and programming appropriate for one community's public library may be very different from what another community needs, and the same community will require different programming over time!

It is much more important to think of library services in the lives of the client population than it is to think of the client population in the lives of the library staff! The parent agency or institution does not exist solely to support library services. The library service that is not user-centered will shrivel, become less and less relevant, and sooner or later will disappear.

It is easy to talk about how the institution needs the "library" instead of "library services." This reinforces the misconception that a library is only a place and a collection, which exist with only moderate tending by someone. The institution's administration can decide to use the space for something else and may regard the collection as nothing more than an accumulation, especially

---

Exercise: The "Whying" Game

One way to explore and define an institution's need for library services is to ask yourself a dozen or so "Why?" questions. Start with the most general: "Why does this institution need library services?" Answer it with several positive statements in simple, plain language. Then, turn each of those statements into a question beginning with "Why" and answer each with several additional statements. Keep going with successive questions and statements until you have enough to write out several paragraphs summarizing what you have discovered. Include in your analysis not only current information services but potential future ones as well.

if it sees the librarian as some kind of guardian of a warehouse of material that people can either use by themselves or else find free on the Internet.

Show How This Profession Supports the Business of the Institution

Knowing how your institution needs professional services and waiting for someone to ask for them is not enough. Real services are much more valuable than potential services, and real clients are much more satisfied than potential clients. It makes more sense to think of the underserved in the institution's population as potential users than as non-users. Everyone in a given library service market should be able to enjoy the benefits of these services. If they do not, the onus is on the librarian to bridge that gap.

So Agile Librarians aren't like wallflowers at an old-fashioned ball, waiting to be asked to dance. Agile Librarians get out of their seats, go to where the people are, and demonstrate what

Exercise: Describe Your Professional Role

The word "librarian" does not have the same meaning to everyone. Most people have a mental image of a librarian based on roles, often stereotypical, in the media or on personal experience, relevant or irrelevant to their real needs. It may be of a shy, or at least dull and boring, person who likes to hide out in libraries. It may be an image of an old practice no longer needed by society in an age of widespread online connection.

In any case, we all need a short, prepared script for describing our professional role on the spot. It has to express both the generalized purpose of our profession and the specific value of your own services in context. It has to be short. Make your most important point in the first sentence. This exercise can help.

1. On the Plane

It's a long flight. You and the stranger sitting next to you have struck up a conversation and she asks what you do. Write out a script, a paragraph of five to seven sentences, for yourself describing your profession, your job, and your role in your institution in terms of positive services for people. Use active sentences. Begin the first one with "I" or "We." Do not begin by describing your resource collection or using "the library" as the subject of the first sentence. Use clear, commonly understood words in place of librarians' esoteric terms such as reference, catalog, ILL, young adults, bibliographic verification, and serials. End with a question about your seatmate's information seeking practices. Later you can demonstrate your expertise by offering positive suggestions and advice. "Have you ever used ABC library services or XYZ database?"

2. At a Cocktail Party or Reception

You are making brief small talk with an acquaintance who says "Don't you work at ABC library?" Write out a script of four to six sentences describing your professional role as above.

3. On the Elevator

You get on an elevator at work with several people. Some you know, some you do not. None are librarians. You recognize at least one as a major administrator, such as a superintendent, president, principal, mayor, or dean, and another as an opinion leader, such a reporter, accreditation official, or board member, for your institution. Someone introduces you or asks what you do. Write three sentences that clearly, honestly, and professionally describe your valuable role in the institution. Reduce that script to two sentences. Someone is getting off the elevator on the very next floor. Make it one simple sentence.

A Librarian at a Girl Scout Career Fair

Another librarian called me one day. She'd promised to go to a local middle school Girl Scout career fair event and represent librarians, but something else had come up. Could I go in her place? I told her I'd be happy to do so and she gave me the number of the event planner, whom I called for instructions. "You don't have to do much, just sit at a table and answer any questions the girls have," she said. "You have to understand that we are really trying to steer the girls away from traditionally female career paths, so you'll be at a table at the far end of the hallway. I hope you don't mind."

Well, I needed more "information needs analysis" than that, so I asked some girls I knew about the annual career fair. They told me that they liked the party with food, music, and games, but that first they had talk to five people and fill out some forms about five careers. "What do you have to find out for the forms?" I asked. "Oh, stuff like, uh, five things: what they do, what equipment they use, where they work, what education they have to have, and how much money they make."

Now I knew how to prepare for the event. I made up a single sheet hand-out with simple, direct answers to the questions, and I printed it on very bright pink paper. I used terms that would be familiar to them, not library jargon. I dressed colorfully, and I added posters and played music at my table. I also brought candy and plenty of library goodies, including big blue library logo stickers.

What happened was that the girls told each other that the cool librarian had their answers all ready for them and was giving away some good stuff as well, so my table was mobbed. Of course, I didn't get invited back to the career fair again. I guess I didn't fit the organizer's image of what a librarian should be. Here's what was on the page I gave them:

LIBRARIAN

WHAT THEY DO

- They find information for people.
- They help people find information for themselves.
- They organize information so that it can be found easily.

WHAT TOOLS THEY USE

- Computers
- Books
- Magazines
- Videos, CDs, and DVDs
- Phones, fax, and the Internet

(Continued)

they can do. Knowing how to do all the steps is worthless if they are never executed!

Agile Librarians proactively demonstrate how their profession supports the organization's business. When Agile Librarians' expertise is apparent, obvious, and beneficial to the employer and to society at large, it becomes much more difficult to substitute someone else for a librarian. Professional information services are too important to be provided only reactively.

Tell the Decision Makers How This Profession Plays a Necessary Role

The Agile Librarian cannot assume that the major decision makers know what is going on, even if "know" and "show" are solidly in place. The Agile Librarian constantly and consistently *tells* them what library services are doing for the organization, whether the decision makers are service users or potential users. The Agile Librarian, of course, wants them to be library "frequent flyers," but they may not be. It is easy for librarians to complain to each other about how decision makers "ought to know" the value of librarians' services, but if librarians don't tell them, who will?

Christine Olson, head of a marketing firm dedicated to information professionals, writes, "Strategies for communicating value should be an integral part of every information service and the products it offers." She continues, "The worth of an information service is an intangible asset determined by a series of value criteria applied by the target market" (Olson, 2002). The Agile Librarian

[Now I would add MP3 players, smart phones, instant messaging, online chat, blogs, and social networking.]

WHERE THEY WORK

- *Special Libraries*—in hospitals, law firms, companies, associations, and other institutions (Many special libraries are not open to the public.)
- *Academic Libraries*—supporting education and research in colleges and universities
- *Public Libraries*—tax supported libraries for everyone in a specific city, county, or other geographic area
- *School Libraries*—in schools for grades K-12

EDUCATION THEY MUST HAVE

Master's Degree in Library and Information Science
A librarian's bachelor's degree may be from any field. Some school librarians have a bachelor's degree in education and other courses in library science. Some special or academic librarians have additional degrees or certificates.

AVERAGE BEGINNING LIBRARIANS' SALARIES

[Here I quoted, with citation, from the most recent beginning salary report from *Library Journal* on special, academic, public, and school librarians.]

finds out what services the users value and need, provides those services, and reminds the users of how valuable they are.

For instance, it is easy for the naïve to believe that with the Internet we don't need librarians and libraries; however, the Agile Librarian will readily explain that it would be just as logical to say that with automatic teller machines (ATMs) and debit cards, bankers and other financial professionals are obsolete. In both cases, automation has freed professionals from processes that used to be tedious, so that now both can do what they do best even better. The Agile Librarian frequently proclaims what these better services are. People tend to ask only for the services they know about. If librarians don't tell them about other options, who will? (McKnight, 2002).

Summary

Everyone needs information. All humans create, gather, store, retrieve, and use information, but professional librarians have the expertise to provide specialized services unavailable elsewhere. They obtain information directly for clients, organize information sources for access, guide clients in their own information seeking, and teach information literacy skills. They have an ethical responsibility to provide such services to their clients and to promote their value to society at large.

Different institutions will need different services. The school librarian with a mission to teach children information literacy is providing a service somewhat different from the archivist developing a collection for future as well as present users. The public librarian's skill at helping consumers find reliable, relevant information about different kinds of refrigerators before making a purchase differs from that used by a university librarian working to build support for the curriculum of the chemistry department. The corporate librarian verifying facts for a news agency with a rapidly approaching deadline works differently from a librarian indexing the documents of a government agency. In any institution, a professional librarian is the bridge between what people need to know and the sources of that information.

Each Agile Librarian clearly knows, shows, and tells the value of these professional services to the organization. Because not every organization has professional library services, librarians must not only know, but also communicate clearly, what the value of a librarian would be to the organization. Administrators may not instinctively understand the value of library services; they must be shown and told about how these services could benefit their institutions. The Agile Librarian may occasionally provide services outside of professional practice, but is wary of becoming the universally helpful servant. The work of the Agile Librarian is to be the professional connection between questions and answers, between people's needs and information sources, seamlessly connecting expert knowledge of both. It is not enough for librarians to know the universe of information sources; they also must know exactly what information their clients and potential clients need and seek. The organization with a librarian does not have to settle for what an amateur can do.

The profession of librarianship, like other respected professions, has professional associations, formal post-baccalaureate and continuing education, a theoretical and practical body of knowledge, commonly accepted codes of ethics for the practice of the profession, and community recognition. Most importantly, it has a deep-seated service orientation.

The Agile Librarian conceives of library services in the lives of the clients instead of the clients in the lives of the library staff. These library services support the mission of the larger organization, be it a school, a community, a university, a company, or some other organization. The Agile Librarian actively learns the clients' needs, demonstrates professional service in meeting those needs, and tells the organization's decision makers exactly how this works.

References

Abbott, Andrew. 1988. *The System of Professions: An Essay on the Division of Expert Labor.* Chicago: University of Chicago Press.

———. 1998. Professionalism and the Future of Librarianship. *Library Trends* 46:430–444.

American Library Association. 2007. *2007–2008 Directory of Institutions Offering ALA-Accredited Master's Programs in Library and Information Studies.* http://www.ala.org/ala/accreditation/lisdirb/lisdirectory.htm. Accessed September 8, 2007.

Atlas, Michel C. 2000. The Rise and Fall of the Medical Mediated Searcher. *Bulletin of the Medical Library Association* 88:26–35.

Beitz, Janice M., Janice Fey, and David O'Brien. 1998. Perceived Need for Education vs. Actual Knowledge of Pressure Ulcer Care in a Hospital Nursing Staff. *MEDSURG Nursing,* 7:293–301.

Cowen, Janet L. 2000. Email posted to MEDLIB-L listserv. April 29, 2000. Archives available at http://listserv.buffalo.edu/archives/medlib-l.html.

Cowen, Janet L. and Jerry Edson. 2002. Best Practice in Library/Information Technology Collaboration. *Journal of Hospital Librarianship* 2:1–15.

Davis, Donald G., Jr. 2005. Ninety Years of Education for the Profession: Reflections on the Early Years. *Journal of Education for Library and Information Science* 46:266–274.

Goleman, Daniel. 1998. *Working with Emotional Intelligence.* New York: Bantam.

McKinney, Renée D. 2006. *Draft Proposed ALA Core Competencies Compared to ALA-Accredited, Candidate and Precandidate Program Curricula: A Preliminary Analysis.* Chicago, IL: ALA Office for Accreditation. http://www.ala.org/ala/accreditationb/Core_Competencies _Comparison.pdf. Accessed September 5, 2007

McKnight, Michelynn. 2002. Professional Hospital Librarians: Doing Better What We've Always Done Well. *National Network* 26:1, 4.

Merriam-Webster's Collegiate Dictionary. 11th ed. 2003. Springfield, Mass.: Merriam-Webster, Inc.

Olson, Christine A. 2002. What's in It for Them? Communicating the Value of Information Services: Establish Value. *Information Outlook* 6:19–23.

Orwig, Darrell. 1991. "Executive Summary" in Special Libraries Association, Task Force on the Enhancement of the Image of the Librarian/Information Professional, *Inter-Association Task Force Report on Image.* Washington, DC: Special Libraries Association.

Oxford English Dictionary. 2007. *OED Online Word of the Day* [email to author from oedwotd@ OUP.COM, December 4, 2007] "profession, n.—Draft Revision June 2007." Oxford, UK: Oxford University Press.

Reitz, Joan M. 2004. *Dictionary for Library and Information Science.* Westport, Conn.: Libraries Unlimited. Also available as *ODLIS—Online Dictionary for Library and Information Science* from http://lu.com/odlis/.

Siess, Judith A. 2003. *The Visible Librarian: Asserting Your Value with Marketing and Advocacy.* Chicago: American Library Association.

United States. Office of the Federal Register. *Code of Federal Regulations.* Washington, D.C.: U. S. General Services Administration, National Archives and Records Service. 8 CFR 214.6 Revised January 1, 2006. Accessed through LexisNexis.com September 10, 2007.

Winter, Michael F. 1983. The Professionalization of Librarianship. *Occasional Papers,* no. 160:1–46. Champaign, IL: University of Illinois Graduate School of Library and Information Science.

Chapter 2

Delighting Your Clients

The Agile Librarian has many delighted clients. These people have more than nostalgic old memories of some beautiful and quiet building or a slightly positive impression of a flashy online system. They have recent memories of getting something yesterday that they wanted yesterday, and the expectation of getting even more of what they need tomorrow. These delighted clients are school children who can hardly wait for library time. They are college students working on papers late at night in dorm rooms who get exactly what they need by using library systems by themselves, with help from librarians, or both. They are community business leaders who know that they can get valuable competitive intelligence from their public library service today. They are nurses working the night shift in a hospital who are confident that if they run into something unfamiliar, they can get reliable and authoritative information without being more than steps away from the patients' monitors. All these delighted clients experience information services going far beyond access to a few expected information containers. As Rick Anderson, a technical services librarian, writes, "Our job is not to manage information, but to deliver it" (Anderson, 2007, p. 191).

When diners enter a good restaurant they are greeted immediately, even if a table is not available yet. When they are escorted to a table, they are immediately provided with water and menus and asked if they want something else to drink. They feel free to chat with each other, continuing the conversation they began outside. The server arrives and asks if they are ready to order. One diner asks if they serve pasta with spinach. The server says, "Yes," and describes several such dishes. The diners order, and when the dishes arrive they not only look very good, but they taste even better than expected. Some tastes are familiar, but others delight them with the chef's unexpected combinations of ingredients and preparation. The evening progresses pleasantly all the way to the point when someone says "Have a good evening!" as they go out the door. They remember the experience and it influences their future actions.

What if no one greeted them and they had to find their own way around the restaurant? What if, when they ordered, the server had said or even expressed with body language, "Hey, you've got a menu. Why don't you read it? You should know that 'Florentine' means 'with spinach.' You're taking advantage of me by being too lazy to read the menu. You need to be taught a lesson about how to behave in a classy place like this." What if, when they did order something on the menu, the server told them it would be ready next week? What if they were served something that only vaguely resembled what they had ordered? Would the diners be likely to return to that restaurant? What would they tell their friends and acquaintances about it? Would they be likely to go to a restaurant with worse food but better service? Of course they would!

The Agile Librarian ensures that clients have a positive experience, as in the first dining vignette. The Rigid Librarian, when asked if the library has a certain book or resource, says either aloud or with body language, "Hey, why didn't you look it up in the online public access catalog (OPAC)? You ought to know to look there first. You're taking advantage of me by being too lazy to use the OPAC instead of talking with your friends. You need to be taught a lesson about how to behave in a library." Or what if the librarian approaches the library visitors not with an offer of service but with a noisy demand that they take their conversation someplace else? If this happens in a public library, how will these people vote the next time there is an election for library funding? Even if they are only teenagers who don't vote, they will remember the negative experience in a few short years when they are old enough to vote!

The Rigid Librarian may have reasons for such feelings of annoyance. A high level of expertise and difficult work went into the creation of the bibliographic retrieval system. It meets very demanding professional standards. The Rigid Librarian may be concerned, even angry, that there are potential service users who rarely or never use this system. Nonetheless, library service users are more concerned about finding what they want than learning the complexities of a system. There are opportunities for information literacy instruction, but every encounter doesn't require a bibliographic lecture. The diner may inquire how a dish is prepared, but the waitperson is not likely to tell diners that they should go cook it themselves so they would know better how it is done.

The Agile Librarian delights clients with service and results that can be found nowhere else. This isn't just about being nice; it is central to the very survival of the library service in that school, community, or business. The effects of good or bad service can come swiftly in a small library, and although it may take longer to be visible in a very large one, eventually funding will shrink or dry up completely for any library service that does not delight both its users and its stakeholders.

Satisfied clients and stakeholders are the key to library survival. Delighted clients are essential to those thriving Agile Librarians with client-centered service.

Client-Centered Service

What is a "client"? Clients are active, participating beneficiaries of professional services. Librarians use and have used many terms to describe their clients, including customers, patrons, users, guests, and students. "Customers" implies an economic relationship; it's a term favored in business over its older synonym "patrons." "Guests" is an appropriate term in the hotel industry, but in stores and other enterprises it is a euphemism as strained as calling members of the sales force "associates." In many institutions, it is easier just to refer to people by their roles in the institution or company, such as "students," "faculty," "employees," or "staff."

"Users" is an awkward term that implies mostly self-help, a situation in which invisible librarians have created information systems for people to use on their own. Like users of illegal drugs, these information users don't know or even much care about the work or risks taken in the production and supply chains. "Users" implies that people are on their own with a collection of information resources or access points assembled by an almost equally anonymous group of "mules." They care about getting what they believe they need any way that they can. In a "user" situation, there is little relationship (often as little as possible) between the creators and suppliers of the system and its users. One may not care about the other, as long as they all play their roles in the economy.

The client relationship respects both parties: the expert, a specialist in information services, and the seeker of that expertise, without depriving the information seeker of freedom of choice. The professionals do organize systems and access points for groups of clients, but they also serve individuals directly. As with the lawyer/client, physician/patient, or teacher/student relationship, there is an expected state of mutual interest, attention, trust, and confidentiality. Some health care providers have taken a stronger stance against referring to their clients as "patients," seeing the use of that term as taking a paternalistic stance and a role of doing something *to*, rather than *working with*, an individual. Thus, some nurses prefer to refer to such individuals as "clients," acknowledging simultaneously the interactive nature of the relationship and the professionalism of the nurse.

However much librarians may enjoy designing and improving information storage and retrieval systems, they must remember that their primary mission is to serve the clients for whom they choose and design systems. Collections and systems exist to support client services and not vice versa. Some systems are designed to be used by librarians, librarians are, in this case, the clients. Problems arise when non-librarians are forced to use systems designed for librarians.

Does a client-centered outlook mean that librarians should be meek and passive? Not at all. It means that professional librarians seek engaged interaction with clients. The professional bridge between the clients' goals and the librarian's knowledge of sources and systems is more important than ever. The client-centered Agile Librarian provides professional service.

Professional Service: What's the Difference?

The Agile Librarian knows that most of the library's print and online information sources are available elsewhere. With home and office Internet access, people can use documents available online or order the delivery of hard copy books and documents. With the Amazon.com® Kindle, they don't even need Internet access for instant delivery of content. Although it is important for adults and children who can't afford books and Internet access to have cost-free access at a library, professional library services must provide their clients with more than they could get even if they can afford access to the documents from another source. Answers to most reference questions that used to require professional help are now available online. As Rick Anderson argues, client-centered services are the responsibility of all librarians, even those who work in technical services and do not see everyday clients using their work. He writes:

> [D]evelopments in the information world generally (and in libraries in particular) over the past decade have conspired to blur the boundaries between technical services and public services. It's becoming less and less

possible to separate the products we provide (books, journals, databases) from the services that patrons use to gain access to them—increasingly, what libraries provide are direct links to content, not just descriptions of content and directions to the content's physical location. (Anderson, 2007, p. 190)

Individuals' successful information retrieval is not just a matter of software, hardware, and paper systems. It requires social resources such as community, institutional, and corporate support for access as well as language and cultural resources. Concepts and language develop in human communities: people write content, organizations purchase systems to access content, and so forth. Little of that is any use without the human resources: professionals to design, refine, and guide the use of all of the above.

Professionals do for clients what their clients cannot do for themselves. In libraries, professional librarians select, store, organize, and provide access to documents and information sources. Commercial services do the same, with a larger range of selections than many local libraries, online and home delivery, and no need to return the material. Indeed, if document access were all that professional librarians provide, there would be less reason for their continued service. What do they do that their clients cannot do for themselves?

One answer is that librarians can teach their clients information literacy: how to recognize a need for information, choose and evaluate sources of that information, and recognize whether or not that need has been met, in a product independent context. All librarians, not just school librarians, are teachers. The risk is, of course, that their students may believe that their own information skills are as good as or better than those of the librarians. What is the librarian's professional expertise?

Just as a reasonably intelligent, informed person with a high degree of health information literacy still needs the interventions of a professional health care provider, the librarian's client needs the intervention of an expert information professional from time to time. Nardi and O'Day, borrowing a term from technology, identify such a professional as an "intelligent agent . . . an intelligent person who helps a client accomplish a goal that either the client cannot accomplish on his own because of a lack of expertise or a goal that needs to be accomplished with less effort on the client's part" (Nardi and O'Day, 1996). In their observational research into reference librarians' practice they described near textbook examples of reference interviews, emphasizing the collaborative refinement of the client's goal. This process, which continues with the collaborative evaluation and retrieval of information sources to meet that goal, is the librarian's unique professional service for the client.

Unfortunately, this service is little known and poorly understood by the general population. Some students enter LIS programs without any personal experience of it, let alone appreciation for its centrality in our profession. Other chapters of this book discuss advertising and promoting this service, but such promotion is useless without the reality of services that truly delight clients.

The school librarian who not only helps a child find more books "just like the one just finished" but also introduces the child to other material that delights that child, has to begin by listening and discussing with the child. The librarian must discover what the child found appealing about the "one just finished." In all kinds of library services, the Agile Librarian not only helps clients to define their desires, but also helps them to learn the terms and syntax necessary to interact more successfully with various information systems.

Even if clients can only use a simple "type a question, hit enter, and get a document" interface, a high level of information exploration is necessary both before and after the successful system interaction. Librarians teach these skills.

The librarian may teach clients that when searching any text-based system without controlled vocabulary, for instance, Google®, they will have more precise retrieval with terms that have few meanings. They may need to come up with different ways to express the concept, and if they are searching a multi-word phrase in some systems, they will get more precise retrieval if they enclose it in quotation marks. If someone wants to identify the kind of spider she just saw in the closet, she has to think of words to describe it, because she cannot take a picture and insert the picture into the search box. If she enters *brown spider* in the search box, she will have more irrelevant hits, currently more than a million in Google®, than if she enters *"brown spider,"* which currently returns about 50,000 hits. After cognitive exploration of pages in that set, including those with pictures, she may see pictures of brown spiders that look like the spider in the closet. She can search again, this time using "brown recluse spider," and the results will be more precise, even if the set is larger, about 200,000 hits. On exploring some of those items, she may learn that the Latin name for this spider is *Loxosceles reclusa,* and that some experts believe it belongs to the family *Sicariidae.* Searching both of those terms will render results from different kinds of information. If her curiosity leads her to seek information beyond "What kind of spider is this?" she now has terms to use that she did not have before.

Using a constructivist approach in which the client builds information, Ruth C. T. Morris writes:

> The term "user-centered" . . . is normally associated with the idea of increased attention to the needs of users of systems . . . [It can] denote a focused approach to thinking about information services and systems: one that regards information as something in part constructed by users, that recognizes common traits which humans share in processing information, and that views the contexts in which information needs arise (and the contexts in which they are pursued) as significant factors in the design of user-centered information systems and services. (Morris, 1994, p. 20)

One practical application of this theoretical understanding is moving from a rule-based standard for source evaluation to a context-based evaluation. The rules for evaluation of a source on the basis of authority, currency, reliability, scope, cost, accessibility, reviews, recommended lists, and intended audience are still valuable, but the context of the client's information pursuit trumps everything. For some purposes, even the Agile Librarian uses Google® or Wikipedia®.

In any case, the information quest is not satisfied with "vending machine" service: drop the right coin in the slot, press the right button, and the complete answer, no more, no less, pops out. The seeker more or less consciously constructs relevance

The Agile Librarian Cuts to the Chase

While writing Chapter 10, Behaving Ethically, I needed to track down the original citable source for a story I remembered reading about Joan Baez many years ago. I thought that it might have been in her early autobiography, *Daybreak* (1969), so I looked for it in my local university library's online catalog. I found that its only copy was in a special collection and non-circulating. The "catch-22" was the library's rule that they would not order a book that they owned through interlibrary loan. So, I e-mailed a librarian there, explaining exactly why I needed this book, even though few clients would go that far in the first contact! She replied that if I would specify a day when I could come in, she would have the book held for me to inspect in the library during regular hours for the special collection. About to leave town for a meeting, I groaned when I read that. Being an Agile Librarian, however, she decided to invest a few minutes in looking at the book herself. She retrieved it and, looking through the table of contents, noticed a chapter title related to the story I remembered. The story was told on the first page of the chapter, so, just a few minutes later, she e-mailed me a scan of the brief excerpt I needed with the complete citation. I was a delighted client!

Her quick thinking saved us both time. She didn't have to go through the reserve process after all. Not only would the Rigid Librarian refuse to take the few minutes to look herself, but if asked to do so she would have dug in her heels, citing library rules. She probably would have reminded herself that she should not let patrons take advantage of her! They have to be taught to take care of themselves! Of course, I was also delighted that this Agile Librarian had been an LSU SLIS student.

criteria during the process, so that even if the vending machine pops out exactly what was requested, it very well may not satisfy. By the time the seeker has the result, the seeker often has a different concept of the information goal developed during the process.

Expert library services that delight clients include both personally aided or mediated information services and superior options for self-service. The same client may prefer a quick, do-it-yourself search in one situation, whereas in another situation that client would be grateful for personalized professional attention. Just as not all information can be contained in one type of resource, Web site, book, or broadcast, not all information services can be based on the same model. The "invisible librarian" or "invisible library" approach of total unaided, do-it-yourself access with very little if any available personalized client service can appear to be, or may even be, little different from what is freely available online. On the other hand, some clients are uneasy about having a librarian seemingly looking over their shoulders at everything they seek; yet even they will reach a point at which direct professional service can save them substantial time and effort.

In some large libraries, formal reference desk service is shrinking as individuals learn to retrieve many ready reference answers online instead of going to the library and waiting for a librarian. Librarians who restrict their personal practice only to passive question answering at such a desk reinforce the perception that their services have become redundant. The assumption made by these librarians and clients alike is that the vending machine systems work so well that contextual expert help is no longer necessary. That's not true. Everyone experiences the helpless feeling of having come to a dead end or an endless loop in a system; in these situations, an expert may be able to find the necessary information immediately. What has changed is the context in which the clients seek information. If people aren't using services and sources around the reference desk, then librarians need to be obviously available in the real or virtual environments where their clients are searching.

Take Action: The Onus Is on Us

The Agile Librarian actively seeks interaction with clients through whatever media, in whatever place, and at whatever time is convenient for the client. Online sources can include "pop-up" offers for personal searching assistance. For some client groups, that may mean providing human service 24 hours a day and 7 days a week.

In order to demonstrate professional service, university library department liaisons may hold office hours not in the library building, but in the departments they serve. They may do rounds of faculty offices, listening and offering professional services. Just as clinical librarians make rounds in hospitals and retrieve relevant sources in context, school librarians might make regular visits to classes, not just to preach library but to listen and directly support lessons, demonstrating their professionalism outside the library.

Delighted clients get more than they expected because librarians have acted to make that happen. Such clients not only are surprised by personal empathetic service, but also by the versatility of the Agile Librarian who doesn't wait for specific requests for service. People don't ask for what they don't expect to get, so delighting clients has to become more of the information service culture than a reactionary wait for requests. "It is available but they don't use it" shouldn't be a surprise to librarians if their clients have no knowledge of "it," don't need "it," or both.

Different clients are delighted by different services. For instance, the school or children's librarian will put series labels on the spines of novels to make them easy for children to find (Burch, 2007). The special librarian develops "value-added deliverables" (Kassel, 2002) and the access services librarian offers self-checkout kiosks in addition to the traditional circulation desk (Driscoll, 2005). The library manager looks beyond the immediate problem to the greater systemic mess that caused it (Lubans, 1994).

The Rigid Librarian fears change that involves moving from rote, task-oriented services to more thoughtful interactions. That may be expressed as indignantly taking offense in terms of clients taking advantage of or asking too much of librarians. Is this because they are anxious about the size of their workload or anxious about change in the services they provide? Some openly say that they don't want clients to know what librarians really can do for them because more of them would ask for such service! Some wonder, "If we change it, will they come?" Gary E. Strong, in his keynote address at the 2005 Virtual Reference Desk Conference, answered that question this way:

> We are beginning to understand . . . that as the world's knowledge becomes a network accessible to a large part of the world, we will not exist unless we too are accessible. . . . If we are truly customer-centered, we will guide customers at their point of need to resources that accelerate the process of identifying and retrieving information for study or personal use any time, any place. . . . (Strong, 2006)

What Do Clients Need and Want?

Agile Librarians offer new, relevant, and needed services for their clients. Some really wonderful new services are appearing all the time. Some new services may not work well at first, but services won't improve without taking that risk. One mark of an Agile Librarian is the practice of agile revision, invention, and reinvention of information services for current clients instead of maintaining services relevant only to past generations. The working culture of many libraries today fosters such growth.

Clients need both proactive and reactive information services based on their real contextual information needs. What does that mean? That means that information instruction, collection and system development, and personal situational services must all be based on current and ongoing professional information needs analysis. Surveys and focus groups may provide some good ideas about group information desires, but direct observation of information behaviors renders greater insights. Insight to delight clients one at a time, one after another, comes from direct dialog with individuals.

Population Information Needs

Because of differences in populations, no two libraries provide exactly the same services, even if they are of the same general type. Librarians in different kinds of libraries offer differing suites of services because of the varying needs of their clientele. Within the clientele of any particular library there are groups with different needs and information-seeking behaviors. Faculty and students express different information needs than do consumers. Practicing professionals demonstrate different information-seeking behaviors than do students or faculty, and full-time researchers may have other information desires. Agile Librarians can use the rich body of information science research literature in such behaviors (Case, 2002; McKnight and Peet, 2000) to help them understand the needs of their clients.

Evidence of Population Information Needs

Focus groups and surveys are useful for gathering data on current opinions and general satisfaction with services. Questionnaires may be useful for general impressions, but not for fine-tuning services to clients' real needs. Generally, most people who will complete surveys or participate in focus groups are people with very strong positive or negative feelings (perhaps stemming from a single incident), and those feelings affect their responses to all questions. Librarians rarely have the opportunity to gather quantitative data from a truly random sample that will yield results that are statistically significant. Focus groups or surveys of various user groups that ask about information-seeking behaviors are frequently used but generally produce inaccurate descriptions of actual behavior. Self-report from memory, even if anonymous, tends to be incomplete and biased even from the most honest respondents. Better evidence of actual behavior comes from observational studies. For an excellent review of such research, see Donald O. Case's *Looking for Information: A Survey of Research on Information Seeking, Needs, and Behavior*, 2002.

That said, focus groups and surveys with open-ended questions can yield useful qualitative or narrative data that can answer some kinds of questions about population information beliefs. Open ended questions that begin with "What," "Why," or "How" prompt valuable, unanticipated answers. Quantitative data, garnered by asking quantitative questions such as "How many," "How much," and "How often," can be gathered with other methods. Also, useful revelations come from studies of a broad range of information activities rather than studies of one particular information system, such as use of a particular library's journal collection or online services (Allen, 1996; Davenport and Cronin, 1998; Maybee, 2007; Palmer, 1999; Tenopir, 2003). Such studies are another example of considering library services in the life of the client, rather than considering the client in the life of library practices.

Although evidence of the ways current clients use library services can be found in circulation and material usage data gathered at the library, it does not describe the information needs that the librarians are not meeting, nor does it reveal anything about potential library clients in the institutional population who are not using library services. In a sense, material use data allows us to study users in the life of the library, but not the library services in the lives of the users. For that, we must go beyond the library to understand clients' information needs holistically. To do so can be as simple as walking into a department, office, or classroom elsewhere in the institution to chat with clients and potential clients, or it may be as complex as hiring an outside consultant to do a major study.

Students

Carol Kuhlthau's excellent research into students' information search processes for writing papers is particularly significant (Kuhlthau, 1988a, 1988b, 1991, 1993). She has identified specific stages of the process that can be observed in students from grade school through post-graduate work. Drawing on her research, Agile Librarians can understand both the emotional and the scholarly stages of Initiation, Selection, Exploration, Formulation, Collection, and Presentation. Feelings of uncertainty and apprehension are very common during initiation. These give way to a brief sense of optimism once the student has picked a direction and begun the work. During the exploration stage, feelings of confusion and doubt increase dramatically and the librarian must be particularly sensitive to the general background exploration the students must accomplish before focusing on a particular point. The librarian cannot demand that a student present a well-articulated, specific search request at this point when it is not yet clear in the student's mind. During the fourth stage, Formulation, the desired theme begins to take shape, and only during the Collection stage can the student best use library systems to gather the material necessary to complete the assignment in an appropriate Presentation. Librarians frequently serving students would be wise to read Kuhlthau's *Seeking Meaning: A Process Approach to Library and Information Services.* (Kuhlthau, 2004).

Librarians serving students must balance providing information services with information literacy instruction, because either providing only literacy instruction with the assumption that all students must find everything for themselves or providing only intermediary information retrieval may do the students a disservice. While students should not be expected to develop the librarian's level of information literacy, the librarian can share the searching process in a way that both helps the student to become a better searcher and provides the student with material unavailable without such help.

Researchers

University libraries serve faculty who often have the dual roles of teaching and research. Librarians in independent research institutions and some corporations serve clients who are full-time researchers. In addition to domain-specific information, they need information for identifying research grant–funding organizations, as well as for writing articles, books, and proposals. Proposal and publication deadlines can be as crucial to them as patient care emergencies are to health care providers.

In university libraries, librarians may develop professional relationships with students that last several years, but they will certainly work much longer with individual faculty members. Delighting these clients is extremely important and deserves careful attention. Departmental liaison librarians make a difference. It is far better to work with faculty as allies than as opponents.

Public Library Clients

Whereas all librarians serve clientele with diverse needs, those who work in public libraries must be the most versatile. Client-centered analysis of the information needs and behavior of the community, and of many groups within that community, is essential to successful service, but it is no small undertaking. Needs of some groups may overlap with others. For instance, students of Spanish and native speakers of Spanish both need Spanish language material, but not necessarily the same material. The interests of some people will be diametrically opposed to those of others, and some clients will need very esoteric information sources. Public library clients need services for all aspects of their lives, including, but not at all limited to, their professional, recreational, educational, health, aesthetic, and financial lives.

Individual Information Needs: Application of the Traditional Reference Principles to Delight Today

Although it is useful to understand generalizations about a library's client populations, ultimately information services are for individuals, preferably delighted individuals. Even the best client-centered system designs are based on evidence from research into the experiences of large groups of clients, not individuals. Clients may be delighted with both the convenience and the utility of do-it-yourself information seeking, but everyone needs individualized service at some time.

The principal steps of the traditional reference interview are important in any interactive context, and are at the heart of personalized professional library services. A reference interview can be conducted through asynchronous media like e-mail or fax, through synchronous media like private online chat or text messaging, and any time or anywhere the professional and the client meet face to face. Some of the most delighted clients are those who have been visited by their librarians in their natural habitats, such as classrooms or offices. When done well, this process will delight clients.

Through what may appear to be a casual conversation, the librarian helps the client refine an information request and retrieve that information from an appropriate source. Perhaps one reason that this service is often unrecognized and undervalued is librarians' success at making a formal interview appear to be a casual conversation. It is the Agile Librarian's primary means of discovering what an individual seeks at any given time.

The goal in any medium is to discover what the client wants and needs well enough for the professional to help the client make the connection between that question and the sources of its answer. The process helps the client clarify goals, a very crucial stage that may be difficult in automated systems. Only after that clarification can the search really begin. Yet, the librarian-assisted search must really reduce the client's search time. As the current favorite speaker's line goes, "only librarians like to search, everyone else likes to find," so the librarian's help really must do more for the client than the client can quickly do with available systems. It can delight the client only if the retrieval truly meets the client's goals, not just those of the librarian. Even if the client appears satisfied with the results at the moment, the Agile Librarian always invites the client to return with any additional comments or requests.

During the opening greeting, both parties establish a channel of social communication. The librarian's first contact with the client is welcoming, even though the client's first request almost never describes the entire information need. These are like the opening moves in a chess game in that they may hint at, but do not reveal, an entire goal, let alone a strategic plan. Whereas in normal conversation it can be considered impolite to answer a question with a question, in a reference dialog the librarian usually will answer the initial question with a question to begin the process of clarification of the initial request.

In an online chat interview, the librarian must convey that a real person is paying attention to the client in the first sentence, for example, "Good morning. I am [name] and I am glad to work with you on your question." On the telephone, cheerful vocal inflections add to the words. Smiling, perhaps into a mirror, affects the tone of voice when answering a call. Answering the phone with a personal name as well as an institutional or departmental title helps the caller to identify who is on the line. In person, when librarians do not know the client, they should introduce themselves even if they are wearing an identification badge. State your name and title, and then call the client by name if an institutional identification badge is visible. If not, clients may or may not introduce themselves by role, name, or both in response.

In person, physical position and body language as well as professional grooming and dress add to the meaning of voice and words. The librarian should look at the client with a pleasant, welcoming expression, even if only briefly while the librarian is helping someone else. If the client approaches a desk where the librarian is seated, it makes sense for the librarian to stand and perhaps even walk around the desk to the client. If the client sits at the desk, the librarian also sits to maintain a relative eye level during the conversation. If not done too obviously, some "mirroring," which means adjusting some body position to match that of the client, helps establish rapport. If the librarian is visiting a client's office or classroom, the same social communication skills nonverbally enable the dialog to continue smoothly.

While the in-person clients may express a reticence to bother or interrupt the librarian's work, especially if a librarian appears to be busy, that happens less frequently in virtual reference. The skillful librarian not only knows that the client is the center of professional practice, but expresses that in words and actions: "That's an interesting question." Indeed, a librarian's lack of attention to the client can result in an inefficient waste of time for both the librarian and the client. Online, a long wait between messages may be interpreted as lack of attention, so the librarian has to keep the client posted. If the librarian does not get it right the first time, there may never be a second time.

Likewise, the librarian going to the client's native habitat may not want to bother or interrupt the client's work. Appointments can lessen that risk. The key is to make a first impression of honest concern and empathy, backed up with demonstrable professional service. The librarian must set a tone that is neither craven nor overbearing. It cannot sound like a vendor's flippant "Can I help you?" nor can it be intimidating. The word "help" may give some clients the idea that the librarian believes the clients to be ignorant. The librarian approaching a user who is obviously searching may better ask "Are you finding what you are looking for?" Indeed, some people may refrain from asking a librarian for help because they see asking as a sign of their own ignorance or incompetence. Early school experiences with library instruction may have left them with the impression that libraries are entirely self-service. They also may believe that their own information-seeking experience has given them an expertise equal to or greater than that of the librarian. If it has, the Agile Librarian would be wise to take an interest and learn from the client before enhancing the client's experience with increased information literacy.

Discovering and defining the real information need is a very interactive process, which can proceed after the opening of the interview. Some refer to this stage as the "negotiation" of the client's request, but it should really be a joint investigation. The librarian asks open-ended questions, and answering them helps the client to develop or focus aspects of the quest. The librarian must concentrate on listening to all the nuances of the conversation and to resist the temptation to start thinking about possible resources before both have a clear understanding of the goal. Eventually, the librarian will paraphrase the client's interest, adding additional details and encouraging the client to edit and refine the question. Sometimes the client's terminology will be new to the librarian, and the librarian should ask for further explanation; sometimes the librarian uses terminology new to the client, which also requires explanation. The librarian has to discover not only what is wanted, but how much, in what format, in what depth, and how soon. The client may have opened the interview with a request for a particular kind of material, such as "Can you find me a Web site that . . . ?" or "Do you have a book on . . . ?" During the discussion it may be clear that the information is more important than the format of the document that contains it. The client expressed the request in terms of how the information is expected to be found, but the librarian may know better sources in other formats. The interview may involve definition of terms, specifications of limitations on the information desired, and other details about what the client's ideal document or documents would be. If the request is for a number, the client may want only a general estimate or need a specific number depending upon how the information is going to be used.

A librarian may ask, "So that I can get you exactly what you want, can you put this in a little more context for me?" or other gently but effectively probing questions. The librarian tries to round out the story as much as possible. It takes skill to elicit some information without appearing to be prying or grilling the client. Of course, listening librarians will not be mentally composing their next question while the client is talking. Overly eager librarians may have to remember to stop, look, and listen. While the client is talking, the librarian not only listens, but also encourages the client with a nod of the head or relatively meaningless words like "okay," "I see," and "uh-huh." Some judicious, attentive waiting can give the client a better opportunity to elaborate on the request. This is what professional educators call "wait time." Agile Librarians often find it useful to ask one more question about the request after they believe that they completely understand it. Some times their entire understanding of the question shifts as a result of that answer.

Late in the interview, the librarian can estimate how much time it will take to retrieve what the client needs. It may be a simple ready reference answer or a bibliographic verification that can be retrieved in a few minutes. It might require an interlibrary loan request, a referral service, a moderate literature search, a comprehensive literature search, term paper counseling, or any of many other kinds of information services. At that point, the librarian can decide how much to do on the spot and how much to promise to deliver later. If the client does not have time to work through the process with the librarian, the librarian may ask the client for contact information and give the client some idea of when to expect the answer or material. Because people are generally more pleased if something takes less time than expected rather than more, it is good practice for the librarian to overestimate how long it will take. Then, if the librarian cannot complete the process within the original estimated time, there still is some room for taking more time without disappointing the client.

This real-time iterative interaction is very powerful. It can be significantly less effective if the request is received asynchronously, for instance through e-mail, voice mail, or a memo. Often the librarian has to follow up such a request with additional time-consuming communication.

The third stage is the search for and identification of documents or other resources that will communicate the needed information. Online or on the phone, the librarian may need to say, "I'm going to do such and such for the next few minutes; you may not hear from me while I am doing this." In person, librarians may begin by describing what they are about to do. If the client follows along, thinking aloud can help the client understand what is happening and even participate as the search is refined. If the librarian is using a computer, it is usually better for the client to be able to see the screen as the search progresses. Citrix® programs and other software utilities allow the online client to see what the librarian is doing, or the librarian can see what the online client is doing, keystroke by keystroke. Some clients would rather not go along for the ride, and that is also acceptable. In any case, the librarian searching for the client must not seem to disappear without a reason once she has understood the quest. Seeing the librarian suddenly typing and scowling into a computer without saying anything, seemingly shutting out the client, is counterproductive!

Information service ranges on a spectrum from completely mediated, expert searching on one end, through joint, professional-client searching, with varying degrees of in-context instruction, all the way to complete, client do-it-yourself searching at the other end. A professional librarian should not practice only at one extreme or the other. The development of user-friendly search systems for the non-information professional has had the effect of raising the complexity of searches professionals do for their clients because the clients are more likely to do the quick-and-dirty searches themselves. Sometimes the quest must be owned by the librarian, sometimes it is shared by the librarian and the client, sometimes it is taught by the librarian, sometimes it is witnessed by the librarian, and sometimes library quests are completely invisible to the librarian (Atlas, 2000). In any case, Agile Librarians never abandon clients to fend for themselves without any alternative, nor do they take all control of searches away from clients.

The fourth stage of the traditional reference interview is the delivery of documents or information to the client. Clients want documents containing the information they need, and usually they will be satisfied with less reliable, full-text documents online more than with citations to better but less accessible documents. The menu is not a substitute for the meal; it is only a finding aid.

An important value-added professional service that delights clients is the management of retrieval. Often the librarian will deliver to the client a range of documents, or perhaps citations and Web site addresses, representing the variety of information available. In some circumstances, based on the earlier parts of the interview, the librarian will filter retrieval to more closely fit the needs of the client. This filtering may include any of the materials evaluation standards practiced by librarians or standards requested by the client. In any case, it isn't based on the personal opinion of the librarian on the subject. Within the limits of Copyright Law and Guidelines, the librarian may repackage documents, highlight pertinent passages related to the client's need, and add material that in some way makes the documents easier to use. For material beyond the client's expertise, the librarian might provide dictionary definitions, textbook explanations, or other background material to help the client understand the findings of an esoteric research study. To carry on the restaurant analogy, the diner is delighted not just with the ingredients in the dish, but with both its preparation and its presentation.

The final stage is often called the "closing," but the Agile Librarian uses it as an "opening." The librarian must find out *from the client* if the material completely answers the question. Without client evaluation, the librarian's perception of the success of the consultation may be completely wrong. Although much briefer, this client evaluation of the results is as important as the original question exploration. During the evaluation, both client and librarian may discover needs that weren't developed during the original discussion. Steps 2 through 4 of the process may have to be repeated before successful closure is achieved.

Equally important, the librarian must make it clear that this professional relationship does not end here and now with the completion of this particular quest. The librarian must emphasize that the client is welcome to ask again and often will back up that offer with a description of when and how the client can reach professional information services in the future. The Agile Librarian may later ask the client again how useful the results were and offer continued support.

At any stage in the reference interview, the professional librarian will avoid the sloppy work of what Ross and Dewdney call "negative closure" (Ross and Dewdney, 1998). Here are some examples of unprofessional neglect of the patron experience: "The librarian may bypass or abbreviate the reference interview. The librarian may take a system-based perspective, saying something like 'Have you checked . . . [library specific resources]?'" At issue is not the patron in the life of the library, but the library in the life of the patron. The professional librarian will avoid the unmonitored referral or sending the client to a source, such as a section of the library, a book, a Web site, a person or another information service, without checking to see if the client's search was successful.

The worst examples of unethical, negative closure are clear expressions of the librarian's desire to get rid of the client. The Rigid Librarian may categorically state that what the client needs does not exist, may send the client someplace else as quickly as possible, or may haughtily imply that the client should have found it without help and not bothered the librarian. In person, this may be expressed more in body language and vocal tone than in actual words. Other examples of negative closure include giving the client more easily found information than what the user really needs, giving up too early in the search without any further referral, and disappearing before the transaction is fully concluded (Kluegel and others, 2003). For further reading, see Ross, Nilsen, and Dewdney (2002), *Conducting the Reference Interview: A How-To-Do-It Manual for Librarians*; Janes (2003), *Introduction to Reference Work in the Digital Age*; and Bopp and Smith (2001), *Reference and Information Services: An Introduction*.

It is no accident that the process of delighting clients begins and ends with information needs analysis, asking clients for their input both before and after providing them with information services. The processes of marketing, quality improvement, and evidence-based librarianship follow the same pattern of asking, studying, acting, and asking again, a pattern not unlike that of scientific research.

Remove Service Rules as Barriers to Client Delight

Are service rules designed to maximize clients' access to information and information services, or are they attempts to prevent the repetition of undesirable behavior of a few individuals? Clients are not some kind of wild things that must be tamed to make life more convenient for library staff. Some policies are necessary to promote good service, but the survival of traditional rules and restrictions that routinely discourage people from using services can and should be seriously questioned. Examples of such rules include severely limiting the number of books a young child may check out and mandating that if a person has a single overdue item, that person may not check out anything else.

Commercial businesses realize that if their customers are not satisfied, they will go out of business. So they study customer behavior and design service delivery models that are better than those of their competitors. Customers will accept a service of lesser quality if it is more convenient than a better one. What can librarians learn from how the business world has used research to improve service delivery?

Location, Location, Location

Location is more than a matter of online sites and branch libraries. Long ago banks and post offices realized the utility of putting mailboxes and ATMs where people spend their time. Allowing the return of physical materials only at the physical library is for the convenience of the library staff, not the convenience of the clients. Some school and special librarians collect materials at pick-up and drop-off points around their buildings. Larger libraries with branches have delivery routes between branches that could include pick-up and drop-off points in other locations. That's more client-centered service.

Professional Web site design includes considerable user testing to develop a user-centric environment. Those same practices are important in the design and redesign of all library service delivery models.

Librarians in any kind of library should take advantage of opportunities to make what could be termed "house calls" or "open house events" to visit their clients where they do the business that the library service is designed to support. When university libraries have blended the collections of small departmental branches into the main library, it has become more important than ever for the subject liaison librarians to spend time, and perhaps even hold formal office hours, in the departments they serve. Any librarian can learn from visiting clients outside of the library space, especially if they make visits that include as much asking and listening as telling and promoting.

Self-Service, Assisted Service, or Professional Service?

It doesn't have to be either one or the other. Some clients need the time-saving efficiency of doing the search themselves using professionally designed systems as tools to meet their goals. But anyone who has ever been caught in the purgatory of FAQ "help" knows how important it is sometimes to chat with an empathetic and knowledgeable person! Perhaps the most important feature of a self-service system is quick and easy access to personal help.

People have a right to learn what they need to know when they need to know it. All librarians have to teach. Instructions in a brochure or on a Web page no more constitute teaching than does giving someone a textbook. That does not mean that there isn't an important role for well-written and accessible client instructions; it does mean that whatever library access service a person is using, they have a right to expert help. Often the truly teachable moment comes not during a lesson or an orientation presentation, but during the time of information need.

People also have a right to know the level of expertise of the person to whom they are talking. Not everyone who works in a hospital is a nurse, and not everyone who works in a library is a librarian. Staff and paraprofessionals provide important services to library clients, but, like the patient who never sees a doctor, they are not getting professional service if they never see a librarian.

People have a right to system interfaces that are friendly to a variety of people. Just as there is no one best dictionary for all uses, there is no one-size-fits-all interface. Catalog and database interfaces developed for regular professional use are very important, but so are interfaces to the same records and data for the professional who is an intermittent user or a novice user of that particular system. By the same token, the naïve user needs interfaces to the same information that are appropriate for his use as a novice, intermittent, or regular user (McKnight, 2008).

Traditions and Habits: Gateways or Barriers?

It is all too easy to mistake habits for lofty library traditions. Frances K. Groen writes that the three values of librarianship that began in antiquity and will continue far into the future are access to information, promotion of literacy, and preservation of the accumulated wisdom of the past (Groen, 2007). The history of librarianship describes many different ways to uphold these values that were invented and discarded in the past, and undoubtedly there will be many new ones in the future.

Are today's service models always designed to maximize clients' access to information and information services, or are they solely means to simplify the lives of staff? Are they remnants of needs and problems that used to exist in library services but don't anymore? One metaphor for practices and procedures that are not only outdated but also counter-productive to upholding the traditional values is what Karen Hyman (1999) of the South Jersey Regional Library Cooperative, calls the "Rule of 1965." The choice of a particular year for this rule isn't as important as is the attitude it illustrates. The rule has three parts: "Anything the library did prior to 1965 is basic; everything else is extra. Any new service must be offered begrudgingly for decades. Patrons must jump through hoops to get it." Her examples include, "You charge handling fees for 'individual services' like interlibrary loans" and "You offer services that you don't publicize because too many people might want them." Most librarians (and, unfortunately, their clients) can think of more examples. Is it any wonder that people in communities stuck with such nonsense pass up libraries for commercial enterprises that do advertise their new, more convenient services? She suggests positive steps to defeating the "Rule of 1965":

1. Remember that the customer is not the enemy.
2. Create a climate in your library that supports change.
3. Survey the environment continuously.
4. Redirect resources.
5. Treat every customer like a person.

Obviously well aware of common objections to the development of new, client-centered services, she suggests five easy questions and their most common answers when librarians are considering offering new services:

Do you have the skills? No.
Do you have the time? No.
Do you have the resources? No.
Is it difficult to manage? Yes.
Can it be abused? Yes

And then she writes "None of the above is a reason not to do something, because the answers are always the same for any significant change" (Hyman, 1999). Think about that last statement for a few minutes.

From a technical services perspective, Rick Anderson, Associate Director for Scholarly Resources and Collections in the Marriott Library at the University of Utah, writes:

> Library services that are designed to meet the problem of information scarcity seem irrelevant to today's user, who sees the information world as a place of dizzying, kaleidoscopic abundance—a place where the challenge is to pluck the answer to one's question from a huge pile of readily available information, not one where the answer can only be found in one or two places and must be laboriously sought out. (Anderson, 2007, p. 190)

He describes his view of libraries and their condition:

> Libraries exist to help patrons. Patrons have alternatives to libraries that did not exist until very recently. If we want to be useful to those we are here to serve, then we have to deal with the fact that we are now in a competitive situation. If our resources and services are less attractive to researchers than the growing array of alternatives, then they will stop using our resources and services. (Anderson, 2007, p. 198)

He tells us we might think that our resources are better than others that appear to be free and easy to use, but he reminds us that "those alternatives are getting better, more comprehensive, and more easy to use every day. Can we say the same for our services[?]" (Anderson, 2007, p. 198).

A long time ago, subscription libraries issued users tokens that they would leave at the library when they took out a book. When they returned the book, they could take out another or receive their token back to use another day. There were no due dates. Recently, when online services that mailed DVDs to their customers introduced a similar system of limited simultaneous borrowing rather than due dates, the store-based DVD rental companies had to change their rental period terms significantly, essentially eliminating overdue charges and replacing them with an automatic purchase after a certain period of time. Meanwhile, library overdue fine policies continue to annoy people who check out many books, without having much good effect at all on clients' patterns of returning borrowed materials (Eberhart, 1999; Heeger, 2007; Pierce 2006).

Have you ever been at a party, and, when introduced to someone as a librarian, seen a look cross his face? Is it the same look that would cross his face had you been introduced as a deduction investigator for the Internal Revenue Service? It's a ghost of a memory of the shame of having had the dreaded overdue book. They don't even have to say the word "overdue." My response is to laugh and say, "You know, the only people who never have overdue books are people who aren't smart enough to [or who never] use libraries," and the ice is broken.

Collecting fines costs many libraries more than they recover while perpetuating the illusion people have that libraries are so inexpensive to run that fines make up a large portion of their budgeted income. In short, fines for keeping borrowed material too long tend to discourage potential clients from ever using library services at all. They would rather pay a charge to a commercial organization to rent or buy material than to risk a usually cheaper fine from a library. New technologies are making it possible for people to download books, movies, music, and serials to various devices for less than the cost of some library fines, or even for free. Potential clients see purchasing a book as making a positive decision up front, whereas they view paying a library fine of lesser value as the library staff punishing them. Such a fine of a few cents or dollars can be very expensive to library services in the long run when the disgruntled victim comes to be in a position that affects library funding. Circulation policies should encourage, not discourage, clients' access to materials in a library collection. Agile Librarians provide clients with more than a circulation service they cannot get from home.

When?

"Banker's hours" were once a barrier to financial services for many people. When bank employees had to spend a lot of time doing calculations by hand or with mechanical adding machines, they could offer public services for only a few hours each day (not convenient for people who also worked during those hours). With automation, they could and did shift their time and attention to individualized services. Now when a person decides to buy a new car on a Saturday, they can explore financing options and complete a borrowing transaction that very day. Like many businesses, their policies for service hours are customer-centric.

Customer-centered businesses schedule more staff for times when their traffic is the heaviest, even if it is not the most convenient time for the staff. Yet many libraries not only keep the same service hours as they did before automation, but also schedule staff more by tradition than by client needs. For instance, some academic libraries have no professional staff available at all on nights and weekends, the only time when working part-time students can use services restricted to the library space. Some Agile Librarians are developing services for students of all ages on nights and weekends, even in cooperative online services. Thinking of library services in the life of the client rather than just thinking of the client in the life of the library removes barriers and makes all the difference.

When the last book of the Harry Potter series was first available for sale, thousands of bookstores stayed open past midnight. Some even opened just before midnight for customers who wanted the book immediately, even though few of these stores were normally open those hours. Some of their customers drove home that Friday night past darkened libraries that had copies of the books in boxes, books that would not be processed until the following Monday when technical staff reported for work, books that might not even be available to check out that day. Only a few public libraries were customer-centric enough to have their own Potter parties and check out copies with quickly done temporary processing that night! What is wrong with this picture?

Writing for technical services librarians, Rick Anderson urges the development of "patron centered workflow . . . designed with patrons, not librarians in mind. . . . Are we putting work on our patrons that the library staff could reasonably do instead? Are we delaying the end result unnecessarily?" He urges procedures that have a high level of efficiency, are cost effective, and focus on the "speed-to-stacks" (Anderson, 2007, p. 193–194). With the existing level of library automation, boxes of Harry Potter books could have been opened just as they were in book stores and checked out in a few minutes.

Ambience and Attitude

Clients are delighted when they have few bureaucratic barriers to what they want and need. So are librarians. Systems, like OPACs, designed for librarians have printers for librarians, yet clients using terminals for the same systems find themselves scrambling for pencil and paper to write down the information they find on the screen! Client-centered librarians not only provide them with intuitively obvious interfaces and some terminals *in* the stacks, but also with immediate print-outs that include instructions for finding the identified items.

Traditional bans against all food and drink in library buildings are good examples of policies that create barriers for clients. Spilled liquids can destroy computer equipment. Fast food leftovers can introduce noxious smells and attract vermin. Everyone agrees that rare archival material and some permanent print collections must be protected from damage that would limit their use in future generations. Yet many large academic research libraries that allow beverages in spill proof containers have discovered that "clean up in stack 4!" is rare and well worth the positive benefits to people who need to work in the library for hours. Small corporate and hospital libraries often encourage staff to bring their lunch to the library, because lunch time may be their only on-the-job opportunity

---

It's Closing Time

It's been a terrible Friday for you at the small Clinton Public Library. The Children's Librarian and a paraprofessional both called in sick today. You've not even had time for a full lunch hour and are glad that the library closes in less than a half hour, earlier than it does on other week nights.

(a) Someone you've never seen before comes in and asks you "Is this the Clinton Public Library?" What should you say and how should you say it?

(b) A few minutes later, a high school student you've helped off and on for a couple of hours comes up to you and says, "I still can't find anything for my paper on teenage parenthood." What should you say and do next?

(c) You've made an announcement that the library will close in 10 minutes. The mayor walks in. He asks for some detailed census information about the city. He's been in meetings all afternoon with the planning commission. They've taken a break for dinner and he wants to go back in an hour with either verification or refutation of some of the information they've been presenting. What should you say and do?

The Rigid Librarian would not delight any of these people, but would take offense at the first and shoo away the other two. The Agile Librarian would understand that the person in situation (a) was just opening a conversation, not making a stupid remark, and the reference interview would begin. The student in (b) and the mayor in (c) both need professional service and they need it now. Even though the doors will be locked and the hourly staff will leave at closing time, the professional librarian will continue working with both of them a little longer. They will both be delighted, and they will remember.

to leave the office or patient care unit. Teachers may gather to eat their lunch in a school library, giving the librarian an excellent informal opportunity to learn what's happening in the school and what specific materials and services teachers and students need. Some larger libraries have successfully added cafés.

Jeannette Woodward writes that although the collections of Carnegie-funded public libraries were originally assumed to be permanent, public library collections today are very dynamic. Acquisition, weeding, and loss ensure that most of the current collection will be gone in a decade. So some rules that grew out of the "permanent collection" tradition may be irrelevant, even counter-productive, today. She asserts:

> If you were to ask many people to describe a favorite pastime, they would picture themselves curled up in a large, cozy armchair, possibly by the fire, with a good book and a favorite hot drink. In other words, libraries check out books to people who take them home and enjoy them in just such an environment. To make matters worse, they are likely to read them with breakfast, lunch, dinner and snacks. If we're honest, we must admit that we do the same thing ourselves. It is really impossible to keep books and food apart unless we never let them out of their hermetically sealed environments. (Woodward, 2005, p. 196)

Delighted clients are more than satisfied with their experiences. They can be confident that services and spaces are for them, not for some ideal angelic being. Through client-centered services, they encounter accommodations instead of physical, intellectual, linguistic, and other barriers.

Agile Librarians think beyond serving clients in a professional relationship, Agile Librarians delight the population of people for which the library service exists. These clients experience information services unavailable anyplace else, with unprecedented accessibility and quality, and they know it immediately, just as they recognize good service in a high-quality restaurant. Services, procedures, and collections must be designed for the clients and not for the librarians' convenience or personal interests. All of the professional, political, marketing, and business skills featured in the rest of this book are meaningless if the clients are not delighted.

Summary

Agile Librarians delight their clients. They extend their services to wherever their clients live and work. They provide information services that clients experience as positive because Agile Librarians know that such experiences are keys to library survival. Libraries exist because of clients' needs, and the client-centered approach emphasizes the engagement of professional services more than just the passive creation of systems in the hope that someone might use them.

Agile Librarians use many techniques to study and analyze information needs of both groups and individuals in their constantly changing, unique situations. Then they satisfy those needs, removing as many barriers to information services as possible. They save their clients' time and tailor their services for their clients not just through reactive responses to requests but through proactive provision of delightful information services.

References

Allen, Bryce L. 1996. *Information Tasks: Toward a User-Centered Approach to Information Systems.* San Diego: Academic Press.

Anderson, Rick. 2007. It's Not About the Workflow: Patron-Centered Practices for 21st Century Serialists. *Serials Librarian* 51:189–199.

Atlas, Michel C. 2000. The Rise and Fall of the Medical Mediated Searcher," *Bulletin of the Medical Library Association* 88:26–35.

Baez, Joan. 1969. *Daybreak.* New York: Avon Books.

Bopp, Richard E. and Linda C. Smith. 2001. *Reference and Information Services: An Introduction.* 3rd ed. Englewood, CO: Libraries Unlimited. [The 4th edition is expected to be published in 2010.]

Burch, Karen. 2007. Tips from Your Colleagues: Series Series. *Library Media Connection* 26:8.

Case, Donald O. 2002. *Looking for Information: A Survey of Research on Information Seeking Needs and Behavior.* Amsterdam: Academic Press.

Davenport, Elisabeth and Blaise Cronin. 1998. Texts at Work: Some Thoughts on "Just for You" Service in the Context of Domain Expertise. *Journal of Education for Library and Information Science* 39:264–274.

Driscoll, Lori. 2005. Technology for Access Services: Patron Self-Checkout. *Journal of Access Services* 3:85–87.

Eberhart, George. 1999. To Fine or Not to Fine. *American Libraries* 30:75–78.

Eldredge, Jonathan D. 2000. Evidence-Based Librarianship: An Overview. *Bulletin of the Medical Library Association* 88:289–302.

Groen, Frances K. 2007. *Access to Medical Knowledge: Libraries, Digitization, and the Public Good.* Lanham, MD: Scarecrow Press.

Heeger, Paula Brehm. 2007. Better Late Than Never: Late Fines Stop Teens from Coming to the Library. *School Library Journal* 53:30.

Hyman, Karen. 1999. Customer Service and the "Rule of 1965." *American Libraries* 30:55–58.

Janes, Joseph. 2003. *Introduction to Reference Work in the Digital Age.* New York: Neal-Schuman.

Kassel, Amelia. 2002. Value-Added Deliverables: Rungs on the Info Pro's Ladder to Success. *SEARCHER: The Magazine for Database Professionals* 10:42–53.

Kluegel, Kathleen, Catherine Sheldrick Ross, Jana Ronan, Kathleen Kern, and David Tyckoson. 2003. The Reference Interview: Connecting in Person and in Cyberspace. *Reference & User Services Quarterly* 43:37–51.

Kuhlthau, Carol Collier. 1988a. Longitudinal Case Studies of the Information Search Process of Users in Libraries. *Library & Information Science Research* 10:257–304.

———. 1988b. Developing a Model of the Library Search Process: Cognitive and Affective Aspects. *RQ* 28:232–242.

———. 1991. Inside the Search Process: Information Seeking from the User's Perspective. *Journal of the American Society for Information Science* 42:361–371.

———. 1993. A Principle of Uncertainty for Information Seeking." *Journal of Documentation* 49:339–353.

———. 2004. *Seeking Meaning: A Process Approach to Library and Information Services,* 2nd ed. Westport, CT: Libraries Unlimited

Lubans, John L. 1994. Sherlock's Dog, or Managers and Mess Finding. *Library Administration & Management* 8:139–149.

Maybee, Clarence. 2007. Understanding Our Student Learners: A Phenomenographic Study Revealing the Ways that Undergraduate Women at Mills College Understand Using Information. *Reference Services Review* 35:452–462.

McKnight, Michelynn. 2001. Beyond Surveys: Finding Out Why. *Journal of Hospital Librarianship* 1:31–40.

———. 2008. Not Just Another Pretty Interface: Expert Information Searching and Retrieval. *Journal of Hospital Librarianship* 8(2):155–174.

McKnight, Michelynn and Martha Peet. 2000. Health Care Providers' Information Seeking Behaviors: A Review of Recent Literature. *Medical Reference Services Quarterly* 19:27–50.

Morris, Ruth T. 1994. Toward a User-Centered Information Service. *Journal of the American Society for Information Science* 45:20–30.

Nardi, Bonnie A. and Vicki O'Day. 1996. Intelligent Agents: What We Learned at the Library. *Libri* 46:59–88.

Palmer, Carole L. 1999. Aligning Studies of Information Seeking and Use with Domain Analysis. *Journal of the American Society for Information Science* 50:1139–1140.

Pierce, Jennifer Burek. 2006. Grassroots Report: A Fine Madness. *American Libraries* 37:45.

Ross, Catherine Sheldrick, Kirsti Nilsen, and Patricia Dewdney. 2002. *Conducting the Reference Interview: A How-To-Do-It Manual for Librarians.* New York: Neal-Schuman.

Ross, Catherine Sheldrick and Patricia Dewdney. 1998. Negative Closure: Strategies and Counter-Strategies in the Reference Transaction. *Reference & User Services Quarterly* 38:151–159.

Strong, Gary E. 2006. If We Change It—Will They Come? *Reference Services Review* 34:333–339.

Tenopir, Carol. 2003. *Use and Users of Electronic Library Resources: An Overview and Analysis of Recent Research Studies.* Washington, DC: Council on Library and Information Resources.

Woodward, Jeannette. 2005. *Creating the Customer-Driven Library: Building on the Bookstore Model.* Chicago: American Library Association.

Chapter 3

Expanding Your Political Influence

Thriving librarians in dynamic libraries have influence in their organizations. People know them and are interested in their opinions. Why are budgets and staff cut for libraries with excellent professional service, strong support for the institutional mission, and delighted customers? They are cut because, at some level, the librarians do not have enough influence. Influence is a factor in any relationship between two or more people, and the more people involved, the greater the complexities of influence.

Serious consideration of politics, the influence that can make changes within the organization and its immediate social environment, is not optional. The librarian who thinks the library is somehow above or unrelated to such issues will be baffled when the axe falls. And yet, "Education for librarians rarely includes guidance on political maneuvering within an organization and many librarians find that such behavior does not come naturally" (Walker, 1994, p. 320).

Just as water and fire can support or destroy life in nature, influence is a basic element of professional practice that can be used positively and creatively or used destructively and negatively. Careful and constant consideration of intra-, inter-, and extra-institutional influences helps the Agile Librarian know when and how to take action. Without that knowledge, the library may be crushed or left behind as the organization changes. "If they cut back on library services, they'll miss what they had and it will serve them right" is not a viable professional political plan.

Organizational political savvy is important for librarians because it directly affects budgeting for all library services, collections, buildings, and programs. "We can't afford that" usually is a political euphemism for "We value other things more than that." Organizational funds are always limited to some extent, and there are influential factors that determine how those funds are allocated. Money may seem hard to get, but influence to increase that funding has to come first. This chapter presents some insights into taking opportunities to build organizational influence before budget crises happen.

Usually, increased influence (perceived value to decision makers) precedes increased budgets. Daniel Goleman, in *Working with Emotional Intelligence* (1998,

p. 163–197), describes the art of influence as making use of the contagion of emotions involved in

- "wielding effective tactics for persuasion"
- "listening openly and sending convincing messages"
- "negotiating and resolving disagreements"
- "inspiring and guiding individuals and groups"
- "initiating or managing change"

These are not minor skills one just naturally stumbles into. People who are good at influence have mastered skills in winning people over; fine-tuning presentations to appeal directly to the listener; using less obvious tactics, such as indirect influence, to build consensus and support; and actually orchestrating events to make a point. They can function well in give-and-take, notice emotional cues, make minor adjustments as necessary, and do not dodge difficult issues. They listen well and handle "tense situations with diplomacy and tact." Such people can "articulate and arouse enthusiasm for a shared vision and mission" and take the initiative to lead no matter what their official position. They not only recognize the need for change, but also remove barriers, bring others into the change process, and make needed changes in themselves (Goleman, 1998, p. 163–197). These arts are essential for the Agile Librarian.

Notice that very influential people who get things done may not have much official power or authority. "*Influence* is the ability to use examples or actions to cause others to change their behavior, something charismatic leaders often can do. *Power* is the ability to do something. *Authority* is the right to do something" (Evans, Ward, and Rugass, 2000, p. 194). Influential people can be found at every level of an organizational structure. An influential librarian can thrive anywhere on the organization chart. Bellman, in *Getting Things Done When You Are Not in Charge* (2001), and Fisher and Sharp, with *Getting It Done: How to Lead When You're Not in Charge* (1998), offer advice on how this can be done.

The darker side of politics, persuasive manipulation of people's good nature for personal or corporate gain, is presented in Robert B. Cialdini's *Influence: Science and Practice*. This is not a treatise on the use and growth of a ruler's power, but rather a discussion of the commercial use of commonly accepted social behaviors to manipulate compliance. These weapons of influence include the leveraged use of societal values of reciprocity, that is, the "free gift" that obligates one to make a purchase or donation; commitment to a course of action even after it becomes obvious that it's a bad idea; social proof that everyone is doing it; trust of a likeable personality; trust of authority figures; and scarcity. An example of artificial scarcity is a toy that is heavily advertised before Christmas but distributed to retailers in small quantities until after Christmas. Children clamor for the toys, which their parents can't obtain. So the parents buy other toys before Christmas as well as the scarce toy after Christmas (Cialdini, 2001). Political literacy includes the ability to discern when such techniques are used. Even nonprofit and charitable organizations use them.

The important thing is to learn how to use influential skills for good. Even some of the classic techniques of propaganda, for instance, repetition, simplification, glittering generalities, euphoria, slogans, and testimonials, sometimes can be used ethically and positively as well as negatively. Others, such as the big lie, scapegoating, and appeals to fear and prejudice, are not so versatile. Jowett and O'Donnell in *Propaganda and Persuasion* (2005) provide an academic study of such techniques.

In *Office Politics: Positive Results from Fair Practices*, Rebecca Luhn Wolfe contrasts the use and misuse of influence with the following good and bad effects:

Strengthen communications . . . or promote power games
Make business deals work . . . or make negotiations difficult
Help people find creative solutions . . . or hamper productivity and creativity
Increase influence . . . or undermine authority
Create an atmosphere of respect . . . or create bad feelings
Help people avoid destructive behavior . . . or encourage vicious smear campaigns
Make employees adaptable to change . . . or hurt healthy corporate climates
Offer competitive career advantage . . . or bring out the worst in obsessive people
Build self-confidence . . . or weaken the naïve and already weak
Foster excellence and innovation . . . or encourage lying and deception (Wolfe, 1996, p. 7)

Furthermore, she encourages professionals to look and act calm even when outraged, to show respect to all people at all levels of work, to refrain from revealing details about personal feelings, to say the right thing always, and to believe that honesty has its own rewards (Wolfe, 1996, p. 5).

Librarians do not build influence or funding by accident, nor can they assume that their services will be appreciated for their own sake. The Agile Librarian does not wait demurely for some benefactor and understands that neither constant vociferous complaints nor unrealistic positive hyperbole will be effective.

Effective Organizational Politics

Wolfe (1996, p. 4) presents five deceptively simple sounding rules that everyone can use in any school or business to build influence:

Understand your corporate system
Know when to hold and when to fold
Believe in win-win situations
Play fair
Think first, act later

Understand Your Corporate System

The first step of influence building and political savvy is to know thoroughly and understand completely the organization and its culture. Every organization has both a formal, visible, influence structure and another informal, and equally powerful, invisible one. It is easier to inspect the first, but we always have to consider the second as well. Both are often in a state of constant change.

In addition to the military hierarchical pyramid, organizations can have many different formal structures. Some in different shapes, such as hub and spokes or concentric circles, have clear lines of authority, whereas others may be organized into more organic teams. The style of the structure within the library may differ from the larger structure of the parent organization. The informal structures of every organization are important but less obvious. Documentary evidence of organizational structure is often out-of-date or out-of-touch with reality. The Agile Librarian observes behavior patterns, rituals, territorial customs such as who gets what office or parking space, and the organization's stories and myths. In addition to the documented mission statements, ethics codes, goals, and statements of values, there are expected styles of conduct and relationships. (Stueart and Moran, 2007).

Who really are the influential people in the organization? Do the "Who's Who and What Have You Done for Me Lately?" exercise shown below. Then explore who some of the influential people are that are not on the organization chart. Some will simply be people whose opinion everyone respects. Some will be effective gatekeepers, such as administrative assistants. Regardless of positions on organization charts, some combinations of people will be old friends and some will have adversarial relationships.

Learning both the official policy and the real values of the organization is a savvy librarian's continuing responsibility. Mission statements are important, but they usually paint a picture of the parent institution's purpose that is a broad, vague, and glittering generality, a common propaganda technique. Keen observation will reveal more than the mission statement.

Not only does the school, department, or corporation

EXERCISE:
Who's Who and
What Have You Done for Me Lately?

1. Drawing and completing the "Who's Who" chart

a. On a blank sheet of paper, write your name and title in a box about two-thirds of the way down the page.

b. FROM MEMORY, write down the names and titles of each person above you in the organizational hierarchy in boxes, one above the other connected by lines. In a public library, this chart should include not only the library and library board, but also the elected and appointed officials of the municipality or county to which the library belongs. Librarians working in school libraries or small branch campuses should include officials in the larger system. Librarians in university, corporate, and state libraries may have more obvious organizational hierarchies. In any case, this who's who will most likely include people you don't see every day.

c. FROM MEMORY, draw lines and boxes horizontally with the names and titles of your peers. These people may be competing for the same funds and resources you are and may be possibilities for building alliances.

d. Draw lines and boxes below your name for the names and titles of the people who answer to you. Surely you can do that from memory!

e. Draw horizontal lines and boxes representing your immediate boss's peers

f. Now, find out and add to the chart all the names and titles that should be there that you don't know. An official organization chart will be useful, but it is often incomplete, out of date, or both. Web sites and printed directories are also often out-of-date. Who or what is your best source of up-to-date "Who's Who" information? An administrative assistant in the appropriate division somewhere probably is more up to date. Administrative assistants are good to know!

(Continued)

have a mission, but everyone who works in its corporate structure has a more specialized and personalized vision of how it ought to work. Each librarian has one, too. The Agile Librarian has to watch, listen, ask around, and consider. It's best to follow policy unless one really is in a position to change it or strongly influence its change. That means that the librarian can influence an administrative ally to share the understood need for change. Librarians have "shot themselves in the foot" by bringing a proposed change to the very person who had opposite goals. For instance, the public librarian who wants to increase the library's circulation of recorded movies won't find an ally in the trustee who owns a movie rental business. A little homework would have prevented that expensive gaff!

Library board and administrative perspectives change. Principals may return from a conference with a changed vision for the school or for how they want to communicate with teachers and staff. Changes can be a matter of style and packaging or they may be deep changes in values. Librarians who have worked in the same place for a few years can easily fall into the trap of believing that how things get done now is exactly the same as how it was five years ago. Even in the rare cases in which the administrators are still all the same people, administrative perspectives change. In "Politics of the Library of the Future," Mara Niels recommends regularly checking to see if the librarian's priorities are consistent with those of the current administration. Ideas that might have been important only a

2. What have you done for me lately?

a. Circle the names of all of those people with whom you've had a pleasant face-to-face conversation within the past three months. Congratulate yourself.

b. Put big stars next to the names of each of these people with whom you've not had a positive face-to-face conversation in the past year. Put even bigger stars next to the names of people with whom you've never had such a conversation. Plan now for how you are going to talk with them in the near future! (See True Story on the next page.) If you work for a library, institution, or corporation that is widespread geographically, you may have to make do with a telephone conversation. In any case, unrecorded synchronous conversation is preferably to one without immediate feedback.

c. Put a check mark next to the names of all of those who have used your professional services. All of the others are some kind of stakeholder and are important potential clients. I like the term "potential clients" rather than "non-users." Ask people you trust to tell you more about them. Start contacting these potential clients to find out what professional information service would help make them look good. If the organization is too big for you to get to all of them, prioritize and go first to those who can most help and be helped by the library. If distance makes face-to-face interaction impossible, use e-mail to make an appointment for a phone call. In any case, make positive personal contact. You know that their ignorance of what library services can do for them is not their fault.

Although not every conversation will have an obvious immediate effect on library services, making some connection is always better than none. Most organizations have a lot of turnover, making it difficult to keep up with who's who; but it is still important. What you *don't* want to happen is to have your first interaction with an influential person, or the first thing they hear about you, to be negative. First impressions do count! If you don't plan a positive interaction, a negative one may happen when you least expect it.

True Story

When I taught the "Proving Your Worth" class mentioned in the Preface, I often asked myself if I was really following my own advice. I took the action in the following story immediately after one of those classes.

I had good relations with and was doing searches for all of the vice presidents of my hospital except one. The word in the building was to keep your head low and try to stay off his radar. His reputation was for micromanagement and making sudden, unreasonable demands. I was perfectly comfortable with my own vice president and ordinarily had no need to deal with this one. I really didn't want to make "the visit," but this was a test of my integrity, the integration of what I said with what I did.

So I initiated my normal routine for new vice presidents, directors, and other administrators. First I called his administrative assistant to make an appointment for 20 minutes of his time. As I expected, she asked the purpose of the visit, and as planned I replied politely that I would share that with him at the time. You probably can get by with this only once per administrative assistant! I arrived for the appointment well prepared, well dressed, and bearing gifts such as a library mug stuffed with brochures and library logo clips. As usual with this kind of introductory visit, the first thing I said was that I did *not* come to complain about anything. At this point the executive usually appeared to relax. I hoped he knew I was on no indignant mission, yet he probably was still a little suspicious of me, wondering exactly why I was there. To put him more at ease, I told him that I realized I hadn't had the opportunity to chat with him much and wanted to know what was on his mind. He relaxed and sat back in his chair. As in a reference interview, I asked some open-ended questions about his vision for the institution and his concerns about its problems. I listened carefully and asked appropriate questions for clarification. Then, when the time was right, I gave some examples of some specific ways we could get him information to support his decisions. I slipped in something about how often we looked up facts for the other vice presidents. He asked, of course, what they had requested, and I answered with a smile and a reassuring explanation that all library information requests are confidential, both his and everyone else's. I jokingly said I wasn't leaving the office until he had set me on a quest. As most people do in this situation, he gave me a challenge. I went right to work on it, networking with a couple of librarians who specialize in the area of his question, and personally delivered the material to his office by the end of the day. He sent me an e-mail saying that it was helpful, I crossed that objective off of my list, breathed a sigh of relief, and went on to thinking about other things. I had done my "know, tell, and show." I could put a check mark next to his name on my chart.

(Continued)

few years ago may seem totally off base today (Niels, 1990, p. 408).

Ferret out and read reports and plans, even if you think that they don't affect the library. Beware of thinking of the library in isolation from other parts of the community, school, or institution. If a department appears to be unrelated, there's an opportunity for growth in that direction. Successful library service really serves and is influential in every corner of the organization.

Sometimes leaders declare organizations to be team-oriented that are, in practice, very hierarchical, and vice versa. In any case, it pays to be aware of organizational cousins, the people and their departments that are parallel to the library. These people and departments are seeking resources from the same pool as the librarians. How are these cousins' goals similar to those of library services? What do they need? How are they different? How can they work with librarians as colleagues rather than as competitors? One thing for sure is that to have any influence at all, the Agile Librarian must understand how library services can, do, must, and should fit in with other perspectives in the community they serve.

Know When to Hold and When to Fold

No one has an unlimited supply of influence or political power. It's an asset one saves or spends. Some activities build a reserve of such capital and some draw on that reserve, so the Agile Librarian has to be careful how it is used. Occasionally, something happens beyond one's control. One cannot and should not try to please everyone at all times, but there is a high cost to being unnecessarily confrontational.

As often happens in the corporate world, there had been reorganization rumors flying around for weeks, and it was not a big surprise when we had a meeting a month later to unveil the new organization chart. Guess who my new boss was? At the first meeting of the people newly reporting to him, I could feel some anxiety in the room. I was pleased when he praised our library services to the others and told them that the librarians would be very helpful in both finding what they needed and in keeping their requests confidential. This vice president and I worked very well together for several years because we started out with a positive history of mutual respect and communicated often.

My important, but not urgent, appointment would never have been effective had it occurred after the reorganization, when it would have been both important and urgent. My boss had been a satisfied client *before* he was my boss, so we started in a position of positive influence with each other that carried us both through the inevitable challenges that followed.

This story has an exceptional postscript. In the normal course of corporate life, this boss moved on to a position of more responsibility in another organization in another state. A few years later, I was teaching a class in that state when a librarian came up to me during the break to ask if I had ever worked for this person at my hospital. She smiled when I said yes. Then she said "So *that's* why one of the first things he did when he arrived was to increase the library budget!"

The pejorative term "politically correct" comes from the valid practice of avoiding unnecessarily offending an individual or group of individuals because of the political and influential expense of such an action. For instance, when unsuccessful job applicants ask employers why they did not get the job, "because you are overqualified" or "because you don't have enough experience" is often a polite political euphemism for "we made the best choice we could from the pool of applicants we had, and you weren't it." The employer does not want to insult or hurt the applicant, and this is a way to avoid the political cost of doing so. Only the naïve job seeker takes such comments at face value. The practice backfires if an influential or politically powerful contingent believes that particular avoidance of offense to be disingenuous, insincere, or unnecessary.

Any group of people can have conflicts and differences of opinion. Personality conflicts and issues are other political euphemisms. Wolfe writes "Knowing when to hold tight to your beliefs and when to concede is a valuable skill. Since neither way is always right or wrong, you must be flexible" (Wolfe, 1996, p. 4). The wise professional actively and carefully picks issues to pursue. They are valuable opportunities for wise decisions that can increase or decrease one's accumulated political capital. Neither fighting every possible battle nor retreating from all possible battles is good to have in the long memory of a group of people. The trick is to make good choices, then follow

Purpose Exercise

On a piece of paper, write down in *one* sentence the purpose and main business of your organization. In a second single sentence describe exactly how the library supports that purpose. Try to be as specific as you can.

Next, inspect the official published mission and vision statements of the organization and of the library. Note the similarities and differences. In casual conversations, ask some influential people in the organization how they would describe it "off the top of the head" without word crafting. See if you can pick up on the subtle meta-message differences between their different descriptions of the organization. Some will carefully repeat phrases from the mission statement; they don't want to reveal too much of their own beliefs at the moment. Others will emphasize the aspects of the organization about which they care the most.

those choices with constructive actions.

Understanding one's own beliefs and the different beliefs of others is not enough to justify a confrontation. It may be a very bad investment. Yet passively letting things happen and then speaking out only in reaction is equally bad. As the Reverend Martin Luther King Jr. said in a sermon entitled "Being a Good Neighbor," "The ultimate measure of a person is not where one stands in moments of comfort and convenience but where one stands in times of challenge and controversy" (King, 1963, as published 1981, p. 30–38).

In poker, choosing to hold (continue playing a hand of cards) or to fold (give up in that round of play) is an active choice demanding astute reading of people and circumstances. Either choice is an active response. At another level, an active response can be proactive or reactive. Stephen R. Covey writes that real responsibility is choosing proactively where to spend time, attention, and energy (Covey, 1989, p. 82–85). Agile Librarians focus on positive actions where they have some influence. Rigid Librarians often ignore opportunities for proactivity because they are too caught up in reacting to situations over which they have no control.

Believe in Win-Win Situations

This may be the most important political skill of all. Professional life is not a sport; apparent conflicts or misunderstandings do not have to end in win, lose, or tie. There is a better way, which is sometimes more difficult. Seeing every situation as a power struggle is counterproductive. In "I win/You lose" or "You win/I lose," we both know that there will be lingering resentment and a probable rematch. If we compromise, we also both have lingering resentments. The creative challenge is to find a solution that everyone experiences as an improvement. One of Stephen R. Covey's *Seven Habits of Highly Effective People* is "Think Win-Win," and he discusses it extensively in his book of the same name (Covey, 1989, p. 204–234). He adds that sometimes No Deal may be an early option before Win-Win is accomplished, because it is better than the other alternatives and leaves the door open to more discussion. One interesting idea he emphasizes about Win-Win is that it encourages a high level of both courage and consideration, a situation of mutual respect with no room for the behavior of a passive doormat or a confrontational school yard bully.

Play Fair

Yes, politics can be fair. Influence can be, and should be, used ethically. People with a habit of using their influence unfairly are good at it, but they will eventually trip themselves up and lose influence and respect. Countering unfair tactics in a given conflict with unethical behavior just sets up a senseless tug of war that the person with more experience fighting dirty is more likely to win. Drop the rope of escalating bad behavior. Take the high road, and there will be no regrets or valid recriminations. Thinking is easier with a clear conscience. One doesn't have to struggle to remember and force congruence between the truth and one's exaggerations or falsehoods if one hasn't used such tactics. People who are known for such integrity will ultimately be more trusted and influential.

Think First, Act Later

Think fast, act later is good political advice in the calmest of situations, but with stress it becomes even more important. Research into how the brain works explains why people don't think well when surprised by a bad or good event or idea. It takes practiced self control to rescue one's mind from the natural "fight or flight" urge to act before thinking. Acting before thinking is often very regrettable. Long-term influential gains can be lost in a few seconds of foolish action. Why do otherwise reasonable people destroy years of goodwill or carefully built relationships in a single outburst or foolish act? In *Working with Emotional Intelligence,* Goleman describes how brain studies show that people under stress can be in a neurological state that severely limits their abilities to sort out information that is important and to understand facts and events as well as they otherwise would. Reasoning and working memory function best when a person's mind is calm, but in an emergency situation, the person tends to revert to habitual responses instead of creative new way of acting. Such habitual responses may seem to work in the short term while undermining the possibility of future creative success (Goleman, 1998, p. 73–74, 83).

Anger solves a problem about as well as a fan straightens a pile of papers. In a crisis, taking the time to stop, look, listen, and think before acting is essential. At the very least, one can choose to act calm even if one does not feel calm. Acting calmly can help to slow down the action long enough to choose a thoughtful action rather than a thoughtless reaction. One can also choose to speak forcefully when the situation calls for strong expression. The wise person is the one who can weigh values independently of raging brain chemistry. The professional librarian can use the professional reference interview process to define the situation and explore options before taking action.

Lessons from the Pros in Government

Aside from campaigns, fund-raising, party politics, legislation, and other aspects of government politics, there are some obvious lessons that the Agile Librarian can learn from the political sphere to build influence in the library's environment. Although most of the professional research done for candidates is not published, by observing the overt behavior of professional politicians, librarians can learn how to increase their visibility and influence in their universities, communities, schools, and corporations. What are some examples of that behavior?

Use Good Information Sources

Professional politicians have to have good, comprehensive information sources about both the good stuff and the bad stuff. Just as information sources used for library services should be current, reliable, and authoritative, so should be the personal information sources the professional librarian uses every day to know what is really going on in the organization or community. The Agile Librarian develops contacts to stay informed, with the understanding of the biases of each. Gossip is, by nature, destructive and unethical, but good organizational intelligence is essential to influence. There is always much more going on in any community or school than what shows up in press releases!

In addition to being a good listener, the Agile Librarian has to actively seek specific information. Building confidence in the librarian's need to know by proactively gathering background material on rising issues requires both tact and action. Sometimes librarians can convince gatekeepers of their need to know by explaining that by the time something, for instance, a new program, does go public, it can be too late for appropriate collection development. Sometimes such information has to be held in confidence, and other times externally verifiable information can be shared with one's best information sources. In every organization there are people who, because of their own awareness, connections, and integrity, are better sources than others. A personal information source can be evaluated just as a published reference source by its scope, viewpoint (and bias), currency, authority, reliability, and accessibility.

Show Up, Speak Up

"Out of sight, out of mind" makes a politician or librarian easy to ignore. Just being at a meeting can be more important than the content of the meeting, and the same goes for professional social events. Even when no cameras are rolling and no one's taking notes, being present at events is important. Deborah Tannen reminds us that "talk at work is not confined to talk about work. Many moments are spent in casual chat that establishes the friendly working environment that is the necessary backdrop to getting work done" (Tannen, 1994, p. 64). Recognition is essential, even, or perhaps especially, out of the everyday work context. Look for opportunities to see and be seen. Make, don't avoid, opportunities to meet new people and build on established relationships.

Always speak up at some point during any meeting of 15 or fewer people. Talk or ask questions that include the interests of most, if not all, people in the room. It's fine to talk about the library or department in this context, but be sure not to express an attitude that implies that the organization chart is in the shape of a doughnut around the library.

If the meeting is dominated by a particularly boring presentation droning on and on, keep alert by mentally composing an intelligent question to ask when the opportunity comes. Sometimes it helps to take notes even if they will go in the trash the same day. The presenter will know the librarian was attentive; the question may be something others want to know; and, like the extra question in a reference interview, the answer may reveal an important detail about the person or the person's presentation.

Learn from the pros and seek opportunities to visit people where they work. Get out of the library. Walk around the building or campus. Greet people by name. Most people like the sound of their own names, and it helps in remembering names. Keep track of which areas or classrooms have been visited recently and also try to visit those that have the fewest regular clients. Eat lunch with different people every day; lunch is not break time, it's opportunity time. Listen to what delights them and what worries them. As John Seely Brown and Paul Duguid write in *The Social Life of Information*, "The way forward is paradoxically to look not ahead, but to look around" (Brown and Duguid, 2000, p. 8). A wealth of useful information is available to those who take the time to look around.

Come Prepared

Before a meeting or professional social event, mentally review who can be expected to be there. Look up names if you might forget them. Think of a kind or interesting comment for each person you expect to see. It doesn't have to be library related. Arrive prepared for small talk in the area of current events, local or national. One only has to ask, one doesn't have to be the first to venture an opinion. Other areas to prepare include humor, such as a non-offensive joke; an idea for a comment about current arts or entertainment events, such as a concert, a blockbuster movie, or a best-selling novel; and, yes, prepare a comment or two current events in local sports appropriate to the current season. You won't need to use all of them at any single event, but with that preparation you will have something to use to launch a conversation, revive one that is becalmed, or change course when a discussion is headed for certain disaster. Susan RoAne's excellent *How to Work a Room: The Ultimate Guide to Savvy Socializing in Person and Online* (2000) includes details about seven steps for planning your "presence" (RoAne, 2000, p. 71–88):

1. Adopt a Positive Attitude
2. Focus on the Benefits of the Event
3. Plan Your Self-Introduction
4. Check Your Business Cards
5. Prepare Your Small Talk
6. Remember to Make Eye Contact and Smile
7. Practice Your Handshake

If you have a point you need to make at a meeting, carefully craft how you are going to say it. Don't use jargon; put it in terms that are meaningful to others. Relate it to their values and concerns. Choose a short phrase to repeat to help people remember. When the time comes to present it, stay on message. Think of possible comments others might make and plan responses. If appropriate, bring documentation, but remember that what you say in person may well be more influential than a quickly forgotten handout or e-mail attachment.

Engage and Balance Responses

Pay attention. Really listen to what others are saying. React appropriately and gracefully. Use the listening and encouraging skills you use in a reference interview. Remember that asking one more question frequently can open a window on

Talking to Strangers

I was at a meeting of a committee that was planning an event for an association meeting. The purpose of the event would be to give a group of librarians who worked, usually solo, in a specific kind of library an opportunity to network with their counterparts from other places. . We were discussing what to serve and how to serve it when I objected to having assigned seats and formal introductions. "But Michelynn," one of the others said, "most of us can't talk to strangers like you can." Does that mean that we need a formal introduction to every library client before we can work with them? Of course we don't, and it should be even easier to talk with people who share the same kind of work environment.

Talking to strangers, whether one-on-one or to a room full of people, is a performance art that all professionals can and must learn, both in principle and in practice. We learned the principles of the reference interview in school and developed our skills in practice. Librarians are especially talented in finding resource information on any subject, and that includes self-help books for talking to strangers.

a whole different view of what the other person is thinking. Though most of your comments will be positive, include a few negative ones for balance. People tend to ignore the complaints of very negative people and not give credibility to those who seem to always be artificially positive. It is good to use a personal story to make a point, but do not respond to everything someone else says with another autobiographical vignette. Sharing is one thing, competitive story topping is another. Maintain both respect for others and self-respect; neither flourishes without the other. For more on this topic, see Nathanial Branden's *Honoring the Self: The Psychology of Confidence and Respect*, 1983.

Constantly Build Positive Alliances and Relationships

No politician, executive, or legislator can make things happen without help from someone. The constant practice of Win-Win goes a long way in building up allies and networks, but so does striking up acquaintances even when nothing is immediately at stake. It is easy to spot people who make the mistake of befriending only the people that they believe can do something for them. People collectors, those who learn to genuinely like others and are liked by many people, have much more flexibility. Whether they know it or not, complaining loners are in a process of political self-destruction.

Build friendly relationships with satisfied clients. Remember who is especially appreciative of a particular service. Make and keep private notes about extraordinary positive service experiences. Also build relationships with influential people, preferably as delighted users of the service. Instead of looking just for library supporters who tend to appreciate a mythological ideal of a library, keep track of those who passionately care about particular services. Consider them as champions in reserve, people who would be willing to voice support for that particular service whether it is under attack or in good position for expansion. Don't wear out the same people by constantly asking for their help. Choose the right person to appear at the right time in the right situation.

Political candidates who complain but offer no solutions get little respect. Be wary of relationships based mostly on dislike of a person or program. That can create adversaries. It can be tempting to pit them against us, but that can jeopardize any future problem solving. It also scuttles any opportunity to work together on whatever common interests may exist in spite of the conflict. Such relationships have another major weakness: when that disliked person or program is gone, the relationship built on dislike will be gone as well, whereas resentments on behalf of the disliked person or program will linger. No one respects a killer. Present solutions to colleagues, not just complaints about problems.

In many settings, "bonding by complaining" is a common social activity, however, as a professional practice, it can backfire easily. Deborah Tannen, in *Talking from 9 to 5*, describes the ritual of "troubles talk," or establishing rapport by commiseration: "You tell about a problem . . . and the other person responds by telling a matching problem. Because troubles talk is more common among women than men, many men are likely to take the statement of a problem as a request to solve it." This leaves the other person, especially a woman, "feeling condescended to and frustrated" (Tannen, 1994, p. 71–72).

Getting Caught in Someone Else's Battle

After the consolidation, Truman and Eisenhower schools were under one administration but still in their own buildings. The Eisenhower school had a very good library collection and service, and the Truman school did not. The Truman faculty, as promised by the new board, wanted to be treated as an equal and not a poor relative, and they demanded a library in their building with a collection and services to match those of the Eisenhower school. The Eisenhower librarian, not knowing of the Truman faculty demand, was shocked one day when the principal walked in and told her to box up half of her collection to be sent to Truman. He didn't realize that a library service is more than a collection. When she pleaded that the Eisenhower faculty wouldn't stand for that loss, the principal told her to make up a purchase list of materials for a new Truman collection. She turned it in, expecting that the materials would be bought out of the Truman school's budget, and was horrified when someone in the office told her that it was going to come out of her budget for Eisenhower. Assuming that it was just her problem, she could have gone to battle with the principal and possibly weakened his already flimsy concept of the value of a library to the school. Instead, she thought about two teachers who used to be at Eisenhower, but took jobs at Truman a couple of years before. She'd stayed in touch with them and they turned out to be real champions in reserve. During lunch with them she found out about the Truman faculty's expectation that the equality promised by the new board included funding for library materials and services, and that that had led the teachers' request to the principal. The librarian realized that she was caught in the middle of a battle about more than her library. The principal wanted to appease Truman without messing with his budget, and this seemed like a quick, low-cost solution to him. The teachers, however, did not want half of the collection and service they had had at Eisenhower. That was not the "equal" they had in mind. These teachers knew exactly what good programs and librarian services they had had at Eisenhower and did not have at Truman. They had never dreamed that the principal would play "King Solomon" and decide to split the living baby. Because it was something that they cared about, they went with other Truman teachers to the principal and the board about their school's need for particular library programs and services. The board members from both schools' districts clearly understood the teachers' presentation, and made sure that equal library services, including a librarian, would be at Truman. The Eisenhower librarian, instead of whining, sulking, and appearing to be personally confrontational, was able to call on champions-in-reserve. She immediately volunteered to help with the search for a librarian for Truman and with plans for that library.

> ### Planting an Idea Seed
>
> It's not hard to imagine the likely sources of client complaints. You can prime influential people's thinking about that possibility with a positive idea seed that may take root and grow. For instance, every time I got a new boss, which happened fairly often in my hospital, at some point I would quip, though actually serious, "You know what? Most of our complaints are from people who want more of what we provide not less." I gave the boss an easy conceptual frame for many kinds of complaints; a frame that would be more helpful than hurtful for everyone.

The influential Agile Librarian is constantly maintaining old relationships and building new ones. Keep in mind the old proverb, often sung as a round by Girl Scouts, "Make new friends, but keep the old. One is silver and the other gold." Remember that an individual's networking reflects not only on that individual, but also on the entire profession. The only librarian in the room is always building up or tearing down the influence of librarians everywhere.

Building Positive Political Capital

The Agile Librarian tries to have a strong positive history with people before a conflict situation arises. That's much easier to do before than it is during or after a crisis. It works better when it is done as important, but not urgent. The Rigid Librarian who lives as a constant crisis manager suffers from this terrible lack of foresight. The crisis manager is constantly putting out fires instead of preventing them. As in the title of Harvey Mackay's book, one has to *Dig Your Well before You're Thirsty* (Mackay, 1999).

Influence building begins during the job interview or even before it, and continues daily into or even beyond retirement. It includes as many daily decisions as does dressing for work. If one thinks of it as an interest-bearing investment, it's easy to see why the crisis manager is always in debt and may go bankrupt.

Does this sound like proactive behavior? It is. It is the opposite of reactive behavior, passively waiting for something to go wrong, such as the sound of a squeaky wheel, and then trying to fix it. "A stitch in time saves nine."

The best investment includes a combination of savvy business networking and demonstrating your professional skills to those who need them. In her article "Becoming the 'Go-To' Person in Your Organization Raises Positive Perceptions of Your Department," Debbie Schachter asserts that every organization has go-to people who are trusted information gatekeepers. They have the personality and communications skills to keep up with what is happening in the organization and are willing to share that information. Information professionals should be naturals in this role. Even though she wrote it for the Special Library Association's *Information Outlook* magazine, the principles she presents in that article work equally well in all kinds of libraries and their parent organizations (Schachter, 2007).

The go-to person always has some important political skills. Jeffrey Gandz describes them:

- They know how their organizations work and how to work their organizations.

- They are politically astute without being corporate politicians.
- They know how to use power when it's needed but seldom use it, preferring to influence and persuade others to get-with-the-program.
- They are consummate negotiators, but getting it done is non-negotiable.
- They use networks of reciprocation rather than deals.
- They think out of the box while acting inside the box.
- They are analytical and intuitive, aggressive and patient, confident and humble, deliberate and decisive. (Gandz, 2007)

Savvy librarians are aware of who their best partners and champions are, or could be. They develop good relationships with people in widely different parts of the parent organization or community, as well as people to

RECOMMENDATIONS FOR LIBRARIANS/INFORMATION PROFESSIONALS
From the *Inter-Association Task Force Report on Image*

1. SELF-DIRECTED
   1.1 Stand purposefully; sit straight; walk briskly.
   1.2 Project competence by organizing your thoughts before you speak.
   1.3 Be decisive by stating a problem in simple, specific, concise language, and then offer optional possibilities toward a solution.
   1.4 Show confidence by talking about challenges instead of obstacles.
   1.5 Exemplify excellence in every service contact.

2. DIVISION/UNIT/DEPARTMENT (e.g., colleagues, subordinates, and supervisors)
Project effectiveness (doing the right thing), as well as efficiency (doing things right). Establish, maintain, and uphold a high degree of departmental and professional standards.

3. ADMINISTRATION (over the library department)
Demonstrate how the department contributes to the achievement of the goals and objectives of the organization and its people. Commission marketing research, focus groups, or user satisfaction research to determine what you are doing well and what the user wants. Utilize them in your departmental planning.

4. ORGANIZATION
Become a project manager over an assignment that has organizational implications. Provide information leadership for your organization. Network with your organization's public relations director and solicit tips on how to promote your department in the organization's house organ [or Web site] on a regular basis.

5. PROFESSIONAL ASSOCIATIONS (library and non-library)
Develop issue-related roundtable programming to bring the two groups together. Exchange speakers between library associations and industry/community-related associations. Develop cooperative projects to address mutual concerns.

6. COMMUNITY
Target community groups that (1) are important to your organization and (2) important to your profession. Become an organizational liaison. Give of your time professionally and personally. Use every contact that is made to promote the profession.

7. MEDIA (library and non-library)
Make a friend of a local reporter, e.g. newspaper, radio or television. Feed them story ideas. Give editors [and web masters] an occasional digest with one-paragraph feature ideas. Offer to produce pieces that alert the community to the library and/or its parent organization.

(Continued)

8. STATE

Institutionalize the observation of a library week or month by asking your governor to issue a proclamation designating such. On the local level, petition the mayor, city manager, or county executive to issue such a proclamation. Develop a library leadership academy for the profession in your state.

9. NATIONAL

Serve on high-visibility committees that receive national recognition. Get your name, title, and organization's name in print. Network with colleagues to get yourself invited to be a speaker at a national conference . . . in another state.

10. INTERNATIONAL

Write an article to submit to journal published in another country. Get yourself interviewed by the editor of a library newsletter in any country you visit. Take a . . . picture of yourself for inclusion with the article. Ask that a copy of the article be mailed [or sent] to you after publication.

Source: Special Libraries Association, 1991, ERIC document ED329267; IR053458, pages 73–74.

whom they and their bosses answer. Then, when a crisis does happen, they know who in the organization is most likely to understand, share, and support their own interests. Like any other political capital, this network must be constantly tended and increased, and spent only on rare occasions when it is truly important. In any case, such networks will inevitably increase the Agile Librarian's sphere of influence.

Advocacy outside the Institution

Whenever non-librarians cut funding for library services, one has to wonder what kind of negative experience or non-experience they had with librarians in their past. Were they once offended by a Rigid Librarian? Is their concept of librarianship more from popular media stereotypes than from personal experience? Do they perceive the industries in which they work to have progressed technologically while library services remained stuck in the mid-twentieth century, becoming obsolete?

Although all professional librarians' associations have active programs advocating for the profession, it all comes down to the fact that in any interaction with a non-librarian on or off the job, the Agile Librarian is, at that moment, the very embodiment of the entire profession. Librarians, like all true professionals, think outside the job. They must remember their ethical responsibilities for professional advocacy. Sometimes these include, especially for librarians in public libraries, involvement in the processes of government. See Turner 2000, *Vote Yes for Libraries* and 1997, *Getting Political: An Action Guide for Librarians and Library Supporters.*

The "Recommendations for Librarians/Information Professionals" (Special Library Association, 1991) provides examples of advocacy on a continuum from the very personal to the global perspectives. The Agile Librarian thinks of and accomplishes many more such acts of advocacy at every level.

Summary

The Agile Librarian's support in the organization and the community grows because of serious consideration of political influence. Even without obvious power or official authority, the positive use of this influence benefits everyone. Agile Librarians are visible and engaged. They build and maintain a strong network of people who know and support library staff and services. They thoroughly understand the organization's structure, culture, and operations and know when and how to act within them. Fair win-win solutions benefit everyone and build positive political capital that the Agile Librarian can draw on when needed.

References

Bellman, Geoffrey. 2001. *Getting Things Done When You are Not in Charge,* 2nd ed. San Francisco, CA: Berrett-Koehler.

Brandon, Nathaniel. 1983. *Honoring the Self: The Psychology of Confidence and Respect.* New York: Bantam.

Brown, John Seely and Paul Duguid. 2000. *The Social Life of Information.* Boston: Harvard University Press.

Cialdini, Robert B. 2001. *Influence: Science and Practice.* Boston: Allyn and Bacon.

Covey, Stephen R. 1989. *The 7 Habits of Highly Effective People.* New York: Simon & Schuster.

Evans, G. Edward, Patrizia Layzell Ward, and Bendik Rugaas. 2000. *Management Basics for Information Professionals.* New York: Neal Schuman.

Fisher, Roger and Alan Sharp (with John Richardson). 1998. *Getting It Done: How to Lead When You're Not in Charge.* New York: Harper.

Gandz, Jeffrey. 2007. Go To People: What Every Organization Should Have. *Ivey Business Journal* 71(1): March/April 2007. Available from http://www.iveybusinessjournal.com/article.asp?intArticle_ID=675. Accessed January 26, 2008.

Goleman, Daniel. 1998. *Working with Emotional Intelligence.* New York: Bantam.

Jowett, Garth S. and Victoria O'Donnell. 2005. *Propaganda and Persuasion.* 4th ed. Thousand Oaks, CA: Sage Publications.

King, Martin Luther, Jr. 1963. *Strength to Love.* Reprinted. Philadelphia: Fortress Press, 1981.

Mackay, Harvey. 1999. *Dig Your Well Before You're Thirsty: The Only Networking Book You'll Ever Need.* New York: Currency.

Niels, Mara. 1990. Politics of the Library of the Future. *The Electronic Library* 8:408–411.

RoAne, Susan. 2000. *How to Work a Room: The Ultimate Guide to Savvy Socializing in Person and Online.* New York: Harper Collins.

Schacter, Debbie. 2007. "Does Your Perception of Your Service Match Your Clients' Opinions?" *Information Outlook* 11:40–41.

Special Libraries Association; Presidential Task Force on the Enhancement of the Image of the Librarian/Information Professional. 1991. *Inter-Association Task Force Report on Image.* Washington, D.C.: Special Libraries. [Accessed as ERIC database document ED329267; IR053458.]

Stueart, Robert D. and Barbara B. Moran. 2007. *Library and Information Center Management*, 7th ed. Westport, CT: Libraries Unlimited.

Tannen, Deborah. 1994. *Talking from 9 to 5, Women and Men in the Workplace: Language, Sex, and Power.* New York: Avon Books.

Turner, Ann M. 1997. *Getting Political: An Action Guide for Librarians and Library Supporters.* New York: Neal-Schuman Publishers.

———. 2000. *Vote Yes for Libraries: A Guide to Winning Ballot Measure Campaigns for Library Funding.* Jefferson, N.C.: McFarland.

Walker, Mary Edith. 1994. Maslow's Hierarchy and the Sad Case of the Hospital Librarian. *Bulletin of the Medical Library Association* 82:320–322.

Wolfe, Rebecca Luhn. 1996. *Office Politics: Positive Results from Fair Practices.* A Fifty-Minute Series Book. Menlo Park, CA: Crisp Publications.

Chapter 4

Pleasing Your Boss

"Efficiency pleases your boss; effectiveness pleases your customer" is an old business aphorism, but in spite of much that is said or obliquely expressed, there's more to pleasing the boss than demonstrated penny-pinching. The very important boss-employee relationship includes many dimensions of personal and organizational mission and opportunity. Let's begin with "Who is your boss?"

To whom do librarians report? Are their bosses librarians? School librarians and special librarians rarely answer to another librarian. Although many public and academic librarians answer to a librarian, at the top of the library's administrative hierarchy a librarian always answers to someone who is not a librarian. This chapter explores building positive relationships between a professional librarian and an individual boss, though some head librarians do report to a board rather than an individual. Of course, the Agile Librarian should be able to apply these ideas to relations with a board's president or chair.

Organizations with different cultures have different structures. Whether they are absolutely hierarchical with a military-style chain of command involving strict orders to report only to the next higher person in the chain, organic with different branches for different purposes, amorphous with no easily discernable structure, or a combination with department-crossing committees and task forces, there still is an individual boss somewhere for almost every librarian. They may see each other every day, occasionally, or rarely, but the impressions they make on each other are vital to the Agile Librarian's ability to survive and thrive in that organization.

It is tempting to assume that a boss who is a librarian will better understand librarian employees than one who is not, but whenever there is a difference in role, there will be a difference in perspective. In any case, a mutually supportive, rather than adversarial, relationship needs to be nurtured and maintained for both to flourish in support of the missions of both the library and the larger organization.

The best professional relationships are not only cordial and cooperative, but also mutually challenging and stimulating. Levels of authority are respected, but so are different perspectives. One clue to the nature of the relationship is in the prepositions. Does the librarian work *for* the boss? Does the boss work *for* the librarian? A high level of blind obedience in either direction is not a good working relationship. Does the librarian work *with* the boss? Does one or both work *against* the other? Kearns writes:

You are more likely to be disappointed and resentful toward the boss when your expectations are implicit because you want the boss to be a mind reader—to miraculously discern your needs and how to meet them. We generally are clearer about what we expect from our subordinates than what we expect from the boss. But any successful relationship . . . ultimately depends on reaching agreement on a core set of shared goals and operating principles. (Kearns, 1997, p. 26)

The Agile Librarian who delights clients with current, factual, reliable, and useful information also recognizes the boss's right to the same standards for organizational, professional, and operational information. Informing the boss appropriately is ethical professionalism. Many fine librarians are sensitive to exactly what and how much the boss needs to know, and they frequently refine that understanding using their best reference interview skills. They take the time to explore the boss's role and perspective within the organization, remembering how much perspective influences perception. For instance, a non-librarian boss looking at a library budget may not understand the interactive relationship between materials purchases such as subscriptions, and purchases of services, document delivery, or interlibrary loan. Falling in different parts of a standard organizational department's budget, they may appear unrelated rather than as different ways of delivering the same information.

A few librarians so much want to avoid obnoxious and unprofessional behavior, often identified as apple polishing, that they will avoid informing the very person they should most keep informed. Some seem to expect the boss to figure everything out without any help. Some see the boss as a Santa Claus who should grant every request on their incomprehensible demand list. If librarians survive in that position, they certainly won't thrive. They must consider carefully their part in managing their relationships with their bosses. "Managing Upward is NOT apple polishing or psychological manipulation . . . is not about being a sycophant or simply adapting your style to match your boss's . . . is not simply a matter of 'going along to get along'" (Kearns, 1997). Managing upward is just as much a professional responsibility as managing the staff one supervises. In fact, solo librarians who have no staff may have even more upward management on their plates.

Occasionally, Rigid Librarians may get so caught up in boss bashing that they sabotage their own professional practice. A clear clue to that myopia surfaces when a librarian changes jobs frequently, but always seems to have the same problems. The same mental furniture is moved into a new house without even being dusted, and obviously not repaired. The results are quite different for the librarian who makes some mistakes in a starter job, learns, and moves on to more successful professional practice somewhere else. If both have worked for three years, one may truly have developed through three years of professional growth, whereas the other may have had only one year of experience three times.

Thoughtful and mindful learning make the difference. The influential attitudes and techniques presented in this book are essential to developing this important relationship with the boss. It is all part of the "know, show, and tell" of professional practice discussed in Chapter 1. The same considerations and techniques, especially "win-win," work equally well with both "the good boss" and "the bad boss."

Understanding Roles and Perspectives

By definition, the boss has different responsibilities and different perspectives on library services. At the very least, the boss lives in a different political environment, experiencing some pressures and influences that are not shared by other employees. Do not expect the boss to be omnipotent and able to make anything happen; no one is.

Roles and perspectives vary with organizational cultures. They vary with individual personalities and expectations, and they vary across time as individuals learn or stagnate. Everyone works in a context of multiple demands and expectations, and everyone makes decisions about what is really important and what is just noise. The rub comes when one person's important issue is another's background noise.

Your Boss Is or Probably Can Be

Your ally
Your mentor
Your mentee
One of your most frequent information seekers
The second most knowledgeable person about what you do
An excellent source of organization information
More aware of what you say to others about your job or the boss than you think

Your Boss Is Not

Your enemy
Your medium, mind-reader, confessor, or fairy godmother
Your only source of organization information
Your ordinary client who should learn to beg, to wait, and to conform to your rules or fear passive or active retaliation like everyone else
Your best topic for bonding-by-complaining conversation with co-workers
Your best friend, mother, father, sister, brother, or lover

When it happens that this person has a non-work related role in your life, you must *both* be conscientiously diligent about keeping those roles separate. Such a relationship can be dangerous, not only for your relationship with each other, but also for your relationships with everyone else in the organization!

If the boss's organizational function is in top administration, ordinary daily operations are not primary concerns unless something goes terribly wrong. Such a person has to look ahead and look around. David H. Freed, president of Overlook Hospital in Summit, New Jersey, writes about hospital chief executive officers:

> They work . . . to reconcile contradictions surrounding mission and [financial] risk and return. . . . They deal . . . in problems and opportunities and these are the two superhighways to gaining a CEO's time and attention. Any other road will lead to business as usual . . . the one thing CEOs are not thinking about. They are alternatively too busy, too confident in their management team or too distant to reflect extensively on what is proceeding reliably. That . . . may appear contradictory from the perspective of consistent performers, who feel punished if their sustained contributions attract much less of the CEO's attention than others' imminent failure or bright ideas. (Freed, 1999, p. 11–12)

The librarian who doesn't appreciate this difference in perspective is doomed to a long string of misunderstandings, open clashes, and suppressed resentment. When top administrators are doing their jobs, thinking strategically, and asking the organization to change in order to take advantage of a new environmental opportunity, those involved in daily operations have to work out the details. They may have a good perspective to see what procedures need to be changed to take advantage of this opportunity, but to do so they have to understand what the administrator sees in this change.

The principal, as the top administrator of a school, not only makes many decisions directly affecting library services, but also, as the person with the greatest power to hire or retain staff, knows best the teachers with whom the librarian must collaborate to be successful. On the other hand, principals' positions are seldom permanent; they answer to superintendents and school boards. The Agile Librarian not only needs to convince the principal of the value of library services in the education of the students, but also must provide the principal with information and success stories that will make the principal look good to the superintendent and the board. Writing for *School Libraries Worldwide*, Lesley Farmer notes:

> In their academic preparation, principal candidates seldom examine the roles of TL's [teacher-librarians] except for legal issues. Usually libraries and librarians are regarded in terms of resources and their use and abuse: plagiarism, circulation records, and copyright violations. For principals, no library news is good news, particularly in an environment where difficult decisions are a daily energy drainer." (Farmer, 2007)

Whether the boss is or is not a librarian, goals and motivations for the boss and the employee will be different. In addition to positional perspective in the organization, there will always be differences based upon life experiences, world views, and beliefs that may not be obvious at all. In any case, each can be an influential ally for the other within the organization, and that's not going to happen without some basic two-way understanding.

Allies, Mentors, and Mentees

Depending on the context, the boss may be a librarian who has had a similar job to that of the employee in the past, or the boss may never have been interested in libraries. Librarian and non-librarian supervisors with the same managerial style may have more in common with each other than two librarian managers with different styles. That is, two democratic managers may have more in common than two librarian managers, one democratic and one autocratic. In any case, it is important to be allies, each supporting the other's role in the organization. As allies, both can contribute and thrive more than either could alone.

The librarian's boss is also a mentor at some level. It may be as little as teaching the librarian how things are done in this organization, or as much as being a complete career counselor. A traditional mentor is an experienced, and usually influential, professional guiding a less experienced professional. Four functions of mentors are teaching, counseling, emotional support, and organizational intervention or sponsoring (Stueart and Moran, 2007, p. 273). A growing professional generally has more than one mentor for different aspects of career growth.

Having the boss as one's only mentor can be shortsighted for a career, but the Agile Librarian pays attention to the wisdom the boss has to share. The boss-employee relationship and the mentor-mentee relationship are never unconditional. One risk of having only one mentor is that one or both parties will imagine that the relationship has parental overtones. Either one may expect unconditional love and emotional support and may even go so far as to perceive, or even foster, sibling rivalries among different individuals reporting to the same boss.

One interesting aspect of mentorship that is often ignored is that this sharing can and should go both ways, depending upon the experiences and perspectives of the individuals. Bosses do not have to know how to do the librarian's job, but they do need to know enough to define the tasks and to understand the job's purpose and goals. The mentor boss who isn't a librarian teaches the librarian about the organization's culture and influences, helping the librarian to see good library services in the context of this particular organization. The Agile Librarian, in turn, subtly teaches the boss what librarians really can do best.

What Does the Boss Want? What Does the Boss Need?

One of Stephen R. Covey's seven habits of highly effective people is "Seek first to understand and then to be understood" (Covey, 1989, p. 235–284). You need to understand your boss's style of management, and there are many styles to choose from. Good bosses practice one fairly consistently; less helpful managers seem to pick and choose different styles depending on the occasion. This practice usually makes employees very uncertain as to how to respond. Most people use individual variations based on their own personalities, experience, education, beliefs, and the stress they are experiencing on any given day in their roles and relationships. If you can share with your boss what management books you are both reading, you can both understand the current management jargon, and this may help you define your boss's style. This can also help you begin to understand what your boss wants and needs. You can also ask directly. Most bosses will be flattered by your interest if you express it as interest and not as accusation.

Use your good reference skills to understand what matters to your boss. Just like some clients, bosses may not articulate exactly what they need; the Agile Librarian listens, asks questions, and paraphrases before moving on to searching and delivery, or in the case of responding to a management task, finding out what the boss really wants. Small changes in the boss's tone and style may be indicators of minor mood changes or of major underlying issues that may or may not involve the librarian. Ex-principal Gary Hartzell tells school librarians:

> You may be the best school librarian to ever grace education, but you won't get the opportunity to prove that unless your principal values what you do. Being ready, willing and able is only three-quarters of the key to your success. . . . Find ways to interact with the principal regularly . . . keep abreast of activities in your school and find ways to show the principal how you

and the library can help deal with challenges and opportunities. How often should you do this? Any time you get the chance . . . pay attention to what the principal talks about—whether it's information shared at a faculty meeting or a seemingly idle remark made in the hallway. Every topic the principal mentions offers you an opportunity to make an impression. (Hartzell, 2002)

Leadership and Management Styles

What matters most to this person? How much engagement is normal for this person? How much attention does one deserve from the boss? Although management is sometimes equated with leadership, many consider them separately. Leadership has many styles ranging along a continuum of control from absolute to laissez-faire. In their book *Winning with Library Leadership*, Olson and Singer note:

> If you believe that your boss is leading from a command and control approach and you are leading from a connecting and collaborating approach, you should at least review some of your own leadership behaviors to make sure that they are indeed different approaches. Sometimes managers rail at command and control bosses and then turn around and repeat the same behavior at their project or staff meetings. (Olson and Singer, 2004, p. 106)

Similar to using different management styles, leaders who are absolute leaders in most situations confuse followers when they switch to a laissez-fair attitude. Many of us behave differently when we are under stress than we do when we are calm. Sometimes this change shows up in times of conflict. Typical conflict management strategies include avoidance, accommodation, competition, compromise, collaboration, or some combination thereof (Bartol and Martin, 1991, p. 580–581).

Micromanagers can't see the mission for the details of tasks. They may closely inspect procedures they believe they understand, such as overdue notices, while missing the more important issue of access to materials and services. Macromanagers haven't a clue how library services fit into their Great Dream Visions. Crisis managers can be "attack helicopter bosses" who are distant and unseen until someone complains about the library. Then they suddenly appear overhead, shouting through a megaphone and shining a bright spotlight on the librarian. At some point, anyone can lean far enough to one side or the other to get out of balance.

Quick Exercise

In a few sentences answer each of the following questions with sweeping generalizations:

What does the boss need to know?
What does the boss want to know?
What do you want the boss to know?
What do you believe that the boss ought to or should know?

Now consider how you are going to gather data to answer these questions more specifically. (Of course, you won't give the boss an examination!) Review these questions again in context just before your next meeting with the boss. Your preparation can save both of you valuable time while enhancing your communication.

Other times, when the interest in overdue notices doesn't appear to have originated in a complaint, what appears to be micromanagement may actually be an attempt to communicate with or understand a librarian using an awareness of one procedure as an opening.

Training, Educating, or "Sharing with" the Boss

Whether or not bosses think they need to know much about librarians' services, they do; and you have an ethical professional responsibility to help them learn. The boss needs to know enough about standards, ethics, and principles of library services to converse about them with both librarians and non-librarians. Whereas the Rigid Librarian may expect the non-librarian bosses to have learned such things independently, the Agile Librarian constantly helps raise the boss's level of information literacy and understanding of the value of professional library services to the organization.

Librarians are fond of gathering service and collection data and delivering it to their bosses as evidence of the value of their services, and in some cases that can be effective. On the other hand, some studies have shown that administrators are usually more impressed by their own experiences of library services and stories of the experiences of people important to the organization (board members, high-ranking faculty, higher administrators) than they are by librarian's reports (Abels, Cogdill, and Zach, 2004, Special Libraries Association 1991, p. 32–42). As the old salesman's aphorism goes "numbers tell, stories sell."

David Drake, director of the Murray Fasken Learning Resources Center at Midland College in Midland, Texas, in "When Your Boss isn't a Librarian: For Library Directors, Teaching Non-Librarian Supervisors to Appreciate the Library is a Big Part of the Job" (1990), writes, "Our bosses' attitudes toward libraries were formed before they became our bosses. They brought to their positions their own vision of what a library is or should be. . . . The person who wields the most influence over the library, whether a vice president, dean, or commissioner, tends to have the lowest knowledge of its operations." He advises librarians to realize that their non-librarian bosses never will have the deep understanding of librarianship that the librarian has, and to accept that such bosses do have a different and definite image of library services. The trick is to accept that the boss's misconceptions are sincere. The boss manages a budget and sees the library as consuming income rather than generating it. The boss's view of the value of library services may be apparent in how much the boss uses such services. He writes:

> Facing the fact that your supervisor doesn't think much of the library is somewhat like facing cancer: Caught early enough, it may be curable. Persuasion is the cure, but your boss will not respond to the same rhetoric that would thrill the heart of a librarian. . . . If you don't promote, you're doomed to defend. (Drake, 1990, p. 152–153)

In general, there are differences between the librarian boss and the non-librarian boss. Nevertheless, there certainly are situations, especially in large libraries, for which Mr. Drake's remarks could be analogically true if one replaced "the library" with "the department," meaning cataloging, circulation, outreach, instruction, and acquisition, among others. In any case, emphasizing the distance with a "them against us" perspective is counterproductive.

Professional library literature includes many articles about why the boss should value library services. They can be mined for talking points in a particular organization, but it rarely does much good just to hand the boss a copy of such an article from a librarians' publication. Such articles may have more credibility for the boss when they appear in a publication important to the boss, particularly if one of the authors has a similar role to that of the boss. In any case, the Agile Librarian actively, but discreetly, teaches the boss and is well practiced in doing so in any organization with frequent administrative turnover.

Like any good educator, the Agile Librarian is alert to teaching moment opportunities. The boss's direct question, "How do you do that?" often presents such opportunities, but so do some remarks such as, "Why do we need these magazine subscriptions when we have all these databases?" Agile Librarians recognize and use such opportunities and to phrase the response more as explanatory guidance than as contradiction. Often the same phrases crafted for clients make sense to bosses as well.

Real teaching is interactive; lecturing is not teaching. It is better to introduce one or two concepts and allow for some "wait time" before a response than to throw out too many ideas and details at once. All good teachers learn from their students' questions and are agile enough to welcome fresh insights or to escape from stereotypical boxes.

For your non-librarian boss, be careful to use plain English instead of jargon or unfamiliar esoteric terms. That often requires more, or at least different, words. For instance, "teaching our students how to find and evaluate reliable information" may communicate more than "bibliographic instruction." Acronyms that spell out words and initialisms, such as "SDI," may not mean any more when the complete words are used. Most will understand "information update service" more easily than "selective dissemination of information." Even librarians will have different understandings of library jargon based on their own education and experiences.

Older librarians tell the story, probably based on a real event now grown into folklore, of the librarian who was working on compiling a list of the serial holdings of libraries in a small consortium when the non-librarian boss walked in and asked, "What are you doing?" The librarian responded, "Working on a union list." The shocked boss went straight to the human resources department with the news that the librarian was involved in some kind of labor organization. "Working on a way to know what other libraries in our consortium have that we can use without our having to buy everything" would have taken a little longer than saying "a union list of serials," but it also would have communicated more accurately what the boss wanted to know.

If students sometimes begin library school without any knowledge of the meaning of reference services, why should a non-librarian boss, even a technologically savvy one, be expected to instantly comprehend the phrase "virtual reference"? A description that makes it clear how a new service will benefit the boss personally as well as the organization is more likely to evoke support. Start from the known and understood, and then move on to introduce the new concept.

Information Services for the Boss

The boss and the librarian each know some things that the other needs to know. Each has a different perspective on political and social issues for the organization and its clients. Each has information-seeking skills and resources, and often can save the other's time by using them appropriately. When it comes to published or so-called knowledge-based information, which is the center of professional library services, it is never enough to just "know" and "tell"; "show," as described in Chapter 1, is just as important. The boss should really experience excellent reference and information services directly, not just vicari-

Educating the Boss

Are there things about your library services that you believe your boss does not understand and should? Make a list, then pick one, only one, to consider now. Consider teaching your target concept with these steps:

1. Pretest previous knowledge. The boss may understand more than you think; subtly ask open-ended questions in context. Paraphrase as you would in a reference interview. For instance, "What have you heard about how libraries can get scanned copies of articles from other libraries?"
2. Simplify complex concepts. Break the information need down into small, easily digestible parts that can be related to what the boss already knows. Present each one over a period of time hidden in the context of other conversations or communication. Be alert for the boss's comments and questions that give you clues about understanding. Follow up on questions. Compliment demonstrated understanding.
3. Ask a carefully structured question. Create a question that requires a synthesis of all of the parts of the whole. If the boss understands it and presents it as a whole new idea, that's great! It's even better if the boss takes the credit for coming up with the insight. You know that there has been progress.
4. Prepare additional information. If the concept is still not clear for the boss, discuss, don't lecture! Repeating yourself more loudly or more slowly won't work. Think of another way to make your point. You just may learn something new from the boss' perspective that will help you. If nothing else, it will help you do a better job of teaching others.
5. Offer a document. Provide one succinct article or textbook chapter on the subject after several personal learning opportunities. Reinforce the boss's understanding. Don't just drop a bibliography, entire book, or stack of articles and run!

ously. The boss, librarian or not, who asks for and frequently receives appropriate information quickly, understands and appreciates the professional's service skills better than the boss who has only been told how wonderful they are. If the boss is not a frequent client, the Agile Librarian seeks and solicits information quests from the boss instead of waiting to be asked. The secret is to pay attention to what is on the boss's mind and then look for good literature about the issue. Even if the boss is a librarian who has the ability to do it without help, everyone likes to have someone else spare them the cost of the time to do it.

Reference and Update Services

The Agile Librarian ensures that the boss gets timely expert information services. It's important for the boss to have this experience, and ensuring this happens is too important

You Want *WHAT?*

I was meeting my new boss for the first time. I thought I had just broken in the last administrator and now I had a new one. I was wallowing in anxiety.

Anxiety is different from fear; fear is a reasonable reaction to present danger; anxiety is telling yourself ghost stories about what might happen in the future. There, in his office, from across the big desk, he said, "I've never heard of a hospital with a librarian before." Unable to think well at the moment I gave my basic "elevator" speech, a short but accurate planned, plain English description of what I did as explained in Chapter 1. He asked a general question, and I responded with the "party" speech, a longer version of the elevator speech, which didn't really answer his question.

Apparently trying to improve the interview, he changed directions and asked what I had been doing that morning. In good old librarian jargon said I'd been "weeding books." Imitating cartoon character Bugs Bunny's nemesis, Elmer Fudd, he replied that he hoped I "weally wead good books." His sense of humor broke the ice, and we went on to discuss the information services I provided for the medical and hospital staff. I stressed how my professional expertise saved my clients' time and my professional ethics preserved their privacy and confidentiality.

I wasn't sure how much he understood reference services until later that afternoon, when I received a formal memo dictated to and typed by his administrative assistant. It said he had an "information need," a phrase he'd learned from me, and he wanted a comprehensive literature search of the recent research and clinical recommendations for a hernia transplant, an obvious medical impossibility. I laughed and my anxiety disappeared. We were off and running, working well together for several years.

His requests became more frequent as he grew to trust my expertise and respect for his confidentiality. Often they began with a smile and "I'll bet you can't find this!" One of those, which I have permission to tell, came on a Friday afternoon. He said he was leaving in the morning to take a group of Boy Scouts hiking in the San Pedro Wilderness in northern New Mexico, and he wanted a good topographical map. That was certainly out of the scope of a health sciences library; but being a well-educated reference librarian, I relied on the old technique of considering "Who else would want to know?" Within 15 minutes I called him back to say, "They're holding one for you at the [name of outdoor outfitter] store in Albuquerque." He became not only of my best supporters of library services in our hospital, but also one of my best mentors for organization politics.

for the librarian to wait passively to be asked. Supplying bosses with good information even when there has been no explicit request helps librarians look good to peers and to their bosses. It demonstrates both the librarian's interest in the boss's concerns and the librarian's professional expertise. The same conversation with the boss that expresses the librarian's genuine interest can double as a pseudo-reference interview. Even if the boss has or could find this information, the librarian saves the boss time.

S. R. Ranganathan's injunction to "save the time of the reader" (1931, p. 336–381) applies to the boss as well as any other client. Nardi and O'Day (1996) have updated Ranganathan's principle by describing the librarian as "an intelligent person who helps a client accomplish a goal that either the client cannot accomplish on his own because of a lack of expertise or a goal that needs to be accomplished with less effort on the client's part." In this case, your boss becomes your client, someone you wish to delight. Providing service for the boss is an excellent context for demonstrating the application of professional ethical principles, including those of privacy and confidentiality. Delivering the boss needed information at the right moment, perhaps even hand delivering it, can really help the boss look good in her sphere of the organization.

Telling the boss how useful library services are will never be as effective as ensuring that the boss has experienced such services. That is always true in any organization, be it a public library, university library, special library, or school library. Former school principal Gary Hartzell writes:

> Teacher-librarians can draw on the Internet and subscription databases to supply principals with up-to-the-minute information on any given topic in planning sessions and prior to any board, faculty, parent or

business partner meeting. Consistent access to such information can only result in improved administrative decision making. (Hartzell, 2003)

She Never Asked!

Mark, an excellent librarian, had to leave his job to move his family closer to an aging in-law who needed care. He was justifiably proud of the growth of and respect for library services in the company since he arrived 10 years before to be the solo librarian. The information needs analysis and marketing projects had gone well, so in addition to adding new useful services, he'd been able to add staff, resources, and space to the library. Most of that was in place when Jones, the current CEO, arrived two years before Mark had to leave.

One day when several of us from different libraries were talking, he said that he'd heard a rumor that the CEO was not going to replace him when he left.

"I think she wants to save the company the cost of my salary," Mark said.

"Did you do searches for her? Did she ever use your services?" I asked.

"No, never."

"What had you told her?"

"I kept telling her about everything. I sent her memos and reports of user data. I even sent her a copy of a presentation I made about the value of the library to companies like ours. I doubt that she even looked at it. She never asked!"

I didn't say anything because it was too late. Mark was always good at "know" and "tell." I knew he had done "show" with previous administrators, but apparently had not yet proactively provided service for *this* one. Because Mark was waiting to be asked, Jones had not experienced for herself the benefits of Mark's expertise. Unfortunately, that made all the difference.

Another colleague said "Well some people will just never get it, no matter what you do. Probably after you've been gone a while there will be an outcry from your satisfied users wanting the service back." This example of bonding by complaining was a way of trying to soothe him.

What was really likely to happen in the long run? Would clients who had their own influence and budgets on their minds spend the political capital it would cost to tell this administrator that they didn't like her decision not to replace the librarian? Administrators in this industry have a high turnover rate. Would *they* proactively ask the next new administrator? Or would they wait to be asked if they wanted a librarian on board?

A Big "Uh-oh!"

A reference librarian in a public library happened to overhear a conversation at the circulation desk. A newly hired member of the access staff was saying "No, I can't help you with your grandchild's homework, and besides, we're closing in five minutes so you should be leaving." Obviously, some of the lessons of new employee orientation were forgotten, so the librarian jumped in to save the situation, as any professional would have for anyone. In the course of providing the right service, the librarian recognized that the grandparent was a member of the library board that was meeting the next week. After the grandparent left, the librarian discussed the service privately with the new employee, emphasizing the positive "script" phrases she had used.

Without specifying which of several recently hired employees was on duty, the identity of the client, or the content of the request, the librarian immediately told the library director about the incident and volunteered to work with the circulation manager on training new circulation staff in referral. With that information, the library director could immediately schedule in-service staff training sessions on service standards, including referrals and positive communication around closing times, training sessions that she would casually mention early in the Director's Report at the board meeting the next week. It would have been wrong to keep quiet and let the director get hit with a surprise complaint during a public meeting. This proactive solution gave the Director an opportunity to express to the board not only how important good service was, but also what specific measures they were currently taking to improve service. It also gave the board member the opportunity to describe the reference librarian's excellent service.

In this case, the reference librarian not only knew what to do and showed what to do, but also told the director enough to make a difference.

In another publication, he specifically tells librarians to notice what topics are on the principal's mind, to look in resources such as *Education Week* and ERIC *Digests* and "[t]ake the first opportunity you have to conduct a quick search for information on that subject. . . . Prepare a report . . . and deliver it to the principal. . . . Imagine the impression you'll make if the principal mentions that he is interested in or worried about topic 'x,' and a half-hour later you put a summary of related research and descriptions of model programs on his desk. Doing this once, or even a half-dozen times, won't reshape your principal's perceptions of libraries and librarians, but by repeatedly taking the initiative, and coupling that with greater contact and visibility, you'll become a fixture in his thinking—and that is the goal" (Hartzell, 2002).

Informing the Boss: The Good, the Bad, and the Inconvenient Truth

The "tell" in "know, show, and tell" is particularly important in managing the boss. Other savvy people who report to the same boss are informing the boss about the important role of their parts of the organization. The librarian who waits to be noticed will become invisible in the shadows of others who step forward. In the article "Doing a good job? Tell the boss. Self-promotion goes a long way," a hospital facilities manager advises other managers to speak up for themselves. (Andrews, 2001). Librarians have to do it, too! But what should the boss be told?

At the very least, the boss should hear library success stories and positive library talking points, especially if the boss can use them in other contexts. Currency is effective; a brief comment in person or in an e-mail may be more noticed than a paragraph in a regular report much later. An ethical librarian would never reveal the origin and content of a confidential information service without permission, but very satisfied clients are often glad to give that permission or to pass on the good news themselves. The Agile Librarian just has to ask at the right moment. For instance, just after a client says, "This is wonderful! It helps me so much!" the librarian can ask "May I have your permission to tell my boss how we helped you?" or "Would you be willing to tell [boss's name] how useful this service was to you today?"

The Agile Librarian demonstrates integrity when telling the boss about things that don't work as well as things that are successful, putting the success stories

How Susan Almost Got Fired

Susan's new boss, who was not a librarian, had the admirable habit of dropping by the library of the small college for a few minutes almost every day. None of her previous bosses had done that, so she assumed that this daily visit would facilitate excellent communication. He'd come in, make some small talk, and she'd present him with her question or points about library services that she'd chosen for the day. He didn't seem to pay much attention to what she was saying, but she persisted in believing that they were communicating well.

It was a time of large-scale remodeling in the building, as small departments were moving into larger spaces and vice versa. Walls were coming down and being rebuilt in different places. Susan knew that the library expansion she had wanted for years was pretty far down the list. She also knew that the replacement of the old heating and air conditioning system was going to involve ducts in the library ceiling and that they were going to have some inevitable disruption. At lunch one day, someone from the engineering department told her that workers were coming into the library the next week, and she wouldn't have access to a large section of the library for at least a couple of weeks. He suggested she act fast to move whatever would be needed from that area before the construction started. Her head was spinning with planning what would have to be moved, how it could be moved, and to where! The library was seriously overcrowded as it was.

The next day, Susan asked her boss again when the construction was going to reach her area, and he told her it would be months or perhaps a year before that happened. So she checked with some of her other organizational informants, who told her directly that the crew was coming into the library the next week.

When the boss came in the following day, she warily mentioned what she'd heard and he got angry. He snapped, "I told you that they are not coming in here for months. Are you calling me a liar?" He saw her remarks as an attack on his authority, and the conversation quickly escalated into a heated argument. He railed on about how she was going to have to change her attitude, while she kept repeating that she had a right to know what was really going to happen. Soon he was threatening to put her on disciplinary leave without pay. In her entire working life, nothing like that had ever happened to her, and she was furious. Needless to say, she didn't sleep well that night.

She didn't know what to do then. So she looked for a source of good advice. Several years before, when she had had a problem with the performance of one of her employees, Marie Williams in the human resources department had helped. Susan had been impressed with Marie's professionalism and wisdom. Not only did

(Continued)

Marie protect everyone's rights and dignity, but she also taught Susan what to do and what not to do through that very uncomfortable period. So Susan made an appointment to see her. Marie listened to Susan's story like a psychological therapist might, showing no sign of her opinions about the behavior of either Susan's boss or Susan. This was not a bonding by complaining session, and Susan was initially disappointed. As one might do in a reference interview, Marie asked Susan probing questions to get at the underlying issues. When they agreed that there were major communication problems, Marie made some clear suggestions. Following the general script Marie had given her, Susan told her boss that she was very pleased that he came by every day and that no other boss had done that. Then Susan said that she had learned that they had different expectations about that visit; he was being nice and building a relationship, whereas she wanted it to be a business meeting. She was willing to stop burdening him with issues when he dropped in if he would agree to an appointment for a short conference in her office every two weeks. He agreed, but said he thought they wouldn't need to do that more than once a month. She should set up the appointment with his secretary, and she should e-mail him before the meeting with an agenda. That was fine with her. He remarked that they probably should have been doing that from the beginning.

Obviously, neither of them was happy with the status quo and both wanted to preserve their own dignity. At that point, each was willing to try something different. It was a "win-win" solution. It worked. He still dropped by every day and they talked about the weather or local sports. She made the appointments and sent him her agendas, which he rarely changed, before each meeting. Sometimes one or the other rescheduled, but they never skipped it entirely. Sometimes she was impatient because there was something she wanted to talk to him about sooner, but she waited for the meeting, when she would have his attention. Budget time came and went without a hitch. About a year and a half later, at the open house for the newly remodeled and expanded library, he thoroughly praised the library's services in general and her work in particular.

Workers did come in to tear up the place to put in new duct work exactly when her sources had told her they would. The workers found old asbestos that had to be removed under specific safety conditions, so a large part of the stacks area was sealed off for more than two months.

She later found out that at the time she had confronted her boss, *his* boss had just told him that they wouldn't get around to the library remodeling for a year or more. Neither he nor *his* boss was thinking about the ventilation project at the time. They had had different perspectives than Susan.

in an honest context. Perhaps more importantly, if something goes wrong, the bosses should hear it directly from the librarian, so that they are aware of it before hearing of it from another source, especially an influential person. It's not nice to let the boss get blindsided with a complaint out of the blue! With the news of a problem, present one or more possible solutions. Take responsibility for problem solving; don't just toss the burden onto the boss. Choosing between a couple of carefully explained solutions gives the boss an input opportunity and a chance to look good; bringing the boss a problem with no possible solutions is like a hit and run accident.

One old aphorism is to "present an umbrella when you hear thunder instead of after it starts raining." This works for general, semi-predictable problems as well as clear and present ones. For instance, saying "most of our complaints come from people who want more of our services, not less" gives the boss

a library-friendly context in which to see complaints.

"How much?" and "How often?" should the boss hear "the good, the bad, and the inconvenient" directly are judgment calls, and the answers will vary with the management and relationship style. But in any case, it's better to communicate just a little too much than just a little too little. The difference can be between support and abandonment.

In addition to providing direct news from library staff, the Agile Librarian encourages satisfied and grateful clients to tell the boss their stories. That also adds to the boss's bank of positive impressions, and sometimes it carries more weight. Communication and marketing principles discussed in other parts of this book apply as much or more to the boss as to anyone else. Don't take for granted or assume that the boss understands more than others do!

When the Agile Librarian Is a Boss, Too

Most professional librarians supervise someone from the first day on the job, even if it is only student, or part-time or volunteer library staff. Others will move into higher level positions, where they will supervise professionals and paraprofessionals as well. The same principles of respectful, empathetic communication apply. Managing up and managing down have similar dynamics. The wise Agile Librarian carefully connects the interests of higher administration officials and library staff, not siding with one against the other. Playing "them against us," in either direction, as a bonding ploy can backfire with terrible results. Apply the same principles of respect for clients to relations with staff. For further reading about library management roles see Stueart and Moran's *Library and Information Center Management* (2007) or Evans, Ward, and Rugaas' *Management Basics for Information Professionals* (2000).

Summary

Librarians and their bosses, whether or not they are also librarians, work with different perspectives within their organizations. Regardless of the organizational structure or culture and the boss's managerial style, this relationship is crucial to the work of the Agile Librarian. Ideally, each will inform and support the other in different ways. The boss is, or should be, the librarian's ally, mentor, mentee, and client. Managing upward is a professional function requiring thoughtful attention. The knowledgeable librarian not only tells the boss how valuable specific services are, but also ensures that the boss experiences such services personally. Such a librarian can subtly determine the boss's own information needs. Even if the boss is a librarian skilled in information storage and retrieval, there will be times when the Agile Librarian can save the boss's time by delivering exactly what the boss needs at that moment. Telling the boss great stories about good library service is important, but so is letting the boss know about conflicts and disappointments before someone else complains to the boss. It helps prepare the boss to look good in the face of otherwise surprising comments from influential people in the organization. Part of that constant preparation is a subtle but effective campaign to educate the boss in information literacy and library values, as necessary.

References

Abels, Eileen G., Keith W. Cogdill, and Lisl Zach. 2004. Identifying and Communicating the Contributions of Library and Information Services in Hospitals and Academic Health Sciences Centers. *Journal of the Medical Library Association* 92:46–55.

Andrews, John. 2001. Go the Distance: Doing a Good Job? Tell the boss. Self-promotion Goes a Long Way. *Health Facilities Management* 17:14–16.

Bartol, Kathryn M. and David Clarke Martin. 1991. *Management.* New York: McGraw-Hill.

Covey, Stephen R. 1989. *The 7 Habits of Highly Effective People.* New York: Simon & Schuster.

Drake, David. 1990. When Your Boss Isn't a Librarian: For Library Directors, Teaching Non-Librarian Supervisors to Appreciate the Library Is a Big Part of the Job. *American Libraries* 21:152–153.

Evans, G. Edward, Patricia Layzell Ward, and Bendik Rugaas. 2000. *Management Basics for Information Professionals.* New York: Neal-Schuman.

Farmer, Lesley. 2007. Principals: Catalysts for Collaboration. *School Libraries Worldwide* 13:56–65.

Freed, David H. 1999. What Your Hospital's CEO Is Thinking About. *Health Care Manager* 18:11–19.

Hartzell, Gary. 2002. Principals of Success: Getting the Boss's Attention Is Crucial to Your Effectiveness. *School Library Journal* 48:41.

———. 2003. Why Should Principals Support School Libraries? *Teacher Librarian* 31:21–23.

Kearns, Kevin P. 1997. Managing Upward: Working Effectively with Supervisors and Others in the Hierarchy. *Information Outlook* 1:23–28.

Nardi, Bonnie A. and Vicki O'Day. 1996. Intelligent Agents: What We Learned at the Library *Libri* 56:59–88.

Olson, Christi A. and Paula M. Singer. 2004. *Winning with Library Leadership: Enhancing Services through Connection, Contribution, & Collaboration.* Chicago, IL: American Library Association.

Ranganathan, Shiyali Ramamrita. 1931. *The Five Laws of Library Science.* Madras Library Association, London, UK: Edward Goldston. Accessed in the Digital Library of Information Science and Technology (dLIST) Classics Project http://dlist.sir.arizona.edu/1220/ on April 11, 2008.

Special Libraries Association. Presidential Task Force on the Enhancement of the Image of the Librarian/Information Professional. 1991. *Inter-Association Task Force Report on Image.* Washington, D.C.: Special Libraries Association. [ERIC Document ED329267 IR053458.]

Stueart, Robert D. and Barbara B. Moran. 2007. *Library and Information Center Management.* 7th ed. Westport, CT: Libraries Unlimited.

Chapter 5

Impressing Decision Makers

Important people who are neither librarians nor librarians' clients make decisions about libraries. These real people have values, responsibilities, and information needs, and they deserve the attention of librarians. Most libraries would not exist without their support.

Librarians with delighted clients and satisfied bosses can and do lose their jobs. Financial support for their libraries and services can shrink or even evaporate. They may be ignored or demoted in reorganizations and remodeling projects. Why? Because other decision makers undervalue their services. The Agile Librarian constantly and consistently impresses such decision makers, ensuring that they personally experience, as well as understand and appreciate, valuable library services long before the time comes when they have to make such serious funding decisions. As Woodward writes, "For the library to prosper, it must be recognized as important by decision makers in the community. That means that either these decision makers have had personal experience with the library themselves or the message has been brought to them by others who regularly use library services' (Woodward, 2005, p. 23).

Who Are These Decision Makers?

People in positions to make sweeping decisions that affect libraries and their financial support often are not users of library services and have not experienced the value of such services firsthand. Some call these people "stakeholders," a term borrowed from the practice in gambling of having someone not in the game, and therefore neutral, to hold the stakes of the bettors. In the business world the term refers to people who have a vested interested in an enterprise, such as stockholders. Just as successful corporate leaders must pay attention to stockholders, the Agile Librarian has marketing, promotion, and service activities specifically for such stakeholders. The first step is to discover exactly who the important stakeholders in the library's parent organization or broader community are.

Depending on the situation of the library, the stakeholders may be individuals elected to government positions, or they may be administrators, principals, presidents, vice presidents, superintendents, provosts, chief operating officers, chief financial officers, or chief information officers. In addition to individuals, there may be groups of immediate stakeholders, such as boards of directors or trustees, finance and strategic

Examples of Organizational Cousins

For a school librarian

Other teachers who deal with students outside the primary class room, for instance music teachers, coaches, or teachers who work with challenged or gifted students.

For a university librarian

Other departments, such as IT, career development, and writing labs, with university-wide responsibilities; this is different from the departments with library liaisons for user services and collections.

For a public librarian

Other community service departments like sanitation, police, fire, and code compliance. For instance, disaster planning should include planning for special professional information services during a community-wide disaster, not just for collection protection and service continuity. Public librarians can work well with local emergency operations centers if such officials understand how librarians can interview individuals and connect them with the specific information sources they need, even while emergency officials are providing the public with general bulletins.

For a corporate or special librarian

Departments in divisions like public or customer relations, marketing, corporate intelligence, and research and development.

For any librarian

Consider any department that might be perceived, or that perceives itself, as some kind of competitor for resources that the library needs or services librarians provide.

Who are some of your organizational cousins?

planning committees, or library committees. These direct stakeholders may be influenced by people outside the organization, such as major donors; community service and religious organizations; benevolent, philanthropic, or scientific foundations; political action groups; professional associations; news media; and any other group that might want to influence the mission and support of the organization and its library.

In addition to thinking about executive decision makers, remember to consider the "cousins" who are in the same division or report to the same administrator as the library. Other institutional cousins answer to other administrators. If these cousins see their needs and interests as dependent on useful library services they can, in turn, influence their administrators to take win-win ideas to the decision-making table. During high-level negotiations, having library service champions from other parts of an organization makes a big difference, even if the librarian has no direct access to such negotiations.

Although who these stakeholders are and what role they play will vary with the type of library and the type of organization, there always are such people. You will need to learn just who these persons are. The "Who's Who and What Have You Done for Me Lately?" exercise in Chapter 3, p. 46–47 is one good tool for identifying some of these important people.

Librarians often have been shocked to discover that another department has purchased consulting services or resource materials that duplicate less expensive services or sources provided by the library. It is often useless to get into a turf battle after the fact. Collection development expertise is valuable to the organization outside the library as well as within it. Smart librarians work with departments to identify and evaluate sources they need and that complement rather than duplicate library services and sources; the departments are often glad to purchase such items with their own budgets. If management frequently uses sports metaphors, then they will value departments working as team members toward a common goal, the mission of the organization, more than departments that function as competitive teams fighting battles within the organization. The Agile Librarian accepts responsibility for impressing the cousins.

Why Are Their Understanding and Experiences of Library Services Important?

"Out of sight, out of mind" can put library services out of support. Ignoring library services is worse than openly opposing them. Many administrators will give lip service to the library, but not follow up words with supportive action for library services. Why? People who consider the library as a venerable antique monument rather than a vital service department can be a greater threat than other equally uninformed stakeholders. They may be people with memories of childhood library experiences that contrast so much with their current online experiences that they cannot imagine what librarians really do today. It is the Agile Librarian's responsibility to make sure that decision-making stakeholders know and have directly experienced vital professional information services.

Decision makers may cut the budget for library services not because of animosity toward libraries, but because other departments or services have been more successful at promoting the importance of their needs for support. Writing for *College & Research Libraries News*, Stuart Basefsky refers to administrators as "The Other Client." He suggests that "Research libraries ought to consider themselves the 'special library' for the university administration. Any library not pushing its client institution forward can be perceived as holding it back" (Basefsky, 2000). The same holds true for all other kinds of libraries.

In a corporate environment, any department that does not directly produce revenue may seem to be less important than those that do. Cousin revenue-producing departments must experience how library services contribute toward their

> ### Proving the Value of Library Services to Administrators
>
> "It is easy to complain about heartless and narrow-minded administrators who do not see the value of the library. But what have you done to prove the value of the library to them? How are you making sure that they see ways that the library can solve *their* problems? Libraries cost money, and if the administrator cannot be shown why spending that money improves the overall health of the organization, then the administrator has an obligation to shut the library down and spend that money elsewhere. That may turn out to be a bad decision, but it is still a rational one" (Plutchak, 2004, p. 294).

Win-Win on a Budget: My Boss, Her Boss, and Me

My hospital library was crowded and uncomfortable. The shelves were overflowing, and there were few places to sit. I wanted to add compact mobile shelving for the print resources and increase our subscriptions for electronic resources. My new boss, a division director, needed to impress her new boss, a vice president, with her fiscal management acumen. Capitol equipment budget time was coming up, and my boss told the managers who reported to her that we could "no longer afford Cadillac budgets" but should turn in requests that asked for a metaphorically less expensive brand of car instead.

I had planned to do some benchmarking comparing our seating and shelving space to other libraries of similar size across the country. Then I listened to what the president was saying and had some general chats with several vice presidents. At that point I wasn't talking about library needs. I was doing more listening than talking.

Our hospital was in a metropolitan area with other competing hospitals. Most hospital income comes from patient care fees paid by Medicare or some kind of healthcare insurance. But patients cannot admit themselves to hospitals; doctors with admitting privileges for particular hospitals do that. Area doctors choose which hospitals' or healthcare systems' medical staffs they want to join for admitting privileges. Another factor is their choice of health care insurance providers. A finite number of doctors bring most of the business, and thus income, to each hospital. Therefore, attracting doctors, even though they neither pay nor receive fees from the hospital, is crucial to the financial health of all hospitals.

Attracting doctors who might otherwise become affiliated with other hospitals was on the minds of top decision makers. Hospital libraries produce no revenue, but library ambiance and useful services can be attractive to doctors. I needed to convincingly tie installing new shelving with administrative concerns. A Rigid Librarian might have just put in a proposal for the shelving and then grumbled when it was rejected, or, because of past rejections, not even put in the proposal because administrators, as usual, kept saying that the budget would be tight this year. I set myself a different group of tasks: looking for internal and external stories and evidence. I did a small, informal survey of doctors that asked them how comfortable they found the library. I told some who expressed discomfort that if we put in compact mobile shelving we could double the seating and shelving space without moving a wall. A few of my "champions" really liked that idea, so I suggested that they talk it up in various influential settings.

(Continued)

goals. Librarians in any kind of library must know, show, and tell the value of their services not only to the organization in general, but to the stakeholders in specific.

Schools, corporations, hospitals, or universities may hire outside consultants to make reorganization plans, but the final decision as to which of the consultants' recommendations will be implemented rests with the organization's top decision makers. Administrators will reject or ignore consultants' recommendations to eliminate higher paid library professionals while keeping lower paid library staff, or to close the library completely if those administrators understand that the supposed savings would be a false economy. If they personally would miss professional library services, they will be less likely to cut such services than they would be if it made no difference in their own lives. Decision makers who have personally experienced expert information services are less likely to heed such recommendations. Their own experiences may have more influence on their actions than librarians' reports of large numbers of satisfied clients.

What Are Stakeholder Concerns?

Agile Librarians discover and value stakeholder concerns. Economists understand that values are more than monetary. Choosing to be attentive to or to ignore something is an expression of value. What must librarians do to get stakeholders to choose to be attentive to libraries? How can they discover these decision makers' concerns?

Library and information science research provides some generalizable evidence of values and information behaviors of groups of people. The librarian who values the concerns of individual decision makers can use social techniques, such as those used during

Next, I made it my business to determine which hospitals the administrators thought were the most important competitors for doctors. Then, with the help of my local hospital library consortium, I gathered benchmarking data comparing library space in those hospitals with ours. As a community hospital, we really weren't competing much on a national basis, so this made more sense than using national benchmarking data. Traditional benchmarking takes into consideration hospital size and many other factors, but in this instance I was concerned only with the availability of medical librarians, collections, and services to local practicing doctors on their daily rounds.

I didn't gather data just about shelving and seating space. I also looked for more expensive facilities and services that our competing hospitals' libraries offered. Then I went to my boss with two lists of capital equipment requests. One I labeled the "Cadillac list." It listed the libraries in the competing area hospitals and then listed expensive things they had bought to delight their physician clients. By contrast, my cheaper brand of car list looked like a bargain. It included the shelving and a couple of other things I didn't expect would be accepted, but all were tied directly into physician satisfaction. I had supportive notes from physicians to that effect.

I won't say that it completely worked the first time, but gradually the support grew and we did get our mobile shelving and our no-construction remodel. The administrators were happy enough with the results to bring prospective medical staff members by the library on their facility tours. My boss got credit for being a team player on two kinds of top administration concerns: keeping costs down and attracting physicians. It was a win-win for everyone.

One of my colleague librarians at another area hospital put our shelving on her "Cadillac" list when she was making a pitch for something else. Our hospitals may have been competitive, but the librarians were very cooperative and mutually supportive.

the reference interview, to discover what these individuals value. You should carefully read reports and memos from decision makers. Asking genuine non-confrontational questions about such reports is not only informative, but is also a positive way to make or enhance relationships with such people. Assumptions and guessing are both dangerous and deceptive. The important thing is for the librarian to discover decision makers' concerns and then successfully explain and demonstrate to them directly how library services relate to their concerns and values. In laudable efforts to express to decision makers their successes in support of particular client groups, the librarian may overlook the individual decision maker's needs and personal experience, or lack thereof, with such services.

Information Technology Cousins' Dilemma

Many decisions that affect libraries are not solely budgetary. People who make decisions affecting libraries might not be in the librarians' direct chain of command. Such was the case with decision makers in my hospital's information technology (IT) department.

System security is an important concern for IT departments in all organizations, but especially in hospitals. IT policy decisions must include serious protection for any systems that might be in any way related to patient records and other confidential information. At my hospital, employees with network access were allowed access only to the hospital's e-mail system and not to any Web-based external e-mail providers. IT said that the main reason was to prevent virus infections from coming in through e-mail attachments. So sites for access to outside e-mail providers were filtered; they effectively blocked access to such sites on the hospital network. At administrators' request, they also blocked sites they considered unrelated to hospital employees' duties, such as gaming and online auction sites; these sites could be serious non-work distractions to on-duty personnel. This filtering issue is somewhat different from that of children's access in schools and public libraries, but the technology is similar.

While eating lunch with IT people, I learned of a conflicting concern. Patients' family and visitors frequently asked for access to Web-based e-mail and unfiltered access to their own business sites. They needed to keep up with relationships outside of the hospital, and telephones weren't enough. It was a serious public relations issue. Also, employees wanted access when they were off-duty.

I needed to use the Ariel® Internet document delivery system to speed up sending and receiving scanned copies of articles from many libraries in the National Library of Medicine DOCLINE® interlibrary loan system. Because Ariel communicates Internet Provider (IP) address to IP address without any intervening servers, it requires an open port through the network firewall. Large university IT departments can more easily work that out than IT departments in hospitals, whose primary IP is shared with other institutions and includes many different system firewalls. I had even written an article about the problem (McKnight, 2001).

The top IT decision makers were concerned with both the hospital network security and patient and visitor satisfaction. I had the hardware and software for Ariel, but without a top IT decision to give the library some kind of open port to the Internet, it was useless. The Rigid Librarian would have insisted that that

Discovering and responding to the information needs implicit in decision makers' concerns is more difficult than the usual client service, but not less important. Marketing services to anyone begins with determining needs and concerns. Reporting useful data helps not only librarians, but also non-librarian decision makers to make decisions when the data directly addresses the concern. The first step is asking, not providing answers.

Some decision makers had excellent experiences of library services when they were in school, but do not understand how different library services relate to their current concerns. They may remember librarians as kind people, but do not recognize the professional expertise on which that kindness was founded. Just like much of the general population, they may believe that library services are good for kids and for schoolwork, but not valuable in other setting. Others may have had bad experiences in the organization or

(Continued)

elsewhere when they sought help finding information. Some are likely to believe that the combination of their own intelligence and their easy access to the World Wide Web precludes any need for the services of a professional librarian. They may have "the outdated impression that 'library work' is vaguely secretarial, instead of more closely aligned with IT or records management" (Tomlin, 2000, p. 20).

Decision makers for schools may see librarians as babysitters more than as instructors. Even school principals may not understand that school librarians can supply information that they need to be better principals. They may compliment the librarian profusely

was the only way Ariel would work. We needed a different solution. After talking with the IT decision makers, I suggested that they a get high-speed Internet access line through a completely different IP obtained from a local cable or DSL service provider. It didn't have to have the large bandwidth of other hospital connections. We could connect a few computers in the library to that service and invite visitors and off-duty employees to have unfiltered access there. Having no connection at all to any hospital network certainly is the best possible firewall. All we asked was that it had the stable IP address we needed for Ariel document delivery. That meant getting a business connection unlike the constantly changing shared IP addresses used by home connections. They agreed, provided we would take responsibility for monitoring use.

This separate access solved their problem with requests for unfiltered access and allowed us to use Ariel. In itself, that was a win-win solution. IT staff and other employees encouraged people who requested access to use the library computers, so it brought people to the library space who might never have looked for it. It gave us the chance to guide their information seeking and once more demonstrated how the library, as an information access service, contributed to the hospital's mission.

One lesson to consider is how much easier it is for us to notice when someone else's decision blocks our service goals than it is for us to notice when our decision blocks theirs. It takes some investment and investigation to generate win-win solutions, but it is *so* worth the time!

What are some decisions your cousins have made that are hampering your service delivery? What concerns did they have that prompted those decisions? Can you think of a better win-win idea?

about the library, but their actions speak much louder than their words. They may not realize how their librarians' expertise can help in their own daily lives as well as in support of the mission of the school in general.

The Agile Librarian recognizes that these decision makers have different information needs in their current roles than they did when they experienced libraries when they were in school. Unless they experience expert service directly, they are unlikely to make the mental connection between the librarian's expertise and their current concerns. The Agile Librarian will work to ensure that not only the boss, but also many of the organization's other decision makers have directly experienced professional service beyond that which they can provide for themselves.

In her article "Reaching Out to Administrators," Anna Beth Crabtree recommends having lunch with organizational cousins to find out what is going on elsewhere. She suggests volunteering to serve on interdepartmental teams to get to know what others are doing as well as to watch for opportunities for library service.

Asking about people's interests and needs isn't nosy, it's necessary for quality service and resources. Once you get to know what's on someone's mind, you can discover ways to make that person a delighted client, and an executive who is a delighted client can be a library champion. Crabtree recommends looking for at least one administrative champion, perhaps even someone not directly responsible for the library. This person can promote library services in meetings that the librarian cannot attend. She writes:

> Be sure to remind your ally when it is time to assist with promotions and give him/her a printed list of key library-related information to disseminate. Following each meeting, contact your collaborator to determine if you can do any follow-up contacts with those expressing interest in library services or training. (Crabtree, 2000)

Actions That Impress

Non-librarian decision makers must have an accurate, relevant, and up-to-date understanding of library services before a crisis happens. That doesn't just happen. If the librarian simply assumes that decision makers ought to know and doesn't act to make sure that they know, the decision makers' impressions of the library's service may be formed by the first people who complain to them.

It can be harder to get opportunities to interact with other non-librarian decision makers than it is with your boss. So you have to make sure that you get them. Because such opportunities may be scarce, it is even more important to (1) find out as much as possible about the other's perspective, (2) develop very clear, non-jargon descriptions of exactly what library services are, and (3) be able to improvise well on the spot when (2) doesn't align with (1)!

Active and Personal Direct Information Services

Reports, newsletters, brochures, Web sites, and blogs can describe library services simply or in great detail. But in all cases they are passive means of communication. These decision makers cannot be expected to seek out every library publication and study it thoroughly. Agile Librarians communicate directly and actively. They communicate much more personally and with more context sensitivity than any automated help system can. Similar to the reference interview, this is a performance art in real time that is developed with frequent practice.

Savvy cousins will also seek decision makers' attention. Decision makers, through experience, develop sensitive radar for thoughtless sycophancy. Anyone who wants effective interaction with decision makers must develop social intelligence (Goleman, 2007).

Savvy librarians are positive without shallow flattery and provide real information service rather than apple polishing. They inform the stakeholders both about what they do, with their words, and by what they do, with their actions. If the individualized personal touch includes services such as hand delivery not generally available to all client groups, so be it. In the long run, the influence gained by such services helps support services for everyone. Information literacy or new resource courses taught to groups can be adapted for one-on-one appointments with administrators and other stakeholders. Better yet, treat administrators to sneak previews of new offerings. If they don't want to come to the library, make an appointment and take the new services to the administrator. Meet them more than half way!

Results may not be immediately obvious, and there is a temptation to give up. It's impossible to predict which small remarks or details will have the butterfly effect of imperceptibly but significantly influencing later decisions. It all comes down to "nothing ventured, nothing gained." Doing something is better than doing nothing!

General Visibility

It is easier to be visible to the boss than to other decision makers. The non-librarian boss directly over the library will accept more responsibility for it than the decision maker elsewhere in the institution. Anna Beth Crabtree, in "Methods for Reaching Out to Administrators," writes:

> Visibility is critical. Keep the library, its services, resources and staff available and visible to all administrators, not just the administrator directly responsible for the library. You never know when someone else's administrator may assume responsibility for the library or have influence in determining the library's budget allocation. (Crabtree, 1999)

Make sure that the library is included in new administrator orientation as well as new employee orientation. Encourage anyone who gives tours of the facility to include the library, and greet such tours with enthusiasm. If the ambiance is right, your organization's dignitaries will not only come by the library to show it off, but may also leave people there that they don't know what to do with for a little while. Use every such opportunity for show and tell.

Get outside the library. The teacher librarian who regularly attends school board meetings and the public librarian who is active in local charitable, faith, or service organizations is visible not only to stakeholders but also to the greater community. In addition to attending professional library meetings that librarians attend, go exhibit or even present at stakeholders' and clients' professional meetings.

Stakeholders' Reports

Find them. Read them. Pay attention. Ask for clarification or elaboration on some points. Notice who appears to prefer quantitative reports, those predominantly consisting of numbers with statistical analysis, to qualitative reports, those predominantly consisting of words with narrative explanations, or some combination thereof. Some will appear to believe that only what can be measured is real, whereas others will agree with the maxim often attributed to Albert Einstein, "Not everything that counts can be counted and not everything that can be counted counts" (Einstein, Calaprice edition, 2000).

Reports are keys to what is important to each decision maker and how each prefers to communicate. Reports are good sourcees of information about values, priorities, and familiar vocabulary.

Administrators may adopt concepts and vocabulary from currently popular "expert" sources, such as speakers, books, blogs, or Web sites. Some are enduring management concepts and some are passing fads. Some will mix jargon and metaphors from different periods in their education and experience. The same is true of pedagogical language in school libraries. In any case, it behooves the Agile Librarian to learn the vocabulary and concepts on decision makers' minds and to minimize esoteric library jargon when communicating with people from a different part of the organizational culture

Your Reports

The Agile Librarian has two kinds of reports. One kind is informal, private, and not published. It includes some kinds of data, evaluations, tentative plans, and wishful thinking. It may contain usage data and private observations. For instance, it might include an "In case of windfall or budget cut, break glass" file, which is a collection of some ideas for what could be purchased or cut on short notice. Some librarians keep a personal journal about library services. Some of these kinds of reports have to be kept in a secure place. This kind of private report can be mined for supportive information for the other kind of report, the kind that goes to a specific administrator or audience.

Reports to others are, in a sense, published information. They are a valuable part of "tell," described in Chapter 1. Even if it is a private memo or e-mail to only one person, there is no way to predict who might see it eventually. All reports, blog postings, and information compiled for others are, at some level, marketing communication and must be thoughtfully composed. Complain respectfully, on the rare occasion that you must, but don't whine or appear confrontational.

I Really Should NOT Have Done This.
(Professional Fool. Don't Try This at Home)

For my quarterly report, after the required numeric data tables, I included pages of lyrical prose about our wonderful library services. I included everything that I thought could possibly interest this administrator; however, I had a sneaking suspicion that he really didn't read it. So one quarter I slipped into the middle of a paragraph several rhyming sentences from a Dr. Seuss book. Having heard nothing about it, I later slipped a direct reference to that passage into a conversation. No response. Well, then I knew for sure that he wasn't reading it. Did I blame him? No. I just changed my style for the next report to short anecdotes that got to the point, the same kind of stories he used in his reports. It worked. I heard him mention in a meeting something he had read in my report.

No matter what the format, communicate clearly and stay on your message. Make the most important point first because the reader may not go any further. Think of the inverted pyramid format used in news reports and articles. The report recipient may not have the time or motivation to read all of it. Remember this principle even if there is a required format for a particular report. Any format can be tweaked; failure to answer a direct question can appear evasive. Librarians tend to rely too heavily on quantitative reports when good stories would present the message more clearly. Start with a hook to get attention, present a problem with possible solutions, and describe good results.

In fact, one should consider whether or not a particular regular report, or some feature in it, is necessary. If it doesn't vary substantially, it will be easy to ignore. Information in an occasional, unexpected announcement or an FYI report will get more attention than writing the same thing in a regular report or newsletter. In a study funded by the Medical Library Association of how institutional administrators and library directors see value in library services, researchers discovered significant differences between what library directors reported and what impressed administrators. Some of their respondents suggested that:

- Reporting should be as needed—LIS [Library and Information Services] directors should avoid preparing reports that will not be read.
- Both qualitative and quantitative data should be used in reports for administrators.
- When LIS directors receive positive feedback from users, they should encourage it to "percolate up."
- LIS directors have to make themselves known by being their own public relations agents.
- It is essential to be proactive about making LIS services known.
- Whenever possible, LIS staff should participate in strategic planning processes for the organization.

The researchers concluded:

Directors of library and information services typically rely on data other than financial impact to communicate their value. Common measures include use statistics, data on the impact of use for individuals and measures of users' satisfaction. . . . Library directors should identify measureable LIS contributions to an organization's mission and goals in consultation with the organization's administrator. . . . Both quantitative and qualitative data may be provided as compelling evidence of LIS contributions, and these contributions should be communicated to administrators using a variety of methods. A combination of formal and informal communication channels were identified as particularly effective. (Abels, Cogdill, and Zach, 2004)

In Chapter 9, you will find descriptions of methods for both private and published evidence reporting, but in and of itself, such activity does not impress decision makers. Data that seems to be important to librarians may be irrelevant to decision makers. Elaborate charts and reports created at high expense in time and effort can be useless if decision makers don't perceive them as supportive of their own conceptions of the mission and value of the organization. Carefully chosen evidence presented in the right context is much more effective.

A writer's maxim is that the best fiction must include well-researched facts, and the best nonfiction will always tell a story. Reports of analysis of numeric data communicate value in the context of presenting a story. Decision makers like to hear and pass on stories that make them and their organizations look good. The librarian who has good relations with the public relations department can ensure that stories of how the library saved the day will spread to the news media. Public libraries get such coverage; other libraries can, too. Reports are very important, but it takes more than reports to impress non-librarian decision makers.

Summary

The Agile Librarian actively seeks those in the organization who make decisions affecting library services, even if they are not regular clients or directly managing the library. Decision makers have different perspectives and concerns and may be unaware of how professional library services can contribute to the organization in general and to their information needs in particular. Such stakeholders' experiences with libraries earlier in their lives may have been negative, or, if positive, may be perceived as irrelevant to current needs. Their influence is too important to be ignored.

As with other clients, the librarian has to constantly gather evidence of what their concerns are. With those in mind, the Agile Librarian will demonstrate directly and personally the applicability of library services for decision makers, as well as report on the utility and value of these services to the rest of the organization. That means ensuring that they have positive, current experience of the best of their librarian's services. The Agile Librarian is clearly visible in the life of the institution and known for win-win solutions to challenges other departments face as well as those faced by the library service. The Agile Librarian stays informed and informs decision makers through many media, including reports, but understands that reports alone will not impress decision makers.

References

Abels, Eileen G., Keith W. Cogdill, and Lisl Zach. 2004. Identifying and Communicating the Contributions of Library and Information Services in Hospitals and Academic Health Sciences Centers. *Journal of the Medical Library Association* 92:46–55.

Basefsky, Stuart. 2000. The Other Client: Information Training for Administrators Pays Dividends for the Library. *College & Research Libraries News* 61:100–101.

Crabtree, Anna Beth. 1999. Leadership Alert: Methods for Reaching Out to Administrators, Part I. *National Network* 24(1):4–5.

———. 2000. Leadership Alert: Methods for Reaching Out to Administrators, Part II. *National Network* 24(3):8–9.

Einstein, Albert. 2000. *The Expanded Quotable Einstein.* (Alice Calaprice, Ed.). Princeton, NJ: Princeton University Press.

Goleman, Daniel. 2006. *Social Intelligence: The New Science of Human Relationships.* New York: Bantam.

McKnight, Michelynn. 2001. Ariel and Hospital Libraries: The Struggle with Firewalls for Internet Document Delivery. *Journal of Hospital Librarianship* 1(4):1–16.

Plutchak, T. Scott. 2004. Means not Ends. *Journal of the Medical Library Association* 92:293–295.

Tomlin, Anne C. 2000. Horn Tooting 101: Building and Using a Portfolio. *National Network* 25:18–19.

Woodward, Jeannette. 2005. *Creating the Customer-Driven Library: Building on the Bookstore Model.* Chicago: American Library Association.

Chapter 6

Choosing an Instantly Credible Professional Image

Librarians have a professional, ethical responsibility to respect their clients, their stakeholders, their profession, and themselves enough to pay attention to image. Good first impressions improve the chances of having continuing positive relationships. In that first instant, people often gather more information from what they see than from words they read or hear later. We know that years of psychological research has documented the snap judgments that people make about other people in just a few seconds (Bixler and Nix-Rice, 1997, p. 4). If the librarian, the Web site, the library, and the information resources look attractive, bright, clear, well prepared, and user friendly, people will gladly follow the first impression with immediate interest. On the other hand, if they appear faded, outdated, vague, unfriendly, neglected, incomprehensible, or downright ugly, people will not take the time to meet, greet, ask, look, listen, read, or browse any further.

Credibility is "the quality or power of inspiring belief" (*Merriam-Webster's Collegiate Dictionary*, 2003). An immediate impression of credibility encourages people to trust your service. You know that you are knowledgeable and dependable and that your information services are reliable. You know you can make them convenient, but can you convey an impression of your expertise, dependability, reliability, and client friendliness in an instant? How does the Agile Librarian instantly inspire professional credibility? No one ever has a second chance to make a first impression. You have choices to make about what that first impression is.

You also have choices to make about the instant image of your library as a place and as an online presence. As Christine Olson writes, "Whether you've carefully chosen your image or chosen to ignore it, your library does *have* an image. Wouldn't you prefer to dictate exactly what that image is?" (Olson, 1993). Image management is both obvious and subtle; what happens in an instant of attention must inspire trust and confidence, or you and your entire enterprise will be dismissed and ignored. Olson continues, "Libraries with poor images fail to attract the attention their skills and resources deserve" (Olson, 1993). People do not have time to make full evaluations of, let alone remember, everything that they see. Everyone uses cognitive attention skills learned in infancy to build conceptions of reality based on small amounts of sensory information. Intentionally or unintentionally, most appearances express values and choices. In short, the packaging has to be attractive enough to convince the potential client to check the contents.

Instant credibility comes from an entire experiential image, not just one piece of it. It starts with impressions made by the sensual, cognitive, and social effects of everything connected with library service. That includes not only you and your staff, but also the building, rooms, decoration, furnishings, arrangement, and contents of the physical library. Some first impressions are made through Web sites, blogs, or social networking services, and they, too, must be carefully planned to inspire confidence and credibility. Furthermore, all of these images have to be compatible. The affect of a beautiful building can easily be negated by an experience of a surly, unkempt library employee. Likewise, the first impression of a neatly dressed librarian disappears in an ugly, messy workspace.

The Agile Librarian takes the time to consider carefully what can be done to create instant credibility. Because of their information retrieval skills, librarians can find abundant resources from experts in real and virtual architecture and design, professional dress, and the graphic arts. Maslow's hierarchy of human needs begins with the physiological (Maslow, 1943) and so do all human avenues of perception. It is not enough to use verbal communication channels; people also learn through sensory channels. Everyday language uses so many sensual metaphors because that is how people perceive the world around them. For instance, "I see" or "I hear you" express understanding; "I feel" expresses belief; and "That's distasteful" implies repulsion. Positive images and impressions begin with positive sensual experiences.

This chapter presents ways to influence what people perceive through their senses. It provides suggestions about presenting the image of a trustworthy professional service in words. But first, it is important to look at the results of research into pre-conceived notions that potential clients may have before they first encounter you or your library.

A Study of the Image of the Library and Information Professional

Some years ago, five major American library associations (Special Library Association, American Library Association, American Society for Information Science, American Association of Law Libraries, and the American Association of School Libraries) and a group of advisory associations (Art Libraries Society, Association of College and Research Libraries, and the Medical Library Association) undertook an extensive two-year study of the image of the librarian and information professional to discover how that image could be enhanced. They formed the Inter-Association Task Force, an expansion of the SLA President's Task Force on Enhancing the Image of the Librarian and Information Professional. It was chaired by Kaycee Hale, librarian of the Fashion Institute of Design and Merchandising. Hale was a former fashion model who taught continuing education classes on the subject of personal image for librarians' associations.

The Task Force surveyed library and information professionals' self-images. They surveyed business and community leaders for their perceptions of librarians and libraries. International perspectives and perceptions of library and information science school students were also included in the study. Finally, a group of management consultants analyzed the results to determine whether or not there was a correlation between commonly accepted image and pay.

With the help of the marketing research consultants, they asked 8,000 leaders in business, academia, government, media, and the performing arts in the United States and Canada about their experiences with librarians. Most of the respondents reported positive experiences and considered librarians to be dedicated, reliable, and good communicators. On the other hand, fewer than 25% of the respondents believed them to be assertive or imaginative. They also surveyed a large group of library and information association members from a number of different countries. The librarians reported themselves to be happy in their positions, but about half of them believed that librarianship has an image problem. Both groups believed that librarians are not well paid (Special Libraries Association, 1991).

Improving Our Image to Increase Our Credibility

Sadly, most of the problems reported by that study are still evident today. Negative stereotypes of librarians persist in popular culture. Librarians have discussed, countered, or supported stereotypical images of librarians in informal conversations, e-mail listservs, blogs such as Petrosino (2008), Web sites such as Absher (1997–2004), and formal articles. Some have raised the practice of collecting appearances of libraries or librarians in movies, television, commercial advertising, or even pornography to the level of a serious hobby. (See Raish, 2008.) One controversial image was that of a toy librarian action figure representing real librarian Nancy Pearl in stereotypical dress and pose (McFee, 2005).

The late 20th-century explosion of online systems easily accessible to almost everyone changed the public conception of personal information literacy. In some areas, online expertise enhanced the image and status of the librarian, but in too many quarters the *content* retrieval expertise has been confused with expertise in building the *conduit* systems (Cowen and Edson, 2002). The Rigid Librarian may believe that providing conduits and containers of content is enough. The Agile Librarian creates environments in which people clearly see and experience professional information expertise as reliable, credible, attractive, and convenient. These environments include more than the appearance and action of the individual librarian or the physical or virtual space. Instant credibility requires everything that one sees to be convincing. One contradictory element can undermine the entire effort.

Color Attracts

The boring negative stereotype of the librarian is colorless, and the colorless surroundings in which some librarians work reinforce unfortunately bland and colorless self-perceptions. One of the more famous stereotypical examples in fiction is Barbara Gordon, better known as Batgirl. She was first introduced in 1967 as a "librarian and daughter of Police Commissioner Gordon" saying, "The whole world thinks I'm just a plain Jane, a colorless female 'brain,'" as she prepares her colorful costume for the Policeman's Masquerade Ball (Fox, 1967, p. 9). After her debut as a superhero, the story continues with "Next Day, Dr. Barbara Gordon tries to lose herself in the mundane world of the library" and reflects on her normal life as "empty and humdrum" (Fox, 1967, p. 11). Even though the author acknowledges her graduate education, he uses the colorless metaphor to reinforce the idea that nothing she does in the library could be exciting or even interesting. The episode ends with her father wishing she were less like a librarian and more like Batgirl (Fox, 1967, p. 22). He and his daughter didn't know how much of a colorful superhero an Agile Librarian really can be at work every day!

Look at products in a supermarket. Attractive color in packaging is the first thing to grab the shoppers' attention. In the produce department, people want brightly colored items. When oranges are picked, their skins have a lot of green and they aren't a very bright orange. Producers expose them to a gas that makes them look more bright orange. People buy more bright oranges because they look better to them, even if they know that the external color has nothing to do with the taste of the fruit inside.

Color attracts and pleases us. Given a choice between something beautifully presented and the same thing indifferently presented, people will usually choose the beautiful, even if it may have less intrinsic value. Thoughtful use of color makes a librarian, a Web site, and a library entrance more attractive. Children express preference for particular colors from an early age, and most adults are aware of their own strong reactions to certain colors. Color can excite, delight, calm, or reassure. It affects how people feel in their homes, their workplaces, and their libraries.

Politicians, newscasters, and actors in advertisements have to create an instant impression of credibility. They will always wear some carefully chosen color. Even if they are wearing a neutral suit, something else is always there that adds a touch of contrasting color to make them look instantly credible. This doesn't happen by accident, and it makes a difference. In our culture, women tend to wear more bright colors than men, but men who have to make such instant impressions often use ties for that tasteful spark of color. Women dressed completely in neutral colors can spark up their positive image with lip color.

Take the time to learn what your best colors really are. What looks good on the rack or on your best friend may not flatter you. By buying only what makes you look good, you will feel good, and you'll save money on your wardrobe for decades. By sticking with a range of compatible colors, you won't have to spend as much on shoes and accessories.

We often make areas for children's services colorful, but color is important to adults, too. The Helen DeRoy Medical Library at Providence Hospital in Southfield, Michigan, is an excellent example of the use of color in a library that serves only adults. The hint of blue visible from the door opens into a vista of different shades of blue from the carpet to the ceiling, and everything in between; even the glare baffles on the light fixtures are a gentle blue. The effect is both calming and stimulating. The stacks radiate in a fan shape from a point just beyond the service desk, and one can see comfortable seating and work spaces at the wide end of each aisle. Of course, the director, Carole Gilbert, coaches the staff on looking instantly credible and welcoming everyone who comes through the door.

A color makeover for a Web site can be done in seconds. A color change for a library space can be done inexpensively with paint and fabric. Borrow ideas from places other than libraries. Learn from professional decorators who provide free home decoration advice on cable television channels. If one can coordinate one outfit of clothing, one can coordinate colors for a room or site. Take a risk. It may very well pay off with increased interest. If it doesn't, changing again can be just as inexpensive as trying it in the first place. Look at unsightly, but necessary, repairs as opportunities to brighten up that area. Look, imagine, and try some color.

Library spaces can be important to communities, organizations, and cultures. Professional librarians' journals have special issues dedicated to library buildings; they are often heavily illustrated with professional photographs of beautiful but unpopulated library spaces. (See *The Library as Place: History, Community, and Culture,* Buschman and Lecki, 2007.) As a piece of clothing on a hanger doesn't fulfill its purpose until someone wears it, these spaces are only successful when they are filled with delighted clients, professionals, and staff.

> ## A Short Discovery Exercise
>
> Watch a television news show and its commercials for 10 minutes. Count each intentional use of color you see on people, in graphics, and on sets. You probably will not have time to notice all of them in one watching, nor will you have time to tally everything you notice. If you can record a few minutes and play it back slowly, you will notice even more, including how color reinforces or even contradicts content.
>
> The broadcast may be much more colorful than you had consciously realized before; however, that colorfulness is the result of psychological research. You can borrow at least some of demonstrated results of that research for enhancing the color experience of library services for your clients.
>
> In the broadcast, no color is left to chance. What would happen if the set were carefully designed, but the anchor walked on set wearing colors that clashed with it? Or what would happen if the person had made good appearance choices, but the set was left to chance?
>
> Try the same color survey with the Web site for a library you don't know well, or walk into a library you've never seen before. What do you notice? If you can be objective, try it with your own library.

"In general, bookstores are not expensive buildings. If you look closely, they are often little more than warehouses. However, they have made a science of appealing to their customers through their senses" (Woodward, 2005, p. 86). In the successful bookstore, the walls, displays, and signs are colorful. They usually look from a distance more substantial and sumptuous than they really are. The scent of coffee or chocolate may be in the air, and one hears the subtle sound of music. Some libraries look like they just happened, with little thought for the sensory perceptions of humans who use them and work in them.

Dress for Your Clients

Dressing for a special occasion shows respect for the importance of the occasion. Dressing for professional service and presenting ourselves well shows respect for our clients and our profession. What someone wears to work is a demonstration of their judgment (Glassman, 2008). With or without formal, culture-appropriate dress codes, managers and librarians can dress thoughtfully and encourage their colleagues and employees to do the same out of respect for clients, rather than for personal comfort and convenience.

When you get up in the morning, you make choices that will directly affect what you look like that day. If you are staying home all day, those choices arise from your own needs and comfort, but if you are going out of the house, your decisions affect everyone who will see you that day. Do you decide not to take a shower or brush your hair? Do you choose the clothing and accessories you will wear to work out of respect for your clients and profession? Do you choose just what feels good to you? Do you grab something and try to ignore your appearance completely, not even looking in a mirror before you go out the door? As Janet Eklund writes in *Library Journal*:

> No matter what one wears to work, in the end, one's appearance is still a reflection of how an institution is viewed by the public. Like it or not, and whether one wants it to be or not, attire says much about the person and plays a significant role in whether one is taken seriously in their job. Sloppy clothes have the potential to convey sloppy attitude. (Eklund, 2002)

Your need to be comfortable is not an excuse for sloppiness; neither is "I don't make enough money to dress professionally." You can feel comfortable in clothes that both fit and make you look good. You can choose what you buy with limited funds and accept that it is more cost effective to wear a few flattering, put-together professional outfits repeatedly than it is to wear a lot of randomly selected pieces from your closet that do nothing to enhance your credibility. Clothing style generally can't be copyrighted. It's okay to look at more expensive business attire and then buy less expensive editions with similar style and color. Sometimes all it takes is a change of buttons, ties, or accessories.

So, what should you wear? Every library is part of a larger organization or community, and the clothing style appropriate in one may be completely inappropriate in another. In the classes I taught in different parts of the United States, librarians sometimes would say to me, "You don't understand, we're more casual here in [name of state]." But I didn't see any difference between what the librarians in that state were wearing and what I saw librarians wearing in other states. "Casual" at work is never the same as "casual" at home or on vacation. Even though few librarians work in a uniform, what they wear does project an image of importance to the organization. In any case, the librarian would be better off dressing more formally than casually. Look around and pay attention to what confident, upbeat people are wearing and contrast it to what you see others wearing.

Tim Gunn makes it all sound simple, and in a sense, it is. "The key to getting your fashion right is the same for men and women. First of all, know who you are and how you want the world to perceive you" (Gunn, 2008). Special librarian Mallory Stark elaborates well on understanding the distinction between one's desired professional image and the perceived professional image in her article "Creating a Positive Professional Image" (Stark, 2005). Gunn continues his direct advice "Understand what colors, what patterns look good on you and the whole interaction of silhouette, proportion and fit. If you can get that right, you'll look good in anything (Gunn, 2008).

School librarians probably should take more dress cues from the principal and district administrators than from the burnt-out teacher down the hall. One wise school principal who was in an inner-city school always dressed as if she expected to be photographed for the cover a fashion magazine. She had once visited a very large school district where she noticed that all the staff in that inner-city school wore dull colors and serviceable shoes. As she visited other schools with fewer children from families in poverty, the clothing of the staff became increasingly attractive. She had made up her mind that no matter what school she was assigned to as teacher or administrator, her children would see an attractive person who cared enough about them to dress well for them. University librarians tend to dress more casually, but they still need to create the impression in the library that they are not students. Again, administrative or management style is a better choice.

Starting out the morning well put together doesn't ensure that you will stay that way all day. Make sure that there is a full-length mirror somewhere in your office or staff room for a quick check, and always have a small clothing repair kit and spot remover handy. Some libraries have a small supply of ties, scarves, accessories, and so forth in their staff rooms for clothing emergencies.

For great advice about personal image for professional men and women, see Bixler and Nix-Rice, *The New Professional Image: From Business Casual to the Ultimate Power Look.* It emphasizes dress more than behavior, but does include a chapter on "Professional Presence." Bixler and a different co-author cover professional presence more extensively in *5 Steps to Professional Presence: How to Project Confidence, Competence and Credibility at Work* (Bixler and Dugan, 2001).

Neatness Counts in the Library

If someone you really care about is going to visit you in your home for the first time, what do you do? You straighten up and put things away that shouldn't be left out. In all cultures people clean up and dress up for special company. Cities hosting the Olympic Games clean up before the world arrives. Neatness welcomes people. Diners expect the table where they are seated to be clean, and they don't want to see a cart full of previous diners' dirty dishes before they've even seen a menu. Librarians' clients are all special company. Carts full of books to be reshelved and trays of dirty dishes both belong out of sight. Stores that are open at all hours do their restocking during the time when the fewest customers are expected; so should libraries.

Librarians never know who will walk in the door, who they will meet on the elevator, or who will visit the library's online space; everything has to be more than just presentable at all times. If a temporary mess like construction, Web site redesign, or shelf-shifting is unavoidable, clients deserve warning and explanation; this acts as a proclamation that they deserve better and will normally get it.

Model interiors in home design magazines may look too good to be lived in; yet there is a middle ground between working and lifeless. Neatness doesn't mean emptiness. Consider the on-camera desks of newscasters and talk show hosts. They generally have clean lines and are expansive, and they are almost never completely empty. Even if the star is using an invisible teleprompter, and perhaps additional screens out of sight under the top of the desk, they usually have a few pieces of paper at hand, which are more than just props. What is missing is clutter.

Likewise, busy Agile Librarians have some documentation on their desks. Many of the clutter organizing principles of magazines like *Real Simple* and some television shows like *Clean Sweep* and *Neat* are directly applicable to the working library or or even the Web site. Make sure that only what you use most or need right now is handy and everything else is tucked away someplace else. And remember, too much obvious work piled on a public desk implies that the librarian is too busy to help anyone now.

It is just as important for your work material to be in organized storage as it is to have the collection organized. Not being able to find something increases psychological stress. The additional anxiety of looking for something that is missing too often may eventually lead to depressive mood swings. It's much easier be in a good mood at work when the environment is neat rather than messy. The well-organized work space encourages pride and confidence in the work place. The principle behind regular collection weeding applies just as well to staff work areas and Web sites with outdated, broken links.

Gardens and collections are weeded so that there is more room for good things to expand. Ranganathan's Fifth Law of Library Science is "A library is a growing organism" (Ranganathan, 1931, p. 382). Constant growth includes constant repair. People who work in a given space every day may get so used to something obviously broken that they don't notice it anymore. But the person who walks in and looks around will spot the crack in the wall and the dirty, worn spot in the carpet immediately. It will distract and detract from any first attractive impression.

That Sounds Good!

In any school or home there are places to enjoy sound, such as the music classroom or the home theater, and places where sound is a by-product of activity, such as the gymnasium or an area for using power tools, laundry appliances, or a sewing machine. The same is true for library space, where there are places that should be silent, places for music, and places where machines create sounds as a by-product of activity.

Some library clients need quiet space for some kinds of concentration. They can share space with people listening privately with ear buds or other personal listening devices. The question is not should libraries be as absolutely quiet as required by the stereotypical shushing librarian, rather, the only question is when and where is the best place for silence, loud noises, and everything in between. Large spaces can be divided into smaller spaces for different purposes with windows or transparent walls so staff can observe activity. Acoustic planning can sound insulate both quiet areas and noisy ones, such as copying areas. As with decorating, there are both inexpensive and expensive ways to do it.

In most libraries today, the only way to ensure absolute quiet is for a person to wear noise-cancelling headphones. Noise-cancelling headphones work on the acoustic principle that certain sound frequencies cancel out other frequencies. That's why people can't hear some sounds over running water, a running appliance, wind, or anything else that generates white noise.

Another attractive way of masking extraneous sounds from the environment is to play music. Music can both set a mood and mask ambient sound, as in a restaurant. Many small special libraries use music to create an attractive ambiance in the library space. The genre, of course, has to be carefully chosen to appeal to the particular clientele. In some hospital libraries, doctors and nurses like 17th to 20th century classical music to help them feel like they are in a soothing oasis away from the stressful patient care areas where they work. In a library open to the public, there are, of course, broadcast rights issues, but librarians who can learn to deal with copyright law and guidelines, as well as issues concerning showing movies in a public library, can also play music properly.

The sound of a ringing mobile phone and the following half-conversation can be a very annoying disruption. Consequently mobile phones may be banned from public spaces. One win-win solution is to acknowledge that people want, and sometimes need, to be able to make and receive calls, so establish a place where they are welcome to use cell phones. People whose work requires them to be available, or parents who need to be accessible to their children, are not going to use library spaces if they don't have a convenient place to use their phones without annoying others.

In any case, the professional concern for the clients is more instantly evident when the Agile Librarian clearly acknowledges and makes arrangements for the needs of different clients. Construction and maintenance sounds may be necessary at times, but ignoring their effect on activity in the library is counter-productive.

As for the library's online presence, the library Web site does not have to be as static as an old photo album, nor does it have to be as quiet as a silent movie without music. It can go beyond just being something to look at and become something to listen to, as well. One good example is the Ocean County Library Jingle available at http://theoceancountylibrary.org/Link2Topic/music.htm#Jingle.

That Tastes Good!

Libraries often have small kitchens in staff rooms. People don't do their best work if they have to go for long periods without food or drink. What is the message to hungry library clients who smell popcorn or coffee aromas wafting from the staff break room when they know that *they* are not allowed to eat or drink anywhere within what seems like miles from the library? Whose comfort comes first? Librarians recognize one kind of physiological need by providing restrooms, or at least directions to restrooms, but what about the human need for food and drink? We need to acknowledge these very real needs either by providing a place where they can be met, such as a coffee shop in the library, or directions to some other nearby place.

In every human society, guests, both strangers and friends, are offered refreshments. For special occasions, places that are not in the business of providing food and drink have refreshments because, to paraphrase a phrase from the movie *Field of Dreams*, "If you feed them, they will come." Indeed, more and more libraries have refreshments for special occasions and celebrations. But what about the average client who may have to choose between grabbing a quick lunch and going to the library? It often is one of the few public places where one can't bring in a covered drink or a bag of chips. Being able to eat in the library could make all the difference!

In *Creating the Customer-Driven Library: Building on the Bookstore Model*, Jeannette Woodward has a wonderful chapter on "Food and Drink in the Library" with many ideas for reevaluating the question. She points out, "You may remember that public libraries of the past did not lend books. Lending is actually a rather new innovation. When most of the old Carnegies were built, books were intended to reside permanently in the library" (Woodward, 2005, p. 195). Books meant to be used in perpetuity had to be protected from all manner of harm; however, most librarians now check out books that will be read in the café down the block, at the client's desk with coffee, over breakfast at home, or even at the beach. Library staff members frequently read library material while eating in the break room, and most staff members who have their own desks in staff areas have their beverage of choice handy. Some client-centered libraries now have cafés on the premises, some allow clients to bring in covered beverages, and most, acknowledging this basic human need, have clear directions for where clients can eat and drink if they are not allowed to do so in other parts of the library.

Every library "thou shalt not" rule should address a current need to increase client access, not an historical or hypothetical one. Some library spaces with special collections, such as rare archival collections, must have a ban on food and drink in those areas for the preservation of those materials. But in many libraries, the ban has more to do with "because that's what libraries do" than with current client needs. In libraries in which the collection is dynamic, with new print material rapidly added and old material weeded at a similar rate, such a rule to protect materials doesn't make much sense. It sounds like continuing a rule left over from the days before electricity when libraries could be open only on sunny days and never at night because of the risk of fire.

Another reason often given for banning food is a risk of attracting vermin, however, any public space has to be regularly cleaned whether or not people eat in it. If people who need to eat and use the library eat there even though it is against the rules, they are more likely to hide whatever they leave behind. And it will be harder to clean up after them than if they were able to eat openly and use a handy trash can. Likewise, a drink surreptitiously smuggled in in a jacket or backpack is more likely to be spilled than one brought in openly.

What does this have to do with creating instant credibility? Everything. A sign on a door describing where people can eat or use their mobile phones is more welcoming and thoughtful than a sign that lists what's banned from the library. That helps to give the client an immediate impression of being safe, wanted, welcome, and, yes, special.

You Don't Look Like a Librarian!

When you take responsibility for ensuring instant credibility, it may well surprise people that you don't fit their old image of a librarian, whether it's based on the stereotype, earlier bad experiences, or both. Your image may even elicit comments like, "You don't look like a librarian," "You don't act like a librarian," or even "This doesn't look like a library." How does the Agile Librarian react to such comments? On one hand they may be meant to be sincere compliments to the individual librarian or library, but on the other hand they feel like an insult to librarianship as a whole. The best answer is to paraphrase Gloria Steinem's famous remark about her age and reply, "This is what a librarian looks like," "This is what a librarian does," or "This is what a library looks like."* Such an answer may include an explanatory adjective, "This is what an active community library looks like," or even, "This is what an Agile Librarian does."

---

* Stienem wrote, "When a reporter kindly said I didn't look forty (a well-meaning comment, but ageist when you think about it), I said the first thing that came into my head: 'This is what forty looks like. We've been lying so long, who would know?'" (Steinem, 2006, p. 9).

Summary

The Agile Librarian has to inspire instant credibility. People, even children, have images of librarians and libraries influenced by many sources and experiences. Before someone can become a satisfied client, a pleased boss, or an impressed decision maker, they have to have an impression of library service as attractive and reliable. Very quickly, a first impression of the library will confirm or contradict the person's previous image through sensory, cognitive, and social perceptions, few of which are recognized at a conscious level.

As with other topics in this book, librarians can learn from examples of the results of research into these questions in other enterprises, even if those enterprises have very different missions from that of the library. The societal image of librarianship can be improved if librarians pay attention to what creates such impressions; it will degrade if librarians choose to ignore it and expect that people just ought to know how excellent their services are. Although librarians may joke about the stereotype with each other, perpetuating it to their clients and stakeholders can eventually be professional suicide. Ensuring that Web sites, libraries, and library staff are professionally colorful, interesting, and attractive does not have to be expensive, but it does require thoughtful diligence. As with collection development or the cognitive aspects of the reference interview, the librarian must anticipate needs in the actual or virtual library environment.

References

Absher, Linda. 1997–2004. The Lipstick Librarian. Retrieved from http://www.lipsticklibrarian.com/. Accessed June 28, 2008.

Bixler, Susan and Lisa Scherrer Dugan. 2001. *5 Steps to Professional Presence: How to Project Confidence, Competence, and Credibility at Work.* Holbrook, MA: Adams Media Corporation.

Bixler, Susan and Nancy Nix-Rice. 1997. *The New Professional Image: From Business Casual to the Ultimate Power Look.* Avon, MA: Adams Media Corporation.

———. 2005. *The New Professional Image: From Business Casual to the Ultimate Power Look.* 2nd ed. Avon, MA: Adams Media Corporation.

Buschman, John E. and Gloria J. Leckie. (Eds.). 2007. *The Library as Place: History, Community and Culture.* Westport, CT: Libraries Unlimited.

Cowen, Janet L. and Jerry Edson. 2002. Best Practice in Library/Information Technology Collaboration. *Journal of Hospital Librarianship* 2:1–15.

Eklund, Janet. 2002. Do Clothes Make the Librarian?: Analysis I: Presentation is Everything. *Library Journal* 27:54, 56.

Fox, Gardner F. (writer); Infantino, Carmine (penciller); Greene, Sid (inker). 1967. The Million Dollar Debut of Batgirl. *Detective Comics* #359, January. DC Comics. Reprinted in Joy, Bob. (Ed.). 2008. *Showcase Presents Batman*, Vol.3, New York: DC Comics.

Glassman, Adam. 2008. Adam Says: O's creative director, Adam Glassman, tells you what your best friend won't . . . about what's wearable at work—and what's not. *The Oprah Magazine* 91(3): 108.

Gunn, Tim. 2008, July 21. 10 Questions. The host of *Tim Gunn's Guide to Style* mentors young designers in a new season of *Project Runway* debuting July 16. *Time* 172(3): 6.

Maslow, A. H. 1943. A Theory of Human Motivation. *Psychological Review* 50:370–96.

McFee, Archie. 2005. The Librarian Action Figure. http://www.mcphee.com/laf/. Accessed June 28, 2008.

Merriam-Webster's Collegiate Dictionary. 11th ed. 2003. Springfield, Mass.: Merriam-Webster, Inc.

Olson, Christine A. 1993. Testing Your Library's Marketing IQ. *Medical Reference Services Quarterly* 12:75–83.

Petrosino, Nancy. 2005. Librarians—the Image and the Myth. http://stereotype-librarian.blogspot.com/. Accessed June 28, 2008.

Raish, Martin. 2008. Librarians in the Movies: An Annotated Filmography. http://emp.byui.edu/RAISHM/films/introduction.html. Accessed June 28, 2008.

Ranganathan, Shiyali Ramamrita. 1931. *The Five Laws of Library Science.* Madras Library Association, London, UK: Edward Goldston. Retrieved from the Digital Library of Information Science and Technology (dLIST) Classics Project http://dlist.sir.arizona.edu/1220/. Accessed April 11, 2008.

Special Libraries Association; Presidential Task Force on the Enhancement of the Image of the Librarian/Information Professional. 1991. *Inter-Association Task Force Report on Image.* Washington, D.C.: Special Libraries. [Accessed as ERIC database document ED329267; IR053458.]

Stark, Mallory. 2005. Creating a Positive Professional Image. *Information Outlook* 9:25–27.

Steinem, Gloria. 2006. *Doing Sixty & Seventy.* San Francisco, CA: Elders Academy Press.

Woodward, Jeannette. 2005. *Creating the Customer-Driven Library: Building on the Bookstore Model.* Chicago: American Library Association.

Chapter 7

Ensuring Positive Communication

We must communicate positively to attract and keep clients and institutional support. Obviously, it is very important not just to create and emphasize client-centered services, but also to communicate that value. Empathy for client needs and positive encouragement goes a long way toward improving the client experience. Thinking about library service in the life of the client instead of the client in the life of the library clarifies the Agile Librarian's perception of what the client needs to experience.

Some potential clients may approach librarians with obvious anxiety or even avoid them altogether because of past negative experiences with librarians. Our positive communication behavior can put them at ease and encourage them to use our services. How do we do that? Without knowing what happened to them or what bad stories they've heard from others, how can we give them a better impression of our services?

Many large service businesses, such as hotel chains, have studied that process and improved their staff training in light of what they have learned about how to make people feel welcome. Their emphasis on knowing how to put the customer at ease makes it more likely that people will return not only to a particular hotel, but will choose the same hotel in different cities as well, confident that they will have a similar positive experience there. The savvy hotel business leaders know that corporate marketing, promotion, and advertising cannot erase an individual's memory of a personal experience of unmitigated bad service. The service has to be consistently positive.

People who work in service professions or industries have to learn to communicate positively with each and every client or customer. This communication style has to be taught and continuously supported by everyone in the organization. Good managers understand that their employees' personal service skills are too important to be left to chance. Management understands that, no matter how good the resources are, the industry or profession will lose customers, clients, or community support if the service is poor. Management invests in communication education and training because it pays off: clients and customers who have a positive experience will come back again, and possibly bring others with them.

Welcome

What the client experiences first can make a lasting impression. What makes a person feel welcome? Woodward (2005, p. 87–90) reports that marketing experts emphasize six needs that should be met for customers *immediately* through their senses:

> They need to be informed.
> They need to be entertained.
> They need a good buy.
> They need fast service.
> They need to feel safe.
> They need to feel special.

Can the clients gather experience and reassurance of all six needs in the first few seconds? You may not be able to give them in-depth evidence that they will be satisfied, but you can provide cues that create the immediate expectation that this professional, this library employee, this collection, this place, or this Web site can satisfy all six needs.

They need information about what is where and who is who right away. To entertain, we make the experience interesting. To provide something worth the client's investment in time and effort, we make it obvious that no one will go away empty handed. To ensure fast service, we minimize waiting time. To promote a feeling of safety, we demonstrate integrity and watchfulness. And, to make clients feel special immediately, someone greets each one personally. On a Web site home page, something emphasizes personal options, such as "Ask my librarian," "My favorites," "My department," et cetera.

Personal Welcome

Large organizations usually have a receptionist who welcomes and pays attention to everyone who walks in the door. The receptionist makes each person feel instantly secure and important. In a small shop where only one person is working, that shopkeeper will be sure to greet everyone who walks through the door. We see smiling, welcoming faces at both expensive restaurants and discount stores because it puts the newly arrived customer at ease.

For the same reason, someone should greet everyone who comes into a library, even if the greeting is nothing more than making eye contact and smiling. Woodward cites some studies that provide evidence that people "perceive a space as unfriendly if they do not encounter anyone who directs or greets them within the first ten feet" (Woodward, 2005, p. 91). It is just as important for a library to have a welcoming system as it is to have a security system; yet the entrance to too many libraries exhibits one and not the other. Retail establishments have to have theft prevention systems in place, but they manage to do it without installing the forbidding entrance barriers and threatening signs some libraries have. Other libraries have volunteer greeters near their doors (Woodward 2005, p. 91). Anyone working within that magic first ten feet should be aware of the importance of cheerfully greeting everyone who enters.

Every culture has a body language for welcoming some people and rejecting others, and this can be apparent even when the person can't actually see you. On the telephone, the same phrase can sound welcoming or rejecting depending on the speaker's tone of voice and inflection. People who smile when they answer the phone sound different than those who frown, or whose minds are really somewhere else. One trick is to keep a mirror on or close to the phone. Smiling into the mirror helps one quickly adopt a friendly sound. After all, sometimes looking in the mirror is thoughtful and considerate, not just vain!

"Do you work here?" It should be embarrassing for a librarian to be asked that question in a library. "Can you help me?" is another indication that something is missing from the first impression. The professional answering the phone immediately gives a name, the newscaster begins or ends with a self-introduction. The presence of the Agile Librarian should is obvious; such a librarian wears identification and seeks interaction with clients rather than hiding from them. The style of dress and identification will vary with the kind of organization and its culture, but it must in some way be instantly recognizable.

Employees in restaurants and stores dress so that customers can immediately see, even from a distance, who can help them. You can always tell who's a crew member and who's a passenger on an airliner. Guests in a hotel getting into an elevator can immediately recognize hotel employees by how they are dressed and by their badges proclaiming who they are and what is their role in hospitality. They are likely to ask a manager a different question than they would ask an engineer and vice versa. Even relatively low-paid shelf stockers in discount outlets wear colorful vests so that they can be identified. Closer up, the customer usually can read the person's name and service role on a badge. The employee's costume is different in different organizations or industries, but nonetheless, it has to exist in some form so that customers or clients can easily pick out whose job it is to guide them. If they can't tell, it might as well be an unattended self-service establishment.

In too many libraries, the only way the client can be certain that someone is there to help them is if that someone is behind the barrier of some kind of counter or desk. If some people believe that everyone who works in a library is a librarian, it is because librarians haven't given them any clues to the different important roles that other staff members play in their service. It is also appropriate for the professional librarian to use the abbreviation for their professional degree, such as MLIS, after their name on their name tag. Clients also have a right to know what role any given employee plays in the library and to understand that they can get different services from employees with different kinds of expertise. With a clearly visible job title they can know who is likely to have a good knowledge of the children's collection and who may have more familiarity with other specialized services. For that matter, in a large library even new employees would be glad for a little help understanding who's who!

Librarians and other professionals like to use name tags at meetings of their professional associations. It saves them from many an embarrassed memory lapse such as "I know I've met this person before but who . . . ?" or lost opportunity, "Oh, you're the person who wrote that wonderful article I like so much!" We should give our clients the same subtle help in identifying us.

If library employees don't want to wear any identification because of anxiety about their personal off-the-job privacy, they certainly can use an alias that the rest of the staff knows. But in any case, clients deserve an easy way to identify the person helping them in the library. With a name they can compliment someone's excellent service to their supervisor or ask for the same person again to ask additional questions or to thank them for their help. They can also identify the employee who treated them poorly, reinforcing the principle that all employees are responsible for positive service. In some organizations, people in some roles wear badges bearing only a first name and not a surname. However, unless it is appropriate for *everyone* to go by a first name only, that practice belittles the first name staff. If people are knowledgeable and important enough to work here, they are important enough to have an adult identity.

Think about this analogous experience: After you've been seated in a restaurant, typically someone comes to your table, smiles and says, "Hi, I'm Bob. I'll be your server today." It doesn't matter whether or not his real name is "Bob," but it does matter that he has greeted you in person, identified himself, and identified his role in your service. You are grateful for the service of the person who escorted you to your table, but you know now that Bob is the person who will be take your order and make sure that you get it. He can help you make choices because he is the person who can tell you about tonight's specials and explain any item on the menu. You know that if you don't see him, you can contact him by telling another employee that you want to speak to Bob. Bob also knows that he is accountable for his service. He knows that you could complain to the manager about Bob. Sometimes you also can specify that a tip go to Bob. People who want to work in a library anonymously should not be in any public service role!

The information professional's goal is to inform, not to intimidate or confuse. The Agile Librarian guides clients to cognitive clarity as soon as possible in spite of the complexity of the information system. Woodward writes that clients want "to find help readily available that will enable them to find their way around and make good choices. This means their first impression of a library must not seem confusing" (Woodward, 2005, 87).

Save the Client's Time

Ranganathan's fourth law of Library Science is "Save the Time of the Reader" (Ranganathan, 1931, 337). This law is even more important in the Internet age than it was eighty years ago. Librarians have the expertise and systems to save readers' time but how do readers know that? If repair and pizza delivery services can promise service in thirty minutes, what can librarians promise up front? At the very least we should make it very easy to tell who's who and what's what even if the person has never used our services. People deserve to have clear cues, in words they understand (not library jargon) about where to start their information quest. While service delays may sometimes be unavoidable, we have to make sure that clients perceive such delays to be the exception and not just business as usual. If people tend to bunch up at some points faster than they can be helped, then the service may need to include take-a-number devices or even beepers like those used for diners waiting for a table at a restaurant. The individual feels acknowledged, has something tangible in hand, and is assured of a fair place in line instead of seeing a gathering crowd as a reason to give up on a service.

A workable staffing procedure used at large stores is to call staff from the non-public areas to come help with check-out whenever lines develop. If stores can use this practice, librarians can cross-train technical staff to help out with circulation when lines get longer, such as just before closing time. For large group events, rope lines at an entrance can make clients more comfortable and crowd management easier.

Where Is It?

People come into a library for many reasons. A library can be a place

---

Exercise

Enter a Library with Fresh Eyes

Try this exercise with your library and with one or two libraries you've never seen before where no one knows you.

Think of a typical question a client of this library might have. Stand in front of the door to the library. If it's your own library, close your eyes. And imagine that you have never, ever been there before. Imagine that you don't speak "librarianese."

Open your eyes; open the door. What colors do you see? What draws your eyes first? How much can you really tell in the first glance about where to go for what you want? Are you confused or are you given clear choices. Does it have too much information or too little? Too much fine print? What do you see first, rules or invitations for services? Is the traffic pattern obvious? Are there some aisles that are larger than others with speed lanes that allow you to fast forward to the department you want? Do you think you're going to get what you want quickly, or is it going to be difficult? What about browsing?

Who do you see? Does someone greet you? Does someone make you feel special and important? Does that person look confident and competent? Can you tell who works here? Can you tell who might have specialized skills to help you?

---

to browse on one's own, a place to get help on a quest, a place to find something or a place to work as a private space in a public space. It can be a gathering place for two or more working together, or for larger group functions. Not only should people be greeted as soon as they walk in, but in that first ten feet they should get some idea of where to go for the reason they came. That takes more than complex signs and directories; it also takes planning about what is in a person's first line of sight. Woodward counsels, "When customers enter a store or library, traffic patterns should be obvious so as to contribute to their feeling of confidence. If, instead of a single aisle that takes them from the front to the back of the space, they must navigate around a maze of shelving and seating areas, that confidence will erode" (Woodward, 2005, p. 87).

Ranganathan's First Law of Library Science is "Books are for use" (Ranganathan, 1931, pg. 1). Nevertheless, people can use only what they can find, so you have to make everything as easy for the client to find as possible. For you, working in a library and using its Web site regularly may make it seem easier to navigate than it is to new clients or new staff. Pay attention to what appears to confuse them and use that insight to make positive changes. Those frequently asked directional questions are a goldmine of opportunities for improvement.

Just like stores, libraries can have well-marked seasonal areas, for instance at tax, term paper, budget, or garden planting time, depending upon the organization. Library visitors need clearly marked paths to materials return, check-out, restrooms, lockers, or, in some small libraries, just a place to hang a coat. And, yes, if we want them to stay, they need to know the nearest place for using a mobile phone or getting something to eat and drink.

Some may come to a library to accomplish an onerous task as quickly as possible; but if it appears and feels comfortable and inviting, they may very well stay longer. That won't happen if the furniture appears to be uncomfortable and the staff suspicious of the individual or group to which the individual belongs. In the early- to mid-twentieth century, people wanting library information services had to approach a tall counter to appeal for help from someone behind it. Getting rid of that high altar-like barrier really improved the welcoming ambiance of many a library! Some areas, such as those meant for quiet reading, should appear restful whereas others should be stimulating (Woodward, 2005, pp. 89–90).

You probably are so familiar with your collection that you rarely need to use signs to find a particular call number area. But for clients who do not know the shelving layout, posting an attractive mass-produced guide to your library's classification system may not be of much use if it is only guide. Call number location signage has to be obvious, clear, accurate, and easily updatable when shelf-shifting. It should include a word or two describing the general subject in that area. If you look in bookstores they have very large signs leading people to the most popular areas.

Finding tools must be integrated with the environment in which they are used. It makes no sense to have all of the OPAC terminals without printers somewhere far from the collection. Some large public and university libraries not only have some stations conveniently located in the stacks, but they also equip them with small printers that print out records on small pieces of paper the width of a register receipt. That way the client doesn't have to transcribe or remember what was on the screen and possibly garble or forget something crucial to the finding process.

Retail businesses use many carefully designed signs to help people find what they want. In large supermarkets or discount stores, the shoppers used to have to look for general departments where they expected to find specific items they sought. Now such stores tend to have more specific signs with large letters hanging from high ceilings, signs that can be read even when there are lots of shoppers, because no people will be in the way. The signs are designed to be changed frequently so, as the stock moves, so do the signs. One can walk for the first time into some well-designed large grocery stores and easily determine in seconds where to find milk, bread, snacks, soda, flour, peanut butter, paper towels, coffee, fresh produce, frozen pizza, and most items on a long shopping list. The same person should be able to walk into an equally unknown library and *see* where to go for that library's primary materials and services. In a public library those destinations might include Internet computers, meeting rooms, special departments, photocopiers, the catalog, fiction, cookbooks, auto-repair, check-out, magazines, movies, travel, "dictionaries, directories, and encyclopedias," or just finding service.

"Reference" isn't an ordinary word in common conversation; it can confuse some client populations because it refers both to a special part of the collection and to a particular professional service. After tearing down the "reference" sign and then later the new "information" sign at the desk where I once worked, I found a simple "Ask me!" to be more effective in that public library. More people did come to the "Information" sign than to the "Reference" sign, but mostly with questions such as "Where is the bathroom?"

"Ask me!" encouraged all questions . . . and some predictable jokes. That was fine; it got the conversation started.

Good signs help the client navigate with both design and data. In addition to carefully chosen words, they express meaning with color, graphics, and even simple pictures. Some signs are absolutely necessary in any library. If clients have to ask over and over again where certain things are, something is more likely to be wrong with directional signage than with clients' intelligence. Most people really don't like to have to ask.

The Rigid Librarian too often believes that everyone ought to know where the signs are pointing, what the numbers on a sign mean, and what every word on a sign means in library terms. Sometimes people ask a question even though they understand a sign just because they need to start a conversation with a real person who can help them more than the sign.

Can you remember being a freshman and overwhelmed with too much information in a short library orienta-

Exercise: Prevent Culture Shock!

A new freshman has been told in class that a book she needs for an assignment is at the library. She might have some confusing or negative experiences trying to get the book she needs. What would you do to improve each of the following six negative experiences for her?

1. Her first challenge is finding the library. Unlike the library in her high school, or the public library in the municipal complex of her small home town, this library, apparently, is a whole building. Studying the map and asking some questions, she finds the tall building with imposing Greek columns in front. Lots of other students are going in and out some doors so that must be the entrance.

2. Inside the building, she has no idea where to go or what to do next. Signs say "reference," "reserves," or "document delivery" but they don't mean much to her. The line of people in front of a desk is long and to the side. The sign over it says "circulation" and there are two people working behind the desk. They look like students and might be able to help her, but that line is awfully long and she doesn't want to waste her time.

3. Meanwhile, students who apparently know where they are going are walking a different direction. She decides to follow them, but it turns out that they are going to a coffee shop. A straight-A student in high school, she thought this would be easier than it is. Following some other students she finds a bank of computers. The library catalog must be there. She knew how to use the one in her high school library. She had worked as a student aide in the library, so this should be easy. Wrong again. The display on the screen is cluttered with words she doesn't understand. She clicks on some of them and is asked for some kind of ID and password.

4. That doesn't make sense so she tries another button and finds a search screen. She types in the name of the book she wants and, *oh, yes*! There's something about it on the screen and she can pick out the call number. But she still doesn't know where in the building the books with that call number are shelved. She asks the student sitting next to her who replies, "You have to go look at the list by the elevator to find out where the books with these letters are." So she writes down all of the letters and numbers and goes looking for the elevators. But where are the elevators? Oh, there they are. Where's the sign? That must be it. Apparently books classified under that letter are on the fifth floor. She goes up to the fifth floor and wanders for ten minutes or so looking for books with call numbers that begin with that letter. Frustrated, she asks someone who's

(Continued)

putting books on the shelves. He says, "Oh, we moved those up to the sixth floor. You have to go up there."

5. On the sixth floor, she eventually locates where the book with that call number should be. It's not there. Now what? She goes back to the first floor again and notices the sign for "reference." Maybe the instructor said something about it being "on reference." She asks the person at the desk where the books with those call numbers are and gets directions. Again she finds where she thinks it is supposed to be and it's not there.

6. She gives up, never knowing that she should have followed the sign to the "reserves" desk. She's spent a bewildering and discouraging half hour in this huge place, and she still didn't get what she needed. If she does figure out that she needs the reserve desk, she may arrive there just after the time that reserve materials may be checked out overnight. The material she needed had been there all the time she was wandering around, and now it is unavailable to her until another day. During her trek throughout the library she passed several professional librarians, but since they looked so much like students in the library, she had no idea that they could or would help and they didn't know that she needed help. Some of the most knowledgeable professionals were hidden away in offices somewhere. If her first visit to the big library was in the evening or on a weekend there might not have been any professionals on duty at all.

Consider what might happen to the student after this frustrating endeavor. What makes the rest of her experience in her library more positive? Why?

7. Our freshman goes back to the coffee shop in the library. Not only can she find it by the stream of students going in and the signs pointing to it, but the aromas are wonderful. Yes, there's a line to get help in the coffee shop, but while she's in line she can easily read the big sign with large letters describing what she can get in the coffee shop. She already feels more comfortable because the colors and graphics on the menu are more attractive and legible than the signs she just saw in the stacks. Some of the combinations of coffee, milk, and flavoring have strange names, but each has below it a description of exactly what it really is. Some information that changes frequently is on a chalkboard that is current. By the time she gets to the front of the line, she knows what she wants. Within five minutes she has it and is walking out of the building. She sits down on the steps where she can call her roommate on her mobile phone. It feels good to hear a friendly voice.

Perhaps she will go to a library orientation session for an hour in a library classroom sometime this semester. Trying to get in as much as possible, a boring speaker talks very

tion? Too much information on the front door or first page of the Web site is equally overwhelming. If clients ignore signs or instructions, it is because the signs or instructions are not giving the client the real information they need exactly when, where, and how they need it. What does someone standing *here* want to know? Test signage and Web site architecture with real potential clients. Read books and articles written about signage in other places, not just in libraries. We will talk about wording on signs later in this chapter.

In any case, signs can never tell clients everything they need to know for every quest. Some large libraries, like some large stores, have phones strategically placed in the stacks, phones that are clearly marked for people to use to call for help with finding something and not just for security.

Negative Actions

The stereotypical librarian is portrayed too often as always saying "no" or "shush." In our blogs and e-mail lists, we are quick to complain about

(Continued)

these caricatures in advertising and dramas. Although we are aware of the exaggerations and stereotypical images of professional doctors, lawyers, nurses, and politicians, they don't seem as personal to us.

Although successful professionals tend to be very positive people, we all know someone

fast, shows some slides, uses some library terms our student doesn't understand, and passes out some handouts. What she hears might be valuable to her at various times during the next four years, but if she can't find out what she needs to know when she needs to know it, the orientation time is wasted. The only information she can use is the information she can find.

Her first impression will be a lasting one. Every university administrator, every member of the board of trustees, and almost every legislator who votes on funding for state universities was once a college freshman.

who really does fit the negative stereotype. Perhaps some people who feel powerless might be attracted to our profession because they believe it will give them the authority to enforce rules. Some seem to relish the idea of punishing people to teach them a lesson. Though such librarians are very much in the minority, too many still live up to a negative image of librarianship. The Agile Librarian knows that real respect for library services and collections has to be earned and cannot be coerced.

Consequently, some potential library service clients are less likely to consider using library services because of past experiences with librarians. These potential clients may even purposefully and pointedly avoid libraries. When forced by some circumstance, for instance, a school assignment, to interact with librarians, they may be guarded or even openly hostile. Agile Librarians give these potential clients particularly positive professional treatment. It may not be easy, but it's important!

In "Negative Closure: Strategies and Counter-Strategies in the Reference Transaction," Ross and Dewdney (1998) report on their observational study of information service encounters gone wrong. They frequently observed negative closures somewhat like these:

1. Responding to an opening question by saying nothing and just starting to type at a computer.
2. Directing the client to a possible source or a very broad area of the collection for the desired information but not checking on whether or not the client finds the source or the information within the source, what they call an "unmonitored referral."
3. Disdainfully saying something about what the client should have done before bothering the librarian.
4. Trying "to get the user to accept more easily found information" even though it is irrelevant to the client's need.
5. Using various strategies just to get rid of the client and the question including using body language to dismiss the client, telling the client that the information probably doesn't exist or is not available before even looking.
6. Going somewhere else, ostensibly to get the appropriate document, but never returning (Ross and Dewdney 1998, pp. 154–157).

The researchers saw clients counter such behaviors by raising the level of the request to a demand, playing dumb, approaching another librarian, or otherwise increasing the pressure for help (Ross and Dewdney 1998, pp. 157–160). The same escalating behavior will arise from "negative closure" to a complaint. Instead of going away, the problem will just grow larger.

Librarians consciously have to know, show, and tell how their services are a positive benefit if they want to be successful. We all dread running into a roadblock on the way to the information we need, and our clients are no different. We want them to have a happy ending to their search. To rebuild trust, we have to maximize our declarations of great service and minimize or eliminate our negative messages.

Verbal Messages: From Negative to Positive

In either oral or written messages, active positive sentences are much, much better than passive negative ones. When we use sentences with active verbs we leave no doubt as to who does what. If we use passive sentences too much, we sound impersonal and evasive. We can transform oral and written messages from negative to positive forms. Rigid Librarians too easily fall into the habit of emphasizing the enforcement of negative rules more often than proclaiming the positive services available and inviting people to use them. A few simple, active, and positive sentences in conversations, signs, brochures, and other media can make all the difference. How can the Agile Librarian improve spoken and written messages?

The "Proclaimer"

James Quinn made a very important point in a message posted March 7, 2001, to the MEDLIB-L e-mail discussion list. At the time he was the librarian at Silver Cross Hospital in Joliet, Illinois, and on this list for medical librarians there had been an ongoing discussion of disclaimers for consumer health information services. Most suggestions were lengthy warnings written to cover every imaginable inaccuracy in the documents, or misuse of the information, for instance, believing that everything in the document pertained directly to the clients' personal health. The suggestions made it clear that librarians were supplying information and were not personally diagnosing, treating, or giving medical advice. As an information referral, librarians can, of course, suggest additional information sources including a professional health care provider. After describing the positive service description he had found on a weight control information site, Mr. Quinn wrote:

> Perhaps the best way to issue "disclaimers" is by positively delineating the services you (or other libraries in your area) DO provide—by issuing "proclaimers" if you will. . . . With the "disclaimer" in mind, how is this as an example of a "proclaimer" for a patient-oriented brochure?
>
> We provide journals, books and computer resources to help you answer your health-related questions. Because every person and situation is unique, the general information we provide cannot substitute for the diagnosis and medical advice of your doctor, but is there to help insure that you as a patient can participate as fully as possible with your doctor and other members of your health care team in meeting your treatment goals. (Quinn, 2001).

What to Say

In the course of providing services we may say things that move the process along or things that bring it to a screeching halt. Our statements that appear to create absolute roadblocks for the client's journey can be worded to become bridges, gateways, or successful detours. Here are some examples:

1. *The library will close in fifteen minutes.*
   May we help you with what you would like to take with you? You have ten more minutes to check out material to take with you and fifteen more minutes to use material here. We will be open again at 8:00 a.m. tomorrow.

2. *I've never heard of that [Web site, book, practice, medium, technology] so I can't help you.*
   That is new to me, but I can look for it for you. I know lots of people and sources that can help.

3. *You are too young to check out this book; it's against the rules.*
   This book seems a little advanced. Shall we see if we can find something a little less technical, or is this really what you need and can use?

4. *We don't have that journal and we don't do interlibrary loan for unaffiliated people.*
   We don't subscribe to that journal, but let me see if that article is available in one of our databases.

5. *I don't like your behavior and you must be more respectful for this conversation to continue.*
   Let's try again. Do I understand correctly that what you want is . . . ?

6. *That is very [fragile, one-of-a-kind, expensive] material and you cannot check it out to take with you.*
   Can I see if we can make a copy of it for you? It is [fragile, one-of-a-kind, expensive] and we have to protect it here so that you and other people can use it again someday.

7. *It should be here, but I don't know where it is.*
   This is its place on the shelves, but it obviously isn't here. It may be checked out or waiting to be reshelved. While I am looking to see if it is, here is something else that may help you on your quest.

8. *I can't understand you.*
   Could you please repeat that a little more slowly or use different words to help me understand your request?

9. *This book cannot be renewed.*
   Someone else has requested this book. If you want another turn, we can reserve it for you to check out again later.

Scripts and the Magic Eraser Word

What about the times when, for one reason or another, you have to say no? Even a refusal can be couched in terms that recognize a client's right to need or to ask. When people hear a two-clause sentence connected by the conjunction "but," they tend to pay less attention to the first clause than to the second. Notice how we just used it in examples 2, 4, and 7. The word "but" can function as an "eraser" word that tends to make the listener practically forget whatever came before it. For instance, in the following unfinished examples sentences, do you *really* believe the first clause is going to be the main message of the sentence?

"You did an excellent job yesterday, but . . ."

"Your hair looks nice, but . . ."

"Librarians are usually very responsible, but . . ."

Notice how the "eraser word" turns the message in the following examples:

"We do this kind of interlibrary loan only for our [employees, students, faculty], but another place where you might get it would be [name of a public library, name of another institution library]. Let me check their catalog with you to see if they have it or can get it for you through interlibrary loan."

"We don't have that kind of [material or service] here, but you can get it from [other institution or business]."

"We don't have the legal right to make forty copies for you to give away, but we can show you how to get permission from the copyright owner *or* we can make copies of your comments about it with a full citation so that people can get single copies for their own use."

"You can't check this out, but you may use it here and also make copies of a few pages you need to take with you. If you find you need more than that, we can get you the information you need to buy a copy or to access it online."

For things you need to say frequently, it is a good idea to use scripts, carefully thought out and composed sentences that convey frequent messages clearly and positively. Every day scripts that we all use are, "How are you today?" followed by "Fine, thank you. And you?" All cultures and languages use them, and so do people who provide services to other people. Just before leaving a patient's room, some nurses may make it a habit to say, "Is there anything else I can do for you? I have the time." They've discovered that delivering that simple positive message, "I have the time," actually reduces the number of times a patient will press the call button just to see if the nurse really is always available. These questions show empathy for what the people may need without forcing them to ask for it. One example of a positive script some librarians use is, "Does this completely answer your question?" Some say "Are you finding what you are looking for?" instead of "May I help you?" because some people don't like to be told that they need help. In a virtual reference service, the librarian might have a collection of such phrases available for copy and paste into a message. Professionals and staff alike can communicate better and save time with such preparation.

Sometimes the "eraser" word doesn't work, especially if, in the first clause, the speaker begins with an overly self-defacing phrase such as "I can't do this well," "This probably won't work," or "This may be completely useless to you." Such phrases from a professional, before anything else is done, are not proof of humility, but, rather, are a different kind of negative closure, like the soldier who shoots himself in the foot so he won't have to march. Having a practiced script, with a few positive, simple, and active sentences, works better. "That's an interesting question" or "I can work on this for you" gets everyone happily moving toward the goal much faster.

What to Write

Generally, you have more time to plan what you write on a sign, in a brochure, in a policy, or on a Web site than what you say in a situation for which you do not have a script. Signs, e-mail, brochures, and other written communication do not have the benefit of the added message from the friendly expression on your face or sound in your voice. So you must take even more care to communicate your message in a context of positivity rather than deprecation. Be especially wary of writing a reactive e-mail, sign, or policy when you are upset!

Restaurant menus list available dishes, not the dishes they don't serve. Good library Web sites, signs, brochures and staff communication are proclamations of great services and benefits. Benefits of using library services can be stated clearly and concisely without being buried under copious descriptions of information sources and restrictions. For instance, here's a message from a public library Web site:

> Your Multnomah County Library card opens the door to a world of information and entertainment.
>
> Use your card to check out a wide variety of materials from any library location and to access the Internet from library computers. With your library card number, you can also access the library's powerful subscription databases [active link] from your home, office or school computer. (Multinomah County Library, 2005).

Of course, we have to warn clients of restrictions and even dangers, but we can do it in non-threatening ways. If you must warn people not to leave their valuables unattended, do it positively. The Ralph Brown Draughon Library at Auburn University once had a sign near a bank of elevators which said it all in two words: "theft happens" (McKnight, 2005). The message was simple and had a wry twist that helped people remember it. In the following examples, notice how you can change an inconsiderate negative passive sentence into a much more positive, active sentence that communicates both information and consideration of the clients' perspective.

1. *Cell phones must be turned off before entering.*
   You are welcome to use your cell phone here in this lobby.
2. *Computers may be used for only thirty minutes.*
   You are welcome to use this computer for thirty minutes, but after that let someone else have a turn.
3. *No food or drink.*
   Use the cafeteria on the third floor or the vending machines down the hall and enjoy your refreshments there.
4. *No talking.*
   Quiet reading here. You can talk in the room to your right.
5. *Don't put any AV material in this book return.*
   Return your books and other print items here. Return your DVDs, CDs, tapes, and other recordings to the people at the circulation desk.
6. *Closed.*
   We open again at 8:00 a.m.

7. *Not open to the public.*
   Services and collection are for employees of [name of organization or institution].
8. *How not to lose your job.*
   Read *The Agile Librarian's Guide to Thriving in Any Institution.*

Here are some useful positive one-liners for signs, posters, sound bites, and e-mail tag lines:

> We answer big and little questions.
> Find the answer fast. Ask a professional. Ask your librarian.
> The more you need to know, the more you need a librarian.
> The only information you can use is the information you can find. We guide you to it.
> You and your librarian: on site, online, and on top of the latest information.
> Librarians save you time.

Transforming Complaints or Confrontations into Opportunities for Positive Innovation

All service professionals experience complaints and confrontations; it's natural that some people will be disappointed, or even angry, about the service they experience. Most librarians want to avoid such experiences, and some will go to extremes to do so. Yet, the Agile Librarian chooses to see most of these negative experiences as wake-up calls and sources of inspiration for good marketing—and also as ways to create and promote improved services based on real client population needs.

Complaints as Reference Questions in Disguise

A complaint, from an individual or a group, is an expression of an unmet need or desire (McKnight, 1996). Receiving a complaint is less pleasant than the average request for information, but the Agile Librarian uses professional reference skills to move the issue toward a positive conclusion. Theresa Jaye Dickson, the Associate Director for Planning and Operations of the Pioneer Library System in Norman, Oklahoma, calls it the "complaint polka" because there are ritualized steps for each party to take, and at least one party has to execute the steps well enough to help the other party have a satisfying experience. Her public library system not only has a policy for dealing with materials challenges, but trains all staff in the steps of the polka. As in ballroom dancing, if the parties don't already know each other, they start by exchanging names and a little about themselves. The librarians have scripted messages they can use during the different parts of the interview, for instance, "Have you read this book yourself or did someone tell you about it?"

> **Exercise: Revising Negative Communication into Positive**
>
> For a week or so collect negative statements from your library. Include statements on the Web site, voice mail, brochures, and signs. Listen for roadblocks and negative statements you and other staff members commonly use. Then try revising them into either positive statements or statements that follow a negative clause with an eraser word and a positive statement.

The librarian must realize that regardless of the packaging of the complaint, it is a professional business transaction and not a personal assault. One cannot control how others act, but one can and must control how one reacts. Complaints are a normal part of a service profession. Sometimes they are prompted by poor professional service and sometimes by perceptions of what that service really ought to be. Occasionally people may be experiencing stress in another part of their life and are transferring anger to whoever is handy.

In any case, no profession practices without any complaints, and all successful professionals must have excellent interaction skills. Having no complaints is not evidence of excellent service. The complete absence of complaints may mean that no one cares or expects anything better. The service is irrelevant. Real complaints usually reflect a need or desire for more service, not less.

Even Agile Librarians may be tempted to assume that they already know the real nature of the complaint and the motives behind it, especially if they have heard the same initial statement before. That assumption is just as mistaken as skipping the interview for any information request. It is an unprofessional and lazy way to dispose of the client and avoid any real interaction. Such assumptions are often wrong and, especially in the case of a complaint, can come back to haunt you or the library. The interview in this situation may be more important than ever. One of Stephen R. Covey's 7 *Habits of Highly Effective People* is "Seek First to Understand . . . Then to Be Understood" (Covey, 1989, pp. 53).

When interacting with a person who is dissatisfied, the Agile Librarian uses superior reference interview skills, starting with the understanding that the client's first statement almost never is the real issue. Only after listening, asking questions, and paraphrasing can you determine the true issue, and only then can the solution process begin. Just as you should not start considering sources before clarifying the reference question, you cannot apologize or ask the angry client to do something until the underlying issue is truly clarified. Just as the person with the reference question may assume that the answer can come from only one kind of source, the irate client may believe that there is only one possible solution to the problem. The skillful professional will probably be able to discover a better solution once the real problem is clear.

Although an interview may seem, to the untrained ear, to be an ordinary conversation, it is not. See the box on page 116 to read about the differences that Ross, Nilsen, and Dewdney (2002, pp. 2–3) have identified.

Stages of the Complaint Interview

The complaint interview needs the same progressive stages as the professional reference interview. It needs an introduction, definition of the question or underlying need, a search for information to answer the question, communication, and positive closure. As with a reference interview, it's best to communicate in person and not by proxy. Too much can be misunderstood by relating through an intermediary. It's also important, if at all possible, to have a face-to-face conversation in private. Reference librarians know how to use their bodies to shield a private conversation from others in the area or to take the conversation into an office or other private place. If face-to-face interaction with all its non-verbal communication channels is not possible, synchronous communication

Conversation	Interview
Participants take relatively equal turns at talking and listening.	The interviewer listens more, especially in the early stages, and responds with body language and short phrases that convey attention.
Statements, rather than questions and answers, dominate the discourse.	The interviewer asks questions, many of which are open ended. The interviewer may answer a question with a question. This practice, which may be rude in an ordinary conversation, demands subtle tact.
The conversation often wanders from topic to topic.	The interview has a purpose and the interviewer may need to guide the interchange to relevant issues.
Repetition and redundancy are drawbacks.	Effective interviewers will repeat and paraphrase with an extending probe to move deeper into the question.
Conversation has no formal structure.	An interview has a structure of four or five stages with possible repetitions of the stages through the process; but, in any case, it starts with an introduction and ends with positive closure.

such as a telephone conversation or live online chat is preferable to an asynchronous exchange of memos or e-mail, or even an abbreviated synchronous medium such as text messaging.

Stage One—Opening a Communication Channel

No matter how the complaint begins, the Agile Librarian never reacts immediately with anything other than attention. Indignation and immediate rejection slams the door on any real communication—so does an immediate apology or acceptance of guilt. In fact, the level of demand, anger, or insult in the client's first statement often is only a reflection of the client's low opinion of library service. Escalation of negative emotions won't improve that at all.

Just as a client's opening question in a reference situation rarely expresses the real need, the first statement of a complaint is likewise an opening move, not a summary of the entire unmet need. Don't react too soon! The first part of the interview is just to open a communication link with some level of trust. If you don't know each other, introduce yourself and smoothly ask who the other person is: "I'm John Jones, the Children's Librarian, and you are . . . ?" and follow the response with "I'm glad to meet you." If you do know each other, "I'm glad we have a chance to talk," emphasizes the importance of the ensuing interview. If you do know each other, a positive "connection" comment helps—for instance, "It's good to see you again."

In the first few seconds, the Agile Librarian begins employing "attending skills" (Ross, Nilsen, and Dewdney 2002) without saying much (51–63). Throughout the interview, open, rather than closed, body language expresses attention. Approach the person at an equal level with both of you standing or both sitting and maintain eye contact, posture, and position. Use open body language, not crossing your arms over your chest in the classic defensive posture. Use a few meaningless but attentive and encouraging phrases such as "oh," "and," "I see," "go on," and "tell me more." If the client begins by asking, "How would you feel if . . . ?" the librarian is wiser to answer with a question about the client's experience than with a personal hypothetical answer.

If the opening statement is angry or seemingly irrational, the professional still listens and waits just as if it had been stated calmly. Wasting mental energy thinking "He just wants attention!" or "No, not now!" just delays any possible resolution. Concentrate instead on discovering the content of the person's unmet need. Sensitivity, tact, and undivided attention to the person is essential before the interview can proceed.

Stage Two—Gathering Information to Frame the Larger Context of the Problem

While traditional outlines of the reference interview sometimes refer to this stage as a "negotiation," the resolution of a complaint cannot be negotiated until both parties understand the larger context. The Agile Librarian will refrain from jumping to any conclusions yet and, instead, ask some open-ended questions that will place the client's chief complaint in the context of that person's life and what role library services can play in it. Your closed-ended questions that can be answered with "yes" or "no" limit the client's expressive options and may hide important aspects of the situation.

The client's opening complaint may be grounded in frustration about having a need that is not met in a particular way. Only after determining the real need can the librarian offer other and perhaps better ways that will satisfy the client's need. A different situation exists when the complaint concerns materials or services the library provides to others, for instance a library's program or book presenting a viewpoint the client finds repugnant or the library's lack of a particular information source the client believes others should use. The larger context here is perception of the mission of the library service in relationship to the school, community, institution, or company.

Stage Three—Working Together to Define and Refine the Central Problem

Like a skilled negotiator in a dispute between a company's management and labor, the Agile Librarian begins the next stage with points of agreement. Paraphrases of the context and issue with a few details added gives the client the opportunity to refine your (and perhaps the client's own) understanding of the issue. At this point, the Agile Librarian may ask probing closed-ended questions or specific who, when, where, what, or why questions. The client must be confident that you are paying attention and understand the concern before the client will accept any suggestion for a solution that you might make.

Stage Four—The Search for Information, Answers, or Solutions

Only after the first three stages have been completed is it safe for the Agile Librarian dealing with a reference question to consider possible solutions or sources of needed information. Just as a client may believe that there is only one source of information when you know several better possibilities, the client may also believe that there is only one possible resolution for the issue behind the complaint. Now the Agile Librarian can propose possible solutions. If the complaint is the lack of a particular resource, another resource may satisfy the client. If the complaint was about poor service not up to the usual standards, an apology and some kind of restitution or service recovery may suffice.

If the problem is a mismatch between the client's legitimate needs and library policy, the complaint may be an opportunity for a review of the policy or a teaching moment for how the policy benefits the client. Library managers carefully write policies for materials challenges and some other complaints. The wording usually is fairly specific, and staff is advised not to elaborate on it or create an impromptu new policy. Pointing to or thrusting a policy into a client's hands, however, is no substitute for empathetic listening to the client's perspective.

Occasionally, a managerial librarian with the authority to do so may choose to bend or go around a standard policy in a particular instance if it helps the client and does no harm to others. Sometimes, just knowing that library staff is aware of the issue is reassuring to the client. In any case, the complaint even from a frequent complainer may reveal an important hidden insight the Agile Librarian can use to improve services for others with similar needs. Carefully considered complaints and comments can reveal new opportunities.

People with complaints believe that library service is important to them, the community, or the institution, and they believe that change is possible—or they would not bother to complain. The Agile Librarian may not like experiencing complaints, but knows that somewhere beneath each is an opportunity to promote and improve good service. As Mara Niels explains, "Someone who is mainly interested in only one aspect of the library . . . can be helpful in packaging that part of your plans" and "the library critic is often someone who cares enough to complain, so you probably have goals in common" (Niels, 1990, p. 410).

Stage Five—Communication, Evaluation, and an Invitation

In their text, *Reference and Information Services: An Introduction,* Bopp and Smith emphasize that "How the interview is brought to an end is every bit as important as how it opened" (Bopp and Smith, 2001, p. 58). Just as in the interview that follows a request for information, the Agile Librarian dealing with a complaint may be able to resolve the issue right away, or may have to work on it for a while before getting back to the client. If it cannot be done immediately, the professional promises—making an informal contract—to contact the client by a certain time and through a particular medium. Even if an immediate answer is available, the librarian may think of another source or solution after the conclusion of the interview and will want to contact the client with an additional solution. In any case, the delivery of a concrete, usable response is not optional.

All effective interviews include two more very important steps. The librarian asks for the clients' evaluation of the response—"Does this completely answer your question?"—and invites the client to make requests again in the future.

Acting Professionally when Feelings Are Intense

Answering anger with anger is counter-productive. Professionals cannot control others' actions, but they must control their own overt reactions. If one's own feelings and fight-or-flight hormones have erupted, one has to act as if they have not. That professional skill is not always so well developed in personal life. This acting is not dishonest; it keeps the conversation focused on the business at hand, the client's needs, and not on the librarian's personal feelings.

That does not mean that one ignores one's own feelings. Daniel Goleman, in *Working with Emotional Intelligence* writes that "awareness—of how our emotions affect what we are doing—is the fundamental emotional competence. Lacking that ability, we are vulnerable . . . to being sidetracked by emotions run amok" (Goleman, 1998, p. 55). Goleman later describes how any time can be "the worst possible time" and multiple crises and pressures both at home and at work are "more than additive—they seem to multiply the sense of stress." The hormones the human body secretes during a moment of stress continue to circulate throughout the body for hours and increase the likelihood that we may overreact to the next stressor. He notes that "Cortisol steals energy resources from working memory—from the intellect—and shunts them to the senses. When cortisol levels are high, people make more errors, are more distracted and can't remember as well" (Goleman, 1998, pp. 75–76).

Acting calm is not the same as repressing such feelings. "[E]motional competence implies we have a choice as to how we express our feelings" (Goleman, 1998, p. 81). Professionals must, "manage . . . impulsive feeling and distressing emotions well, stay composed, positive, and unflappable even in trying moments [and] think clearly and stay focused under pressure" (Goleman, 1998, p. 82). We have a personal responsibility for our own state of mind and we cannot work well if we don't accept it. Goleman continues:

> Moods exert a powerful pull on thought, memory, and perception. When we are angry, we more readily remember incidents that support our ire, our thoughts become preoccupied with the object of our anger, and irritability so skews our worldview that an otherwise benign comment might now strike us as hostile (Goleman, 1998, pp. 81–83).

If a librarian needs to take a break to deal with a rising personal feeling, there are ways to do it without expressing a rejection of the other person or the conversation. One is to offer the person a beverage that must be retrieved outside of the room. Another is to say, "This is important and I want to give it my fullest attention. I have to go to the bathroom at this moment; please sit down, (or wait here, or don't go away). I will be right back." And then come back quickly. In the meantime, the other person might also have calmed down or left. In the latter case, the librarian can call or try to contact the person the next day, but should not chase the person down immediately. That person may also need a little break. The return call expresses the librarian's interest and concern and has no hint of punishing the person for making the comment or for leaving the interview.

Common Ground and Innovative, Mutually Beneficial Solutions

Professional service is not professional football. One team does not have to lose in order for the other team to win. Some people behave as if all complaints are a tug-of-war-style power struggle; they expect and even enable the other party to pull on the other end of the rope or give up entirely. That doesn't solve anything; if both parties increase the tension eventually both parties fall in a heap. There is another way.

After listening enough to thoroughly understand the need, the Agile Librarian goes into the creative process of engaging the client in joint problem solving. Often, that starts with reiterating points of agreement before further examination of the point of conflict. Then the conversation moves into the synergistic realm of working out a perhaps new and unexpected way to satisfy the client. This cannot possibly happen if both parties cling to their differences like distant corners of a boxing ring. The Agile Librarian can interrupt such a pattern by courageously and respectfully stepping to the center of the ring. An assertive move like this is neither aggressive nor passive.

Stephen Covey describes six possible conflict outcomes: Win/Lose (I win, you lose), Lose/Win, Lose/Lose, Win, Win/Win or No Deal. He lists seeking Win/Win as one of his *7 Habits of Highly Effective People* (Covey, 1989, pp. 204–234). Win/Lose and Lose/Win are both variations on the sport paradigm. One would rather win than lose, but someone has to win. If one loses, one can envision a revenge rematch and the winner may expect it. Conventional wisdom suggests compromise as reasonable, yet that leaves both parties feeling less than satisfied; it's really a Lose/Lose outcome. Win, by itself, implies that one does not care what happens to the other party so long as one gets one's own way. These four options create lingering resentment and loss of respect for all involved; those memories will stick. Like all-out war, it may never really be "over". The fifth possibility, Win/Win, is the successful solution.

No Deal is the respectful acceptance of disagreement which includes the possibility of a Win/Win at some time in the future. By looking at needs and resources from several different angles, the Agile Librarian and the client can suggest possible solutions different from the few that seemed to be available at first. Together, the client and the librarian may reject some of these possibilities, but at least they are both looking in the same direction, toward a Win/Win resolution, as they do so. Both have stopped keeping score. In short, sometimes No Deal at the moment makes it possible for the parties to come to an eventual "Win/Win" in the future.

Covey describes these outcomes as levels of communication reflecting varying combinations of trust and cooperation as "Defensive" (Win/Lose or Lose/Win), "Respectful" (Compromise), and "Synergistic" (Win/Win) (Covey, 1989, pp. 269–274). The primary distinction between a positive suggestion or request and a negative complaint or demand is that the interaction begins at the defensive level. Although attempts to force the complainer to be respectful are counter-productive even if the complainer changes demeanor, it is imperative that the librarian not escalate the conflict by entering the exchange at the low defensive level.

Covey describes the escalation of conflict from distant stances by stating:

> [It's] like trying to drive down the road with one foot on the gas and the other foot on the brake . . . [and] instead of getting a foot off the brake, most people give it more gas. They try to apply more pressure, more eloquence, more logical information to strengthen their position. . . . Insecure people think that all reality should be amenable to their paradigms. They have a high need to clone others, to mold them over into their own thinking. They don't realize that the very strength of the relationship is in having another point of view. Sameness is not oneness; uniformity is not unity. . . . Sameness is uncreative (Covey, 1989, p. 274).

Just as the wise teacher who is surprised by how many students miss a particular item on a test knows that her teaching in that area needs some attention and improvement, the Agile Librarian finds in complaints some excellent evidence of inadequate promotion of service or the necessity of adding a different kind of service. Thus, complaints are wonderful opportunities for new and useful information not otherwise available. Even differences that cannot be resolved are important. As Covey writes, effective people understand the limits of their own perceptions and value understanding others' different perspectives because it adds to their knowledge. Because no two people have had the same conditioning life experiences, there will always be differences in perceptions. Unless we value those differences, value other people, and accept that it is possible for different perceptions to be right or even that a third viewpoint is better, we will never be able to see beyond our own experiences (Covey, 1989, p. 277).

Resulting Promotions and Innovations

Commercial advertising campaigns for services sometimes are based on accurate assessments of people's most common complaints about the service and turning them into opportunities for proclaiming. One example of turning a perceived weakness into a strength was the MasterCard "Priceless" campaign developed by McCann Erickson Worldwide. Their market research in the mid-1990s showed that, at the time, Visa and American Express were seen as more upscale services for the rich to use for their lavish spending. In an astute analysis of potential client values, they designed a campaign built around what money could not buy (Arens, 2003, pp. 608–617). It didn't matter that consumers could, for the most part, use any of the three cards to charge similar purchases, what mattered was the proclaiming by this service provider. The promotional campaign emphasizes spending relatively small amounts of money to obtain what the ads called "priceless" benefits. Likewise, library clients have many competing sources of information. What do they *not* know that the library card in their wallet can do? We need to ensure that they know they can get from their library information sources or entertainment that they would have to pay for directly somewhere else

Prioritizing Your Own Complaints

Like too much sugar or too much salt in a dish, either extreme—constantly positive or constantly negative—is unpalatable and diminishes value. The wise Agile Librarian will pay attention to times to use the salt. Every complaint has a political cost. During times when you should spend some of your political capital to complain, you always must consider how to spend it wisely.

A librarian participating in the Proving Your Worth course, on which this book is based, said that she found it impossible to be positive because she found so much of what her clients believed and what her colleagues did to be very wrong. She wanted to point out all of their faults frequently for their own good. I asked her, "Which is more important to you, expressing your indignation or changing their beliefs and practices?" When she answered, "Changing their beliefs and practices," I told her that she was going to have to pick and choose which faults were truly the worst and then select one or two to discuss, per year. If she complained too much, nothing she said would be taken seriously. She would be known only as the person who always complains. That would destroy her ability to work effectively with any of these people.

A Tale of Two Closed Libraries

Two small one-librarian libraries in the same city were closed in the same year. Both librarians had lost all credibility with the decision makers in their organization, and both were deeply and personally hurt by the closures. Neither saw it coming. One, known for her twinkling smile and constant cheeriness, had continued doing exactly the same things she had done for years and wasn't aware of the major erosion in the usefulness of her services to her clients. The other implemented many changes, but constantly grumbled to anyone who would listen. Nothing was ever good enough to suit her. If she got new equipment and materials it wasn't enough; if she received praise for something she did, she disdained it. In both organizations, people not only quit hearing anything the librarians said, but actively avoided them.

Both institutions were involved in consolidations. The collection of the first library was given to another and the second was closed. Within months, however, the second was reopened with a new professional librarian in charge; one with positive people skills. She had much less experience, but she was a breath of fresh air to everyone who needed those library services.

Although one complaint per year may be an exaggeration, she probably had already established herself as The Complainer in this environment. She had a strong negative reputation to revise if she was going to bring about any real improvement. Many of her complaints may have been valid, but she was wasting her breath and destroying her credibility when she couldn't control the compulsion to express each one whenever it crossed her mind.

When You Should Complain

Knowing when to and when not to complain is both a personal and a political skill. On a personal level it requires two-way respect. The weak, doormat person with no boundaries and the blustering bully have a common trait: low self-esteem. Both have chosen to take the lazy way out of conflict by eliminating the need for thinking about what their reaction should be. Neither is willing to work for Win/Win solutions. Neither has real skill in assertiveness; they are either aggressive or passive. Without self-respect, they also are very unsuccessful at empathy.

All service professionals must be skilled at empathy. They cannot fake it because most people are very good at recognizing "pseudo-empathy." People who understand others listen with attention. They are able to pick up even very small clues and deliver their helpful service based on understanding others' needs. Manipulative people often feign empathy. Forced friendliness rings hollow and, when recognized, backfires (Goleman, 1998, p. 142). The famous physician and teacher of physicians, Frances W. Peabody put it this way: "[T]he secret of the care of the patient is in caring for the patient" (Peabody, 1927, p. 882).

Summary

Substantive positive communication is very important in any service, but especially in librarianship where the stereotypical image is an unsmiling person saying, "Shush," or a sign saying no. That stereotype is perpetuated whenever librarians and staff appear to emphasize rules more than service. Negative closure experiences reinforce this perception and cause potential clients to avoid librarians and libraries.

The Agile Librarian works to remove roadblock messages from clients' experiences, messages that bring the clients' pursuit of information to a complete stop. Services, procedures, and collections have to be designed with the library in the life of the client in mind more than the client in the life of the library. Professional proclaimers are more useful than negative disclaimers. Active, positive sentences convey both more information and more helpful empathy than negative ones do. Fortunately, a necessary negative roadblock statement can become a positive helpful statement with the addition of the eraser word, "but," and an additional clause that offers options.

Complaints contain clues to how client-centered service can be improved. They may seem like uncomfortable nuisances to the librarian, but if treated like a reference question in disguise, there can be a happy resolution for everyone. Professional exploration of the real information need leads to opportunities that are impossible with unfounded assumptions. An essential professional skill is the ability to be aware of—but not express—strong negative emotional reactions to a complaint. It is a business transaction, not gladiatorial mortal combat. Resolution of complaints should be "Win/Win," or perhaps "No Deal," that is, a respectful agreement to visit the issue again later—not win, lose or compromise.

Such interviews may appear to be an ordinary conversation, but there are some significant differences. In an interview, the librarian listens more, asks more questions, and paraphrases to reach an understanding of the issue. The interview stays on topic and progresses through logical stages towards a mutually satisfying resolution. People discount statements from any librarian who appears to be a constant whiner or a constant Pollyanna. Both are too boring to be interesting. The Agile Librarian carefully weighs which issues to pursue.

References

Arens, William F. 2003. *Contemporary Advertising*. 9th ed. Boston: McGraw-Hill Irwin.

Bopp, Richard E. and Linda C. Smith. 2001. *Reference and Information Services: An Introduction*. Englewood, CO: Libraries Unlimited.

Covey, Stephen R. 1989. *The 7 Habits of Highly Effective People*. New York: Simon & Schuster.

Goleman, Daniel. 1998. *Working with Emotional Intelligence*. New York: Bantam.

McKnight, Michelynn. 1996. Complaints: Reference Questions in Disguise. *National Network: Newsletter of the Hospital Library Section of the Medical Library Association* 21(2): 10–11.

———. 2005. Personal observation. November 14, 2005.

Multnomah County Library.2005. My Account and Card. http://www.multcolib.org/catalog/card/. Accessed July 29, 2007.

Niels, Mara. 1990. Politics of the Library of the Future. *The Electronic Library* 8:408–11.

Peabody, Francis W. 1927. The Care of the Patient. *The Journal of the American Medical Association* 88:877–882.

Quinn, James. 2001. Proclaimers,. E-mail to MEDLIB-L mailing list. March 7, 2001. http://list.uvm.edu/cgi-bin/wa?A0=MEDLIB-L.

Ranganathan, Shiyali Ramamrita. 1931. *The Five Laws of Library Science*. Madras Library Association, London, UK: Edward Goldston. Retrieved from the Digital Library of Information Science and Technology (dLIST) Classics Project. http://dlist.sir.arizona.edu/1220/. Accessed on April 11, 2008.

Ross, Catherine Sheldrick and Patricia Dewdney. 1998. Negative Closure: Strategies and Counter-Strategies in the Reference Transaction. *Reference & User Services Quarterly* 38:151–163.

Ross, Catherine Sheldrick, Kirsti Nilsen, and Patricia Dewdney. 2002. *Conducting the Reference Interview: A How-To-Do-It Manual for Librarians.* New York: Neal-Schuman.

Additional Suggested Reading

Branden, Nathaniel. 1983. *Honoring the Self: The Psychology of Confidence and Respect.* New York: Bantam.

Goleman, Daniel. 2006. *Social Intelligence: The New Science of Human Relationships.* New York: Bantam.

Griffin, Jack. 1998. *How to Say It at Work.* New York: Prentice-Hall.

Seligman, Martin E. P. 1990. *Learned Optimisn: How to Change Your Mind and Your Life.* New York: Pocket.

Tannen, Deborah. 1994. *Talking from 9 to 5: Women and Men at Work.* New York: William Morrow & Company.

———. 1990. *You Just Don't Understand: Women and Men in Conversation.* New York: William Morrow & Company.

Chapter 8

Marketing, Advertising, and Public Relations

Library and information professionals use the term "marketing" frequently, but loosely. H. W. Wilson's *Library Literature and Information Science* database has about 2,500 records representing articles with the word "marketing" in the title. EBSCO's *Library, Information Science and Technology* includes about 1,700. A Google search of "librarians" and "marketing" produces more than 2 million hits! Title words and Google searchable text are, of course, uncontrolled vocabulary, and even casual inspection of this retrieval shows the use of the word to be out of control.

Some hits with the word "marketing" in the title are really about advertising. Advertising is important in the marketing process, but it is not the entire process. Advertising without doing marketing research is like handing a client a thesaurus without first determining what the reference question is. If the client needs a map, the offer of a thesaurus won't be a useful service! People won't use library services they don't know or care about, so advertising has to speak clearly to potential clients' real lives to encourage them to seek such services.

Rigid Librarians may object to using business marketing techniques because they don't see libraries as organizations that sell products. They may be offended by the thought of using techniques developed by profit-making organizations. Nonetheless, no service is truly cost-free, and responsible professionals will use their resources as effectively and efficiently as possible to best fulfill the mission of the institution. The Agile Librarian understands that that responsibility includes learning techniques developed for other service-oriented organizations rather than wasting time reinventing the wheel or completely ignoring disconnects between what clients need and what librarians do.

In an article in *Library Trends*, "Trends in Marketing Services," Linda Gorchels writes, "Service marketing differs from product marketing due to the fact that services are intangible and typically require more personal interaction with the customer" (Gorchels, 1995). Henry Beckwith (2001, xvii) talking about commercial services points out that:

Products are made; services are delivered.

Products are used; services are experienced.

Products possess physical characteristics we can evaluate before we buy; services do not even exist before we buy them.

125

> Products are impersonal . . . things with no human connection to us. Services, by contrast, are personal.

On reading Beckwith, the Rigid Librarian might react with "Aha! 'Buy' means that even with services, the issue is monetary!" Yet so-called "free" library services are not really "free" even to the client and even if a larger organization is covering the expenses in the library budget. The cost to the client includes time, attention, and "hassle factor," as well as the cost of transportation to a place or connectivity to a site. So, for library service, the client often does "pay" for the service before receiving it, and will be disappointed if it turns out not to have been worth the price.

Real Marketing

Marketing, like good librarianship, includes finding out what people want or need, researching where that can be found or made, and providing a strong, active connection between the two. Agile Librarians can build on their best one-on-one skills to learn to really market entire services. Christine Koontz (2002) writes, "It is a lot easier for a librarian to learn about marketing than vice versa!" Telling people that you have a great new service or source for them is useless unless they really need or want that service or source. Susan Webreck Alman, in *Crash Course in Marketing for Libraries*, writes, "Often librarians have a great marketing idea, and they expend a lot of time and energy developing it without ever considering whether the project or program is relevant to their community" (Alman, 2007, p. 2, 4). Their time and energy could be better used had they taken the time to do their homework first.

Marketing is client centered and research oriented. It isn't just an amusing diversion for the staff; it is absolutely necessary for the Agile Librarian to thrive. As Denise Chochrek writes, "No matter how talented you are, you can never avoid marketing and still be successful for the long term" (Chochrek, 2000). The process of marketing is complex and includes continuous research. It is always rooted in a deep understanding of who makes up the client and potential client populations and their constantly changing needs. Clients live in a world that is bigger than just the library, and information market analysis includes not only awareness of library services in the clients' world, but also their other information services. Marketing library services include (1) research; (2) invention, the continuation and modification of services to meet both changing and constant needs; and (3) a set of tools including advertising and promotion activities to communicate with clients and stakeholders.

In that set of tools, good *advertising* directly influences service demand. *Public relations* is not necessarily related to a particular service, but it directly promotes and influences the image of an institution. *Advocacy* promotes something beyond the individual institution, such as endorsement of the value of libraries in general or support of a library service other than one's own. Advocacy is an important function of professional associations. Kirchner (1999) states that public libraries have "more actively promoted the need for advocacy programs than have academic and research libraries," but that may be because of their higher general visibility. All work toward the increase and improvement of client services and client satisfaction.

What are the important elements of marketing? They are often described in four, five, or six words beginning with *P*. Judith Siess, in *The Visible Librarian: Asserting Your Value with Marketing and Advocacy* describes library marketing as "the right *product* at the right *price* in the right *place, promoted* in the right way to the right *people* at the right *point* in time" (Siess, 2003, p. 20). For librarians, "product" includes service and "price" includes convenience, complexity, and the hassle factor for both client and staff. However many *P*s one counts, the thoughtful Agile Librarian does have the power, another *P*, to change, or at least tweak, each one. In this chapter, we will cover the *P*s first and then discuss the marketing research cycle.

The Right People: Who Are the Clients and Potential Clients?

For every library there is a definable population of clients and potential clients, the "people" part of marketing. A library's collections, services, and practices are for a specific population. In an ideal world, library collections, services, and practices would vary from library to library more because of the needs of the particular populations served than because of the interests and personalities of the librarians.

Librarians can have a natural tendency to develop collections and services more for the current clients than for the potential clients within the specific population. They may also continue services and policies more suitable to former clients than to current clients. Only a continuous marketing process can help them avoid these traps.

The Agile Librarian thrives by being inquisitive about the needs of potential clients. Marshall Keys warns, "Only by transforming ourselves to handle the needs of emerging users will we be successful in the future." He further points out that many younger cohorts "value community over privacy, want to be able to personalize the technology they use, and carry more technology in their pockets than libraries provided users just a few years ago" (Keys, 2006).

The organization and library mission statements set boundaries for the potential client population, but really knowing the population requires deeper exploration. That starts with gathering demographic data from appropriate sources. Librarians in public libraries might use census data. Librarians in university or school libraries can get student and faculty profile data from the institutional administration, and librarians in other organizations can begin with information from the organization chart and human resources department. A little rough sampling of actual clients will usually show variation, even a gap, between the demographic profile of the actual clients and the potential clients. That gap suggests a population whose needs the librarians should study in addition to the needs of the current clients.

Grace McCarthy points out that "non-users are not necessarily anti-library; they may just have different ways of getting hold of the information they need." She continues by describing four types of non-users: "influencers and second-hand users," "non-users to whom the library has little to offer," "non-users with own access to information sources," and "non-users with demands for non-traditional library services." She prefers personal conversation to impersonal surveys for getting to know her "non-users" (McCarthy, 1994). In personal conversations with potential users, the Agile Librarian will find examples of all four types. Note that for this informal study, the conversations should be with a representative sample of potential clients. It is not a controlled experiment, and a randomized or convenience sample of people might miss completely a group of people you need to know about!

Market Segmentation

An example of marketing for specific populations is *market segmentation.* "*Market segmentation* is the process of breaking down a large, widely varied (heterogeneous) market into submarkets or segments, that are more similar than dissimilar (homogenous) in terms of what the consumer is looking for or is presumed to be looking for" (O'Guinn, Allen, and Semenik, 2003, p. 25). A market segment may be defined by demographic characteristics, geography, professional roles, political preferences, hobbies, or just about any interest in entertainment or information services. By targeting different segments with different services and messages, advertising for even the smallest of library services need never become stale.

There always are subgroups of people within a potential client population who have interests and needs that differ from those of other subgroups. Not only will students and faculty in a secondary school have different interests, but students and faculty in one university department will have different interests from those in another department. Librarians in public libraries have long recognized the interests and needs of a group they call "young adults," by which they mean early teens—not people between 18 and 30, for whom the term is most commonly used outside of libraries. For hospital library services, nurses, social workers, and doctors will all have different interests and needs. Decision makers and stakeholders who are not necessarily clients of library services make up another market segment that can be targeted by specific advertising messages. Service differentiation marketing can enlighten them about what only your library services can do for them!

Relationship Marketing

Relationship marketing (RM) is more personal than public relations or branding and less directed toward increasing the number of transactions than is advertising. (Arens, 2004, p. 243). In RM, the service provider maintains personal contact with clients. Relations with particular clients may continue amicably for years. Clients trust such relationships with "my doctor," "my beauty consultant," or "my librarian." Companies like Avon, Harley-Davidson, and Mary Kay Cosmetics have

---

Market Segmentation Exercise

Professional advertising agencies invest heavily in research, not only in the creation of television ads, but also in placing them where they will most likely influence the target group of people. Compare the advertising messages in the breaks of several different television shows, shows that you assume would interest different segments of the viewing audience. Keep a log of each ad as you watch each show and watch for patterns. Pay close attention to the difference in ads for the same product placed during different shows. What are the different messages presented in these 30-second dramas? What can you learn from them that could help you develop creative messages about a specific service that would speak to different client groups?

prospered largely because of their relationship marketing (Besant and Sharp, 2003). Clients who have a relationship with a representative of the brand or institution may expect to develop a relationship with another such representative somewhere else, for instance, after a move to a new place, school, or job. Some of the issues in earlier chapters, such as delighting your customers and pleasing your boss, can be part of RM. Librarians in small special libraries usually become particularly adept at RM, but clients of large libraries may also enjoy continuing interactions with a particular librarian. Besant and Sharp (2000) write, "The true value of RM is in building real relationships and not pseudo-relationships. . . . A cardinal tenet of RM applied to libraries would be that relationships, broadly defined, thoughtfully categorized and painfully prioritized, become the engines for achieving the library's main values or contributions to the parent institution's purpose" (p. 20). All such relationships require thoughtful nurturing.

The Right Product: What Services Should We Provide?

Even the Rigid Librarian can rattle off a list of services a given library provides. The harder question is "What service do these clients *need?*" The Agile Librarian defines services in terms of *what the client gets*, rather than *what library staff does*. What the librarians and staff do are practices and procedures to provide the services, and not ends in and of themselves. The Agile Librarian can consider not just service in general, but must also regard specific services as the marketing *P* of "product" for a particular group of "people," actual and potential clients for those services.

Although data on the use of current services provides evidence of what current clients use, it provides no insight at all into their unmet needs, nor does it reflect anything about what the potential clients need. Undoubtedly, some of them would use existing library services if the services were promoted to them at the right point in time and available from the right place at the right price. But no matter how much such services are advertised, people will not use them if they don't want or need them.

One of the reasons for Google's great success is that it appears to be a convenient way to get any kind of information at all. The simple search box creates the illusion that it demands little effort from the user to get good results, and people may believe that it is more comprehensive than it is. The hidden cost is in missed sources and the time it takes to sort manually through irrelevant results to find relevant ones. Few users will actually pay (in time and effort) to go through more than the initial page or two of results (Price, 2003). Another user cost, of course is the lack of metadata or source evaluation.

Strategic Marketing

The strategic marketing process begins with understanding the mission of the institution and how library services contribute to that mission. That mission may change subtly over the years, but occasionally it changes suddenly when schools consolidate, businesses move into new areas, or the community experiences a disaster. This strategic marketing includes careful identification of which information services the client population needs to meet the organization's goals.

Librarians can easily make the classic managerial mistake of defining their role in the organization too narrowly. They may define their roles in terms of collections, and even in terms of traditional services, instead of in terms of meeting clients' current information needs. Fifty years ago, Theodore Levitt described the decline of the rail industry as "marketing myopia." Specifically, he pointed to their lack of concern for the very real needs of their clients:

> [R]ailroads did not stop growing because the need for . . . transportation declined. That grew. . . . [R]ailroads are in trouble . . . not because the need was filled by others . . . but because it was *not* filled by the railroads. . . . [T] hey assumed themselves to be in the railroad business rather than in the transportation business. (Levitt, 1960, p. 45)

It doesn't take very much imagination to apply that paragraph to some libraries in decline. Only two words need to be substituted, "libraries" for "railroads" and "information" for "transportation," for it to apply to some librarians playing institutional roles that are far too narrow. Even if librarians don't see their roles as that narrow, there are plenty of others willing to stuff them into that box! Only librarians can market larger roles for library services. If a service is no longer useful to library clients, advertising it more will not only be unproductive, it will also divert the attention of both librarians and clients from better services that should be developed. Kelso (1995) lamented in a report, "The most commonly used element of marketing is still promotion" (p. 3). And in one of his *Library Journal* "White Papers," Herbert S. White decried librarians' lack of understanding of real marketing, "Libraries do not market; occasionally they advertise what they already provide" (White, 1997).

We can and *must* use effective marketing to expand our roles in our organizations. Many have moved beyond promotion and advertising to marketing what we really can do. The Agile Librarian's service is not just providing access to books, collections, online sources, or even providing "access to information." It is empowering people to pursue effectively whatever information they choose to seek, find, study, or enjoy. That is an active professionalism. In societies with access to "too much" information, the librarian's role in increasing information literacy is becoming more important than most people know. It takes serious marketing, not just haphazard advertising, to encourage people to both seek and use this professional service that they so desperately need.

The Right Promotion: Advertising, Branding, and Public Relations

For libraries, *advertising* uses communication media to promote the use of particular library services. *Branding* connects advertising particular services with the name of the particular library itself. *Public relations* promotes positive images of the library's mission in general and may also use media, but for more general ends. *Advocacy* promotes the mission and image of other libraries or librarianship in general. Thus professional associations all are involved in advocacy for the profession. As Coult writes, "Put in the crudest sense, marketing is about creating markets for products, advertising is concerned with increasing sales and PR is about creating understanding" (Coult, 1999, p. 30). So for libraries, marketing is about creating markets for services and resources, advertising is about increasing use of services and resources, and PR is about creating understanding about what we do for the organization and community.

Advertising

"Advertising is fun. . . . Advertising is also business" (O'Guin, Allen, and Semenik, 2003, p. vii). Advertising is important communication. Doing all the research into the information needs of groups of people and developing services still doesn't work if the clients never know what is available. It would be like doing the reference interview and determining what material would best answer the client's question—but not telling the client.

Indeed, advertising without good market research process can be counterproductive. It can perpetuate inaccurate images of good library service or even strengthen perceptions that libraries are irrelevant. Gorchels presents the example of IBM's failure to develop their market even as their sales increased. The company's emphasis on advertising and selling may have helped the company for a while, but eventually it hurt it. Gorchels contends, "IBM had a 'world class' sales force, but neglected innovative product development which resulted in a loss in competitive standing. Like many large companies, it became a market-share manipulator—its defense of existing markets took precedence over the creation of new ones." She explains how service providers can fall into the trap of emphasizing advertising what they have done in the past over market research into how they can improve what they provide for people now and in the future (Gorchels, 1995, p. 502–503).

Advertising just for the sake of advertising can be wasted effort. According to O'Guinn, Allen, and Semenik (2003), most effective advertising hopes to achieve one or more of the following:

Promote brand recall
Link a key attribute to a brand name
Persuade the consumer
Instill brand preference
Scare the consumer into action
Change behavior by inducing anxiety
Transform consumption experiences
Situate the brand socially
Define the brand image
Invoke a direct response (p. 366)

A particular library within a particular institution or community is a "brand" of information source, and in this sense the "consumer" is the client. Note that advertising can actually transform the experience of using library services. And, to be effective, it must do so within the entire marketing process.

The actual effects of advertising will be different for different people. At the very least, advertising should make most people who encounter it aware of what is being advertised. A generally smaller portion of the audience will comprehend the message, and a still smaller group will be convinced. Some of the convinced will move from comprehension to desire for what is advertised, and the smallest fraction of the audience will actually act as a result of the advertising. Arens (2004, p. 251, 392) illustrates the number of people effected by advertising new products or services as a pyramid somewhat like this:

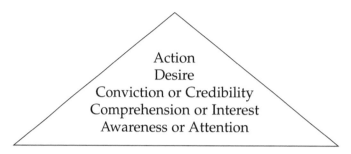

The Agile Librarian's desired result from advertising library services is that people do take action to use or support those services. The rest of the effects of advertising are mental; they may change attitudes, but the goal is to create a desire strong enough that it leads to behavior and even to changing habits. Non-librarian decision makers, stakeholders, and potential clients may all say nice things about a particular library, but interest, credibility, and even desire aren't very useful unless they lead to the intended positive action.

An easy-to-observe example of carefully crafted advertising is the 30-second television commercial. Teams of experts research and develop these mini-dramas in which every detail in sight and sound is designed to capture the attention and credibility of hundreds of thousands of people. They work so well that corporations are willing to spend large sums producing them and even millions of dollars just to get them on the air. A single 30-second ad costs at least $3 million to air during the Super Bowl National Football League Championship (Thomson Reuters, 2008). Such a short commercial presents very little of what the librarian would consider verbal content, but what viewers see and hear is enough to convince some in the huge audience to seek the product, service, or Web site. At the very least, these little dramas get a lot of attention. A smaller part of the audience interacts with it to the levels of interest or credibility. It will evoke desire for the product in only some, but, of course, the advertisers' goal is to persuade a small part of the audience to take action. These ads are so expensive because during the Super Bowl they reach a very large number of people, and the small percentage of those people who are moved to action will more than pay for the ad with their purchases.

Although librarians can't spend that much on advertising, they can learn lessons about image, color, design, and persuasion that orchestrate instant sensory, social, and cognitive appeal. Sloppy advertising and bad publicity can create a different kind of attention and interest, can increase negative kinds of conviction, and can stimulate desire that leads to very harmful actions against library services. When an arrest of someone owing a large library fine makes national news, it is not likely to increase circulation of print material nationwide. Even worse is dull and boring advertising that leads to apathy or reinforces beliefs that library services are irrelevant.

Communicate frequently what the clients and potential clients want and can get from library services. Advertising just "The Library" often assumes too much understanding; it assumes that people encountering the advertising already know all they need to know about library services in their own lives. Promoting "The Library" may be part of public relations (covered later in this chapter), but it is no substitute for client-centered advertising of particular useful services. The word "library" is not derived from a verb, and therefore not related to any action. It can describe a personal collection of books or an information service that provides clients with books, instruction, electronic resources, and personal professional services. The personal professional services may not often come to mind for most people getting the "Use the Library" message. Too much of this kind of advertising can hide rather than promote librarians' real services.

What can we learn from other enterprises about what to advertise? The word "bank" also denotes a place where a service is performed. Much like how a "library" can be a personal collection on a shelf, a "bank" can be a piggy bank on a shelf where someone stores loose change. Such banks or libraries provide no services. On the other hand, like a professionally staffed library, a bank can be an institution that provides a wide variety of value-added services. Banks' service products are different from those of libraries, but in both cases advertising the value of the service to the client can be more effective than just advertising the place.

"Use the Bank!" or "Use the Library!" may in a sense be branding, but they are not client-centered messages. Banks' professional advertising agencies learned a long time ago that they must advertise what the bank can do in the lives of its clients. They learned that banks cannot thrive if they expect all of their customers to come physically to the bank anytime they need service. The same goes for libraries.

Banks advertise their customer services and refer to themselves as "full-service" banks. They advertise services that are convenient for individuals, rather than the amount of the banks' deposits, investments, and loans. Librarians need to advertise "full-service" libraries. Individual potential clients don't care so much about the size of the collection as they do about getting what they want when they want it.

Client-perspective advertising, like client-centered service, makes a big difference. Take, for example, the advertising history of Healthtex children's clothing. By the 1990s, the long-established brand was losing sales to some very savvy competitors. Internal processes could be improved, but it would take a long time for such changes to reach public awareness, if ever. So the company's advertising agency studied the real concerns of the potential customers. They found that ads depicting cute, spotless, well-behaved children did not reflect mothers' real daily experiences. Ads that described how the product would help with their real concerns were far more effective in changing behavior. For instance, the copy for one was "Your baby's naked. Your phone's ringing. And your mother-in-law's walking up the driveway. Let's talk snaps" (Arens, 2004, p. 205–208). The message of the effective Healthtex advertising was a direct result of marketing research.

Every piece of advertising does not have to carry a complete message about the entire enterprise. The Healthtex ad emphasized just one aspect of the product—the snaps made it easy to dress the baby quickly. The unstated implication was that other purveyors of similar goods might not accomplish the same thing. The advertising technique of *differentiation* has as its goal "creating a perceived difference, in the mind of the consumer,

What *Are* You Trying to Say?

Librarians' publications, listservs, blogs, and conversations often describe promotional activities. For instance, National Library Week is an appropriate opportunity for both advertising and public relations activities. Such communication can create interest, credibility, and desire that may result in action. On the other hand, some library or librarian-centered advertising is downright counterproductive. Some such advertising contains vague messages. Some includes library or librarian-centered messages that can make people feel ignorant or unwelcome. For instance, consider the message of each of the following contest activities:

1. Guess which baby pictures are pictures of library staff members?
2. From a list of library services, pick the one that librarians here do not offer. (Make the answer quickly and easily available and make it a service planned for the future.)
3. Guess how many books are checked out in a year.
4. Every 10th person who comes in the door or uses a particular service gets a useful prize; every 50th gets a really nice prize.

The message of the first one must be that everyone on the staff was once a cute baby. So what? How likely are clients to encounter people outside of the library who never were babies? Most people reading the second challenge on the list may be surprised and interested in services they could use—if the service is described clearly in non-technical language. As to the third, librarians may care about how many books they check out as a service measure—but what does that mean to anyone else? I don't care how many transactions my bank successfully processed last year, I just want to know that they won't mess up *my* account. Also, number three sounds like one of those contests in which one person is a winner and everyone else is a loser. Are the "losers" likely to change their behavior because the winning number was more or less than they guessed?

The fourth promotion welcomes everyone and might encourage people to use a service with their friends because the larger the group, the better the chances are that someone will get a prize. Consider also the message carried by the prizes. Some library-themed gifts are more appropriate for librarians than for clients. Not everyone wants an afghan with a picture of cats and books. The advertising pros know that people are more likely to hang on to a branded object that is useful or interesting to them. The office worker is more likely to use a binder clip with a library URL and phone number than a stack of colorful bookmarks. Exactly the opposite would appeal to a young child just learning to read books. Whatever you do to get attention, you want it to be interesting and to move people to credibility, desire, and action.

between an organization's brand and the competition" (O'Guinn, Allen, and Semenik, 2003, p. 25). Librarians who are well aware of the advantages of their services over other services can advertise those differences without directly naming the competition. For instance, public libraries who circulate DVDs, tools, and art as well as books can advertise that their service is free to people with library cards. That is a valid differentiation from other ways of renting or buying the same things. The message is not confrontational if it does not name the businesses that charge. Likewise, it is valid for the video businesses to advertise that they guarantee that certain movies are always available to borrow or download without having to mention that the local library service can't do that. (Of course, that advertising might prompt an Agile Librarian to figure out a cost-effective way to offer the same service!)

Differentiation is a technique of *selective demand stimulation*. Advertising professionals also promote different things for different reasons.

Primary demand stimulation intends to stimulate demand for a new product category in general (for instance, touch screen mobile phones) by educating people about the value of the entire category rather than something specific in that category. Advertising professionals know that "Primary demand stimulation is challenging and costly, and research evidence suggests that it is likely to have a perceivable impact only for a new product category in general" (O'Guinn, Allen, and Semenik, 2003, p. 29–30). The American Library Association "Read!" campaign is an example of primary demand stimulation. Compare the client centricity of the Healthtex message to the message of posters of famous people reading books librarians like. The message of the celebrity posters isn't negative, but the celebrity transfer propaganda technique is likely to connect to the concerns of ordinary clients only if that particular individual celebrity is important to them.

Locally, the "Use Your Library" message is an example of primary demand stimulation and not likely to move a community to use library services that have been known and available in the community for a long time. It might work very well when the library is new to the institution, for instance, when a school or company first opens its own library service. On the other hand, "the true power of advertising is shown when it functions to stimulate demand for a particular company's brand" and that constitutes *selective demand stimulation* (O'Guinn, Allen, and Semenik, 2003, p. 29–30). People need and use hundreds of information sources every day. To make a difference, the Agile Librarian's advertising message states clearly something that is better for the client in library services than in other (unnamed) services.

People in a library's community may well know that the Internet can be useful. What is it about using the Internet in the library that is better than using it other places? "Use the Internet here if you don't have access at home or at work" is a valid message for one segment of the community, but what should the message be for those in the community who do have access at home or work? Is it the same self-service experience, or do librarians offer some value-added enhancement? Lots of news organizations, agencies, and companies have self-promoting Web sites. What does the library Web site offer people that is not available from other sites? Is it obvious?

Direct response advertising asks for immediate action. "Click here to register for this service" is a request for a direct online response. Fear appeal or anxiety-lessening ads may also elicit immediate action, for instance, they may promote consumer income tax information in late March and early April or disaster relief information when a disaster suddenly changes the concerns and interests of an entire community. *Delayed response advertising* encourages action in the near, but not immediate, future. It may rely more on imagery and message themes, emphasizing the benefits of a particular library's "brand" and encouraging trust in it. (O'Guinn, Allen, and Semenik, 2003, p. 4–40) In the appropriate context, Agile Librarians can use all of these advertising techniques.

Branding

Integrated marketing communication (IMC) ensures a consistent message in a wide variety of contexts. Arens (2004) describes IMC as how "Everything we do (and don't do) sends a message" (p. 247). He cites Duncan and Moriarty (1997, p. 78–90) in describing brand-related messages as planned messages (designed advertising), product messages (inferred messages from policies, packaging, etc.), service messages (statements made during interactions with clients), and unplanned messages over which the organization has little or no control (gossip, news stories, comments by the competition, etc.). IMC includes the positive communication discussed in Chapter 7, branding and public relations. Schacter writes, "Branding is a modern term for a very old concept, often using symbols to elicit consumers' emotional responses leading them into making positive associations and building consumer loyalty" (Schacter, 2007). Symbolic branding is just as effective in literate societies as it was in preliterate societies when a symbol on a sign at the door of an establishment proclaimed the nature of the establishment's business. The American Library Association's National Library Symbol, originally designed by Ralph E. Devore, works very well as such a sign and is included in the U.S. Federal Highway Administration's manual for highway sign standards (American Library Association, 2008).

Integrated brand promotion (IBP) is the use of the same branding in all different kinds of organizational promotions. Branding is the creation of a strong, well-known identity for a library and is represented by a graphic design and perhaps a slogan. It is a common theme that runs through all advertising and communication from and about a full service library. Branding provides clients, potential clients, and stakeholders a handy and recognizable mental label for the entire complex suite of materials and services that is a library. It also is part of the connection between specific advertising and generalized public relations.

The brand graphic design identifies media used for advertising and public relations. It includes not only a logo, but also specific colors (even specific shades) consistently used in all promotion. A style sheet sets standards for typestyle, color, and the logo. The visual brand is prominent in the library Web site, newsletter, stationery, flyers, signage, and perhaps even in the color of walls and furniture in the physical library. It is important enough to hire a designer, if at all possible, to do it right. (Wolfe, 1997, p. 39–47). The Agile Librarian takes responsibility for describing the needs of clients and stakeholders to the designer. Clients and stakeholders may be involved in early tests of brand designs.

Peggy Tumey's article "Developing a Cohesive Image for Your Special Library" presents principles applicable to any library:

> A logo is a visual representation of an organization . . . through words, an image, or both as a symbol for the product, service or organization. . . . An icon is a visual representation of a thing (a book, money, etc.). Because icons and logos are representations, they are as uniquely tied and identified with the image of a product, service, or corporation as is its name. (Tumey, 1991)

Once developed, such an icon or logo should be used consistently wherever possible. In the very simplified form of the "brand," it should appear on every Web page, piece of paper, blog, and e-mail signature file provided. It can be on every brochure, flyer, newsletter, and even pads of note paper. It can be large and obvious both inside and outside the library.

Frugal librarians can gather advertising pads, pens, mugs, and other small items from vendors, especially in meeting exhibits. These items can be quite useful *in the librarians' home.* In the library or the library office, everything that can be branded should identify *the library.* It keeps the message repeating; anything else confuses and dilutes. The message clients see should be what they can get from library services, not what the librarians can get from the vendors.

If a particular library has a terrible reputation that needs to be improved, or if the mission or services are changing, it may be time for some rebranding. The extent of the rebranding depends upon the extent of the change. It can be as little as tweaking communications and service delivery, or as big as designing a new logo, slogans, and a completely new campaign. In some environments, the change will be very welcome, whereas in others, "neophobia," or the avoidance of the new, may be a problem. Schacter (2007) explains, "If you decide to change your successful brand, loyal clients may become unnecessarily irritated with you, defeating the purpose of the exercise." Branding, like everything else, has to be client centered.

Library branding should be a strong component of marketing's selective demand stimulation. As such it has to make a promise and keep that promise in every client interaction. Dempsey (2004) writes, "Lines are blurring as alternatives appear for what has traditionally been the sole domain of the library . . . elements of Borders' 'Stay and Explore' strategy have been inspired by libraries." As a component of selective demand stimulation, branding is much more than the design that expresses it. Kenneway (2006) adds, "When developed to its full potential, your brand should help define and communicate what it is that you can do better than anyone else, what distinguishes you from other services and what is most relevant to the needs of your customers."

Public Relations

Good public relations promotes the image of the library through the use of public service announcements, coverage in local media (which reaches more people than most library newsletters do), programs, exhibits, and so much more. Evans, Ward, and Rugas (2000) define *public relations* as "an art form through which the library informs and persuades its service community to support its activities," and it "encompasses everything that a library or archive does, from staff interacting with customers on a daily basis, to published guides on how to use services, from online catalogs through annual reports, to exhibitions mounted within the facility" (p. 90). It is closely related to Integrated Marketing Communication.

Large school districts, universities, and corporations employ staff specializing in advertising and public relations for the entire organization. Large libraries often have one or more people with similar responsibilities for the library. Those without such a department may use consultants for help with advertising, public relations, and media training.

The Agile Librarian in a small library within a large organization fosters good relations with the public relations department. Working closely with the organization's PR department provides many win-win opportunities. For instance, providing factual back-story for people who write news releases and newsletter copy helps to develop not only a supportive relationship, but also a firsthand experience of library information services. In time, the Agile Librarian learns the kinds of stories that PR wants to tell and can supply PR with great stories of library services. With permission from everyone involved, such stories can improve the image of both the larger organization and the library.

In a broad sense, public relations includes practicing professional skills, delighting clients and stakeholders, making good impressions, and promoting the library's image and brand. It is both proactive (often using advertising media and techniques) and reactive in efforts to recover from negative publicity and events. Thus the public relations part of marketing also includes SWOT analysis, which examines both internal strengths and weaknesses and external opportunities and threats (Stueart & Moran, 2007, p. 102–107).

Most people have acquired sensitivity to baseless hyperbole, the propaganda technique of "glittering generality." They can see that the emperor has no clothes. Nevertheless, this and other classic propaganda techniques do still work *if* they are used discreetly and honestly. The "bandwagon" technique implies that many other people are on board, so you should join them. Some messages use "loaded words" with strong emotional connotations. Presenting a "plain folks" image implies that there is something for ordinary people; whereas at the other end of the propaganda spectrum, "transfer" or "testimonial" techniques employ beautiful, successful, or famous people to appear using the service or to endorse it.

Good public relations is easier to achieve if excellent "know, show, and tell" are already ongoing. A major publicity campaign may temporarily improve public image, but it won't revive half-hearted service. Adverse publicity may spring up at any time from surprising sources. The Agile Librarian makes sure that the library's public hears and sees more positive publicity than negative.

The H. W. Wilson company sponsors annual John Cotton Dana Library Public Relations Awards for "outstanding library public relations, whether a summer reading program, a year-long centennial celebration, fundraising for a new college library, an awareness campaign or an innovative partnership with the community" (H. W. Wilson Company, 2008). The company has presented awards to exemplary winners of the competition since 1946. Brief descriptions of the winning projects since 2001 are on the company Web site.

The Right Point in Time and the Right Place:
When and Where to Advertise or Provide Service

Effective advertising will appear when people need it and where they will easily encounter it—and so should services. That may not necessarily be "the way we've always done it." Ideally, the right point in time is the moment of need. Term paper counseling services advertised to students when they are first assigned term papers will be more meaningful than at the beginning of the semester when they don't yet have any assignments. The right place is simply where people will be when the suggestion will be interesting and useful. It's fine to post flyers about library programs in the library, but they should also appear away from the library in places where larger numbers of people will see them, especially people from the market segment for which the program is intended. Placement counts.

Monthly calendars of events for different kinds of people may help librarians demonstrate that they are busy. But they may also give the individual the impression that "there's nothing for me here." In other words, children's programs at a public library should be most heavily advertised when and where they will best reach parents and their children, whereas programs for other groups should be advertised at other times and other places important to those groups. Otherwise, such advertising might perpetuate the myth among adults and teens that public libraries are more for kids than for adults.

Deciding which media to use for advertising depends upon the answers to the what, who, where, and when questions. Learn from the pros; use the media that are most likely to reach the target population for a particular message. "Advertising media are strategies, not objectives. . . . Your advertising media goals may be to reach a certain number of persons with a certain frequency and with some impact. . . . If you establish the use of certain media as part of your goals, you are setting out on your trip without knowing where you want to go" (Kelley and Jugenheimer, 2004).

Indeed, not only are different media generally appropriate for different organizations, but the Agile Librarian knows that always using the same medium for advertising can generate boredom and apathy. Beware of the "law of the instrument," the temptation to use only the medium to which you are accustomed. Both Colby (1963, p. 178, in reference to use of technology) and Kaplan (1964, p. 28, in reference to research methodology) illustrate this "law" with the example of how a two year old, given a hammer, will believe that everything needs pounding.

A new contest (which purportedly involves some kind of skill) or sweepstakes (with randomly selected winners) is likely to attract more interest than one that is a regular, recurring event. The same goes for premiums or "freebies." The Agile Librarian gets positive attention by doing something different! Some mass media may appear to be too expensive for a given library budget, but endorsement or minor sponsorship of a non-library event can get the library's brand or message into a broader media range than the library can afford for promoting its own events. Carefully chosen, such collaboration provides win-win opportunities.

Marketing Research: Discovering the Right *P*

For each *P*, what exactly is the right *P*? Marketing without research is just playing games with traditional or personal ideas. Legitimate research does not have to be time consuming or expensive. Alman (2007, p. 4–19) describes the use of surveys, focus groups, nominal group technique, and environmental scans by librarians with a little or a lot of time and with a little or a lot of money.

Most of us had research courses, or at least had the opportunity to take research courses, in our masters' programs (McKnight and Hagy, 2009). If you didn't, or if, like most of us, you've forgotten some of it, take the time to review some of the readings at the end of this and the next chapter.

Real market research includes the possibility, the risk, that you might find out something you did not want to know. On the other hand, you might learn something desirable that you would really like to know. It's uncomfortable for Rigid Librarians to discover that what they like to do best is not necessarily what their clients want most, so they tend to avoid activities that might reveal such embarrassments. That may explain some librarians' preference for advertising and public relations activities over market research. Even Agile Librarians will sometimes avoid research because of the change it may suggest, and only a wet baby always likes change. On the other hand, without doing the research, librarians might never know that there is something new that they really would *like* to do and that their clients would *prefer* them to do! The surprise results of research can go either way.

The research component of the marketing process has a similar outline to the reference interview. This process has steps in common with service quality improvement, evaluation, and evidence-based librarianship, which will be covered in the next chapter. What do they all have in common? All must start by formulating a question. All must continue by deciding what kind evidence would answer that question, choosing a method of gathering and analyzing relevant data, drawing conclusions from that evidence, taking action, and questioning again. All of these processes are derived from scientific methods of producing evidence to answer questions, rather than using only tradition, hearsay, or unfounded guessing.

Thus, the client–based, research-oriented marketing process includes periodic study of the current the potential client population (the right people), what services and resources they need (the right product) and when and where those services should be provided (the right point in time and the right place). It includes periodic study of how to minimize the clients' costs, including time and inconvenience, as well as the organization's costs (the right price). With thought and attention, professional librarians can study each of these Ps in relation to their own practices.

The librarian's skill in individual information needs analysis can be thoughtfully scaled up to community information needs analysis. The reference interview, like marketing, has to start with a question about user needs and desires, and it isn't over until the professional is certain that the user is satisfied by asking an additional question. Marketing has to include research both before and after new service development and promotion activities.

Without such before and after data gathering and analysis, it really isn't marketing. It's analogous to the teacher who cannot be certain that learning has taken place during an activity without using *both* a pre-test and a post-test. Without having used a pre-test before the activity, there is no way for the teacher to know if the educational activity had any effect because the students might have already known the material. The test may, indeed, reveal what students know, but without a baseline for comparison, there is no evidence that the teacher's efforts facilitated their learning this content.

Another error happens when someone tries to plan a research project without clarifying a question first. The question is more important than the research method, and the research method has to fit the evidence needed to really answer the question. Overeager would be marketers may come up with and use a survey before they've defined what they want to find out. The items in the survey may function only to proclaim what they want, the people who complete the survey may not be representative of any particular population, and the results won't necessarily be useful evidence for anything.

So marketing research, like the reference interview, starts with defining the question and ends with proposing a new question. In between those two points we have to decide both what kind of evidence will answer the first question and which method to use to find that evidence. In the study phase, we gather and analyze the evidence before we act on it. Then we act on our conclusions, gather evidence about the results of our actions, and ask another question.

What Evidence Would Answer the Question?

What *kind* of data will answer the question? For instance, one would expect a question such as "How many people live in the city?" to be answered with a number, but other questions, such as "What is the name of the city?" or "Why is English the official language of this city?" will be answered with one or more words, a narrative response. The first question requires quantitative, numerical data for an answer, whereas the others require qualitative or narrative data. Confusion sometimes arises when people mistake research into *quality* with *qualitative* research. Quality as value or excellence may be evaluated with a number of methods, some of which use quantitative data, for instance LibQUAL. *Qualitative* research, however, is the analysis of data expressed in words or concepts rather than numbers or quantities. Some questions require quantitative or qualitative kinds of evidence, and some require a combination of both. Qualitative research can also refer to naturalistic, holistic research methods that are different from experimental research methods (Cresswell, 2009).

Gathering and Analyzing Data

Someone using the results of sophisticated statistical data analysis to answer a question will be seriously misled if the data set is not really relevant to the question. I have read studies that claimed in their titles and abstracts to be about *practicing* physicians' or nurses' information-seeking behavior, but the reported results came from analyzing data gathered from medical or nursing *students.* Other examples of amateurish and inaccurate research include analyzing data from an uncontrolled convenience sample (whoever is handy) using techniques designed for a randomized sample. Another example is using no control group in a hypothesis-testing experiment. The choice of information to study and the method used to analyze it has to fit the question, the circumstances, and methodical rigor, and not the favored method.

Questions about people's opinions usually require research methods that ask them their opinions; questions about peoples' behavior can be better answered by observation. For instance, a survey question about client opinions on when a service should be available (for instance, virtual reference) might produce different data than observations of when the same clients actually use the service. Asking individuals how often they use a particular service requires a self-report of unrecorded, uncounted memories, memories that can be distorted by many experiential factors. Making such a survey anonymous does not ensure objectivity, especially if the person believes they ought to use a particular service more or less often than they actually do. They might think, for example, "As a responsible professional, I should keep up with the literature in my field." "As a good student, I should use the library a lot." "As an expert in my field, I don't have to look up anything."

Drawing Conclusions, Taking Action, and Asking Another Question

Only after you have analyzed the research data can you attempt to draw conclusions from it. Just as some material that we expect will answer the client's question won't, the results of some research data analysis will be inconclusive. At that point in the reference interview, and at that point in the research, you have to come up with another strategy. After using the new search strategy, you ask the client again if it answers the question. After gathering and analyzing data another way, you may have evidence that better answers your marketing question. When you have valid, reliable, and appropriate information, you can draw conclusions and take action based on that information. Then you look for another question and the process continues. Just as you are not finished when you've helped one client answer a question, you don't do one marketing study and then decide you don't have to do another.

The Agile Librarian can also research what information sources and services people use that aren't from the library. You can use service differentiation advertising to proclaim how library services are different from the competition. Look at the marketing *P*s for a particular service. What would be useful for people to know? If the librarians in a particular institution offer a *product*, a service for a particular group of *people*, and your market

Win-Win Marketing

Ruth, a hospital librarian, heard something interesting over lunch in the cafeteria. A finance director was complaining about how much money the hospital was wasting on duplicate publication subscription renewals for departments throughout the organization. Ruth mentioned that she dealt with only the library's subscription, but that like most librarians, she knew a lot about the subscription process. She asked him how much the hospital was spending on other subscriptions; he gave her a general estimate on the spot. When she e-mailed him later, showing an interest in his concern, he gave her a more exact figure.

Of course, Ruth had experience working with a subscription service for the library subscriptions. She also knew that taking on the hospital's department subscriptions would take time that she simply didn't have. Instead of throwing in the towel then and there, she went to work gathering data about costs. Then she wrote a complete business plan in a format she knew the finance director would understand. Her pitch was that if the hospital hired an additional librarian and the library took over the management of all hospital subscriptions, they could save the hospital more than the cost of the new librarian's salary and benefits. The finance manager was willing to try it for one year, with the understanding that if the savings didn't materialize, the position would not continue. He approved the budget change for the next fiscal year.

Ruth helped write the position description for the additional librarian and worked through the hiring process. She began a survey of departmental manager satisfaction with the current subscription process, looking especially for elements that could be improved. The new librarian continued that market research even as she planned the subscription processing transition. At the end of the year, the librarians were able to report that they had saved the hospital almost twice as much money as they had projected. The finance director was more than satisfied, but they didn't stop there. They repeated the departmental manager satisfaction survey and could also report a clear increase in service satisfaction to complement the report on the financial savings. The administration made the new librarian position a permanent one.

research shows that many of them don't know it, *promote* it. Likewise, relevant information about the low *price* of convenience and convenient *place* of service access could become promotions useful to potential clients.

Similar Processes

The processes of the reference interview, marketing, quality improvement, evidence-based librarianship, and proving the value or worth of library services all use stages of the scientific method as illustrated in Table 1. At their simplest, all begin and end with a question. In between those two questions are various kinds of study and activity. The reference interview begins with helping the client describe an information need as a question and ends with another question about that need; in between those two questions the librarian considers possible sources of that information, gathers data from those sources, and evaluates its relevance to the question. Marketing begins and ends with research and evaluation, but it also includes planning and promotion. Quality improvement (QI) is an organizationally introspective business practice leading to better service, and evidence-based librarianship (EBL) uses externally published research literature to address practice in individual libraries. Some see all managerial decision making as proceeding logically in the same stages (Barton and Martin, 1991, p. 261), although most would agree that such a model is used only selectively. Each of these processes can become quite time consuming, but the Agile Librarian learns how to make data gathering and analysis for one purpose contribute to another purpose. We'll discuss these and other processes in Chapter 9.

An Example of a Marketing Study

The Marketing Study—Ask (Define the Question)

Begin with a question chosen from a universe of possible questions relating to the right *P*s. Many library marketing studies begins with a question concerning clients (people) and services (products). The choice of a question to pursue is somewhat subjective, but the definition of the question must be objective. In any case, it must be important enough to warrant the time it takes to study. The main question may have related questions, but it's best to limit your inquiry to one question at a time. You can pursue related questions in later studies. After the current question is clear, the Agile Librarian considers what kind of data would answer that question, and only after describing the needed data does she move on to planning a study.

There are many reasons why some clients use library services and why potential clients do not. Marketing research questions may address whether or not

> People really need the service
> People actually expect good service
> People know and understand what the service is
> People find the service easily available
> People prefer getting the service from another source
> People prefer a different service to meet their needs
> People find the service affordable on several levels
> People find the service to be easy to use

Table 1
Comparing the Stages of the Reference Service with Those of Marketing, EBL, Quality, and Value Assessment

	ASK Define the Question	*STUDY* Estimate where the answer may be found	*STUDY* Choose a method for finding out	*STUDY* Gather the data	*STUDY, ACT* Analyze the results	*ACT, ASK* Propose questions for further study
Reference Service (satisfying one person)	Conduct a reference interview to understand the question	Consider possible sources for the answer	Consult the sources	Retrieve documents	Choose relevant documents	Deliver to client and ask client if this completely answers the question
Marketing (satisfying a group of users or potential users)	What is the service?	What is the population of users or clients for this service?	Design a study to find out what the users or clients want and need from the service	Carry out the study	Analyze the results	Design, promote, implement, and evaluate service improvements
Evidence-Based Librarianship (searching for and applying the results of relevant published research)	"Formulate a clearly defined, answerable question that addresses an important issue in librarianship" (Eldredge, 2000)	"Search the published and unpublished literature, plus any other authoritative resources for the best-available evidence with relevance to the posed question." (Eldredge, 2000)	"Evaluate the validity (closeness to the truth) and relevance of the evidence" (Eldredge, 2000)	Formulate an action plan based on the evidence; "Assess the relative value of expected benefits and costs." (Eldredge, 2000)	Implement a plan of action	"Evaluate the effectiveness of the action plan" (Eldredge, 2000)
Quality Improvement (improving internal processes)	Find a process to improve	Who should be on the team to improve this process?	Gather data on the current process and identify the desired improvement	Plan and implement the process change	Gather data on the process after the change and compare to the before change data	Evaluate the effectiveness of the improvement and suggest the next process to improve
Proving worth (externally demonstrating evidence of value to the organization)	What are the organization's values	Choose a library service that corresponds directly to an organizational value	What data would illustrate how that service is part of that value? Choose a method to gather data relevant to that value	Apply the data gathering method chosen	Analyze the data and summarize in an appropriate report.	Distribute the report to relevant officials. Ask those officials if this report convinces them of the library's contribution to that value. If so, choose another value to study. If not, seek a different service, a different evaluation method, or both.

For instance, if you are a school librarian wanting to be ready to help students with their assigned papers, you may feel frustrated because you may not find out about the assignments until the students walk in. You want to be ready to provide the service at the best point in time. One way to deal with the situation would be to tell the teachers you want to know earlier. But the teachers are also your clients, and you need to know something about how they work before asking them to make changes to their plans. In this case, a strategic marketing question might be "When and how do the teachers choose the topics for assigned papers?" If some teachers *are* already in touch with you during the process, who are they, how many of them are there, and what is different about the teachers who are not in touch? Another reasonable question is "Why do some not use the existing service?" Pursuing this question must logically follow the first question for client-centered (rather than library-centered) strategic marketing. The Rigid Librarian will ignore the out-of-touch teachers or make assumptions and preach to them. You will want to study the non-client teachers' processes and practices before explicitly offering or even changing your services.

What do we know to begin with? We know who the teachers are. The teachers are all either current clients or potential clients. We know that in this case, the best service for the teachers and students requires that the librarian understand the assignment well enough and far enough ahead of time to ensure that the collection or selected site links are appropriate for the assignment. All of the teacher clients for this service have patterns for making the assignment, but those patterns probably differ from teacher to teacher. Those who don't use the service may have different patterns than those that do. For instance, they may wait until the last minute to improvise a topic, they may need different services for their students than you provide, or they may be unaware of what you really can do. They may have tried and disliked the current services, or they may not be convinced that your services would save their time and improve their students' learning. One question cannot cover all of the possibilities. Let's start by asking if the teachers who don't tell you what they are assigning have different ways of planning such assignments than others do.

The Marketing Study—Study (Estimate Where the Answer May Be Found)

Where might the answer be found? There might be evidence about the work habits of teachers elsewhere in published research, and the wise librarian will do a quick literature search for such studies, perhaps in the ERIC database. There will also be examples of how others gathered similar needed information. Data about "when" will be quantitative, and data about "how" will be qualitative. Also, you'll want to gather some data before you start about which teachers do contact you in time for you to prepare for their students' projects. For this question, you will want to pay attention to those who do not.

The Marketing Study—Study (Choose a Method for Finding Out)

The best data about when and how these particular teachers work will come directly from individual teachers, even though other teachers will be glad to offer hearsay evidence. Human behavior can be studied directly, through observation, or indirectly, by asking people to describe what they do. You will only rarely, if ever, be able to observe these teachers' work processes, but you easily can survey them. The next choice is how to do such a survey. E-mail or paper surveys are easy to send to many people, but the response rate tends to be quite low and the data is often unreliable. The formal survey itself may be a negative message to potential clients. The librarian must not appear to be grilling or judging the teachers. In a small school, a simple visit over lunch that includes an open-ended question during conversation may elicit more information than a battery of questions in a formal interview or paper survey. Most people will respond to questions that show real, nonjudgmental interest in their work.

The Marketing Study—Study (Gather the Data, Analyze the Data)

As soon as is practical after such a conversation, you make notes on what was said, trying not to jump to any conclusions too soon. As you gather more evidence from different conversations, new insights will suggest slightly different questions to ask. Eventually you will have enough data to see some consistent patterns.

The Marketing Study—Act and Ask

Those patterns can suggest new services, changes in the service, or changes in how you promote the existing service. They may suggest a one-size-fits-all service, or they may reveal that different teachers need different kinds of support. These findings help you to design, implement, and promote new or changed services, or perhaps, simply change promotion methods for the current service. The marketing cycle is not complete until you check again after the change to see if it did make a difference. After the changes have been implemented for a while, track how many teachers are contacting you earlier now. You're gathering quantitative data to compare to what you had before you made the change. That is one way to evaluate the effectiveness of the change. You also might want to know how the newly changed or newly promoted services fit in with the teachers' work patterns. For that, you gather qualitative data, descriptions, to help you understand. Then there will be new questions to pursue.

This example of an informal study has all of the elements of a full, professional marketing study: planning, execution, analysis, application of results, and evaluation of the resulting change, but does not require the investment a lot of your time.

Summary

The Agile Librarian knows that marketing is essential to thriving service. It is a continuing client-centered and research-oriented process. Librarians have expertise that can be used for marketing, and they can easily learn and apply good marketing skills. Principles of marketing developed in the commercial sector work very well for librarians. Advertising, public relations, and research methods are tools for the marketing process, but by themselves they are not the whole process.

Real marketing results in getting all of the *P*s right. That means getting the right *product* or service to the right *people* with the right *promotion* and the right *price* or convenience in the right *place* and at the right *point* in time. The Agile Librarian has and uses the *power* to at least tweak or maybe change any of the other *P*s.

The right people includes both the actual and the potential client populations. Marketing usually includes market segmentation, understanding and marketing for specific segments of that population. Relationship marketing promotes trust between particular clients and particular professionals. The right product refers to the right services and right resources for the right people. Strategic marketing uses the mission of the institution to shape how library services contribute to it. Agile Librarians define their roles neither too narrowly or too broadly.

The right promotion includes tailored advertising to promote the use of services and sources, as well as branding, which connects particular services and sources to a particular library in clients' minds. Public relations promotes the positive image of the particular library's mission in general, and advocacy promotes the mission of other libraries or of librarianship in general.

Advertising will evoke different reactions from different people, but its ultimate aim is that at least some people take action. Advertising will capture the attention of many people and lead some to comprehension and interest. Of those interested people, some will be convinced, and some of the convinced will desire to use the services and sources. Advertising is effective not just if it gets attention, but if it results in action.

Different kinds of advertising lead to different actions. Primary demand stimulation is advertising for something completely new in people's lives. Selective demand stimulation moves people to use something from a particular source. Without using a library, people have access to many kinds of information; selective demand stimulation will move them to use library services instead of other services. Direct response advertising is meant to lead to an immediate response, and delayed response advertising is meant to encourage people to do something soon, but not necessarily in this very minute.

Branding, or integrated brand promotion, uses consistent imagery for integrated marketing communication. It connects all kinds of communication to the strong image and identity of one provider. Public relations improves the positive reputation of the library and, in a sense, can include every point of interaction between people and the service.

The right place and point in time to advertise, like the right place and time to offer services, is based on the place and time when people most need the advertised service. Advertising term paper counseling is more effective before papers are due, and library service hours are more effective when they are set for clients' convenience.

Marketing research is a continuous process of discovering each of the right Ps for a particular library. "The way we've always done it" can be a counterproductive trap unless it really provides the right P. Blind assumptions are stumbling blocks that research can remove. Like the reference interview, marketing is a cyclical process of defining a question, deciding what evidence will answer the question, choosing a method to gather data, analyzing data, taking action, and questioning again. Marketing and the reference interview go through stages similar to the quality improvement and evidence-based librarianship processes discussed in the next chapter.

References

Alman, Susan Webreck. 2007. *Crash Course in Marketing for Libraries.* Westport, CT: Libraries Unlimited.

American Library Association. 2008. *National Library Symbol/Library Symbol Highway Sign.* ALA Library Fact Sheet Number 30. http://www.ala.org/ala/aboutala/offices/library/libraryfactsheet/alalibraryfactsheet30.cfm. Accessed March 22, 2009.

Arens, William F. 2004. *Contemporary Advertising.* 9th ed. Boston, MA: McGraw-Hill Irwin.

Bartol, Katherine M. and David C. Martin. 1991. *Management.* New York: McGraw-Hill.

Beckwith, Harry. 2001. *The Invisible Touch: Four Keys to Modern Marketing.* London: Texere.

Besant, Larry X. and Deborah Sharp. 2000. Upsize This! Libraries Need Relationship Marketing. *Information Outlook* 4:17–22.

Chochrek, Denise. 2000. Market the Value of Your Competitive Ingelligence: An Added Role for the Information Center. *Information Outlook* 4:32–35.

Cresswell, John W. 2009. *Research Design: Qualitative, Quantitative and Mixed Methods Approaches.* 3rd ed. Thousand Oaks, CA: Sage.

Colby, Kenneth Mark. 1963. Computer Simulation of a Neurotic Process. In Silvan S. Tomkins and Samuel Messick (Eds.). *Computer Simulation of Personality: Frontier of Psychological Theory.* New York: John Wiley and Sons.

Coult, Graham. 1999. Raising the Profile: Promoting Information Services. *Managing Information* 6:29–35.

Dempsey, Beth. 2004. Target Your Brand: Build an Identity That Works in the Age of the Superstore. *Library Journal* 129:32–35.

Eldredge, Jonathan D. 2000. Evidence-based librarianship: An Overview. *Bulletin of the Medical Library Association* 88:289–302.

Evans, G. Edward, Patricia Layzell Ward, and Bendik Rugas. 2000. *Management Basics for Information Professionals.* New York: Neal-Schuman.

Google. Database available online. Mountain View, CA: Google Inc. www.google.com. Searched July 29, 2008.

Gorchels, Linda M. 1995. Trends in Marketing Services. *Library Trends* 43:494–509.

H. W. Wilson Company. 2008. John Cotton Dana Library Public Relations Award. http://www.hwwilson.com/jcdawards. Accessed September 6, 2008.

Kaplan, Abraham. 1964. *The Conduct of Inquiry: Methodology for Behavioral Science.* San Francisco, CA: Chandler Publishing Company.

Kelly, Larry D. and Donald W. Jugenheimer. 2004. *Advertising Media Planning: A Brand Management Approach.* Armonk, NY: M. E. Sharp.

Kelso, Helena. 1995. The Marketing of Special Libraries to Their Parent Organizations—A Study of Selected Melbourne Institutions. *Australian Special Libraries* 28:3–21.

Kenneway, Melinda. 2006. Branding for Libraries: Communicating Your Value to Increase Reader Awareness of the Library Service. *Serials* 19:120–126.

Keys, Marshall. 2006. Chaotic Transitions: How Today's Trends Will Affect Tomorrow's Libraries. *Serials Librarian* 50:9–36.

Kirchner, Terry. 1999. Advocacy 101 for Academic Librarians. *College & Research Libraries News* 60:844–846, 849.

Koontz, Christine. 2002. Stores and Libraries: Both Serve Customers! *Marketing Library Services* 16(1):3–5. http://www.infotoday.com/mls/jan02/koontz.htm. Accessed July 29, 2008.

Levitt, Theodore. 1960. Marketing Myopia. *Harvard Business Review* 38:45–56.

Library, Information Science and Technology. Ipswich, MA: EBSCO Publlshing. http://www.ebscohost.com/thisTopic.php?topicID=205&marketID=20. Searched July 23, 2008.

Library Literature and Information Science. New York: H. W. Wilson. http://www.hwwilson.com/databases/liblit.htm. Searched July 23, 2008.

McCarthy, Grace. 1994. Getting to Know Your Non-users. *Library Management* 15:30–34.

McKnight, Michelynn and Carol Rain Hagy. 2009. The Research Imperative Connection: MLA Policy and the Curricula of Schools of Library and Information Science. *Journal of the Medical Library Association* 97:134–136.

O'Guinn, Thomas C., Chris T. Allen, and Richard J. Semenik. 2003. *Advertising and Integrated Brand Promotion.* Mason, Ohio: Thomson South-Western.

Price, Gary. 2003. What Google Teaches Us That Has Nothing to Do with Searching. *SEARCHER: The Magazine for Database Professionals.* November/December 11 (10):35–37.

Schacter, Debbie. 2007. Info Business: Does Your Perception of Your Service Match Your Clients' Opinions? *Information Outlook.* 11:40–41.

Siess, Judith A. 2003. The *Visible Librarian: Asserting Your Value with Marketing and Advocacy.* Chicago: American Library Association.

Stueart, Robert D. and Barbara B. Moran. 2007. *Library and Information Center Management.* 7th ed. Westport, CT: Libraries Unlimited.

Thomson Reuters. 2008. Super Bowl 30-Second Ads to Cost $3 million in 2009: Report. May 6, 2008. http://www.reuters.com/article/televisionNews/idUSN0644484220080507. Accessed June 22, 2008.

Tumey, Peggy. 1991. Developing a Cohesive Image for Your Special Library. *Special Libraries* 82(3):165–170.

White, Herbert S. 1997. Marketing as a Tool for Destabilization. *Library Journal* 122(3):116–117.

Wolfe, Lisa A. 1997. *Library Public Relations, Promotions, and Communications: A How-To-Do-It Manual.* New York: Neal-Schuman.

Additional Suggested Reading

Baker, Sharon L. and Karen L. Wallace. 2002. *The Responsive Public Library: How to Develop and Market a Winning Collection.* 2nd ed. Englewood, CO: Libraries Unlimited.

Bingham, Beth. 1998. Library Advocacy. *Louisiana Library Association Bulletin* 58:86–88.

Bussey, Holly J. 1991. Public Relations vs. Marketing: The Information Professional's Role as Mediator. *Special Libraries* 82:154–8.

Claggett, Laura. 2002. Identify Your Brand Before You Market. *Information Outlook* 6:13–16.

Germain, Carole Ann. 2000. 99 Ways to Get Those Feet in the Door: How to Develop a Public Relations Campaign. *College & Research Libraries News* 61:93–7.

Gupta, Dinesh K. and Ashok Jambhekar. 2002. What is Marketing in Libraries? Concepts, Orientations and Practices. *Information Outlook* 6(11):24–26.

Karp, Rashelle S. 2002. *Powerful Public Relations: A How-to-Guide for Libraries.* Chicago: American Library Association.

McCarthy, E. Jerome and William D. Perreault, Jr. 1984. *Basic Marketing: A Managerial Approach.* 8th ed. Homewood, IL: Richard D. Irwin.

Olson, Christine A. 1993. Testing Your Library's Marketing IQ. *Medical Reference Services Quarterly* 12:75–83.

Sass, Rivkah. 2002. For the Cost of a Latte a Week, Your Library Brings You the World: Marketing the Worth of Your Library. *Library Journal* 27:37–38.

Siess, Judith. 2004. Marketing without Much Money: You Don't Need Big Bucks to Get the Word Out. *Information Outlook* 8(1):29–31.

Van Loo, John. 1984. Marketing the Library Service: Lessons from the Commercial Sector. *Health Libraries Review* 1:36–47.

Wolpert, Ann J. 1999. Marketing Strategies: Lessons for Libraries from Commercial Brand Management. In *The Future of Libraries in Human Communication: Abstracts and Fulltext*

Documents of Papers and Demos Given at the [International Association of Technological University Libraries] ITUL Conference, Chania, Greece, May 17–21, 1999, 19. See IR 057 443. http://www.iatul.org/conferences/pastconferences/1999proceedings.asp.   Accessed October 22, 2008.

Zmuda, Allison and Violet H. Harada. 2008. *Librarians as Learning Specialists.* Westport, CT: Libraries Unlimited.

Chapter 9

Gathering and Using Evidence to Support Decisions

Librarians, clients, and administrators make decisions based on beliefs, feelings, and evidence. Beliefs and feelings are unavoidable, but you have to look for evidence. Earlier chapters in this book emphasized techniques for influencing the beliefs and feelings of non-librarian decision makers. Evaluative research to discover useful evidence is a constant in good library services; and, as Rosalind Farnum Dudden (2007) writes, "Evaluation is all about making decisions and then defending the decisions within changing, even turbulent, environments that are influenced by both tradition and the politics of the day" (p. 3).

The continuing education class that led to this book was called "Proving Your Worth," but that title that wasn't exactly accurate. Whereas mathematicians use the word "proof" in the sense of solving equations, librarians and information scientists rarely use it. Scientists regard the results of research to be *evidence*. The more reliable, valid, significant, and important the evidence, the more useful it is in guiding decisions.

Research

The Agile Librarian is at various appropriate times a consumer of research evidence, a contributor to research evidence, and a disseminator of research evidence. *Evidence based practice* refers to the use of published research evidence to inform professional practice. Contributors to research evidence carry out formal and informal research projects. Sometimes contributors disseminate results of well-designed inquiries as publications that benefit others and increase evidence based understanding.

Librarians often help clients make informed decisions by helping them find published reports of relevant research. Thus, the clients are consumers of research evidence and librarians facilitate its dissemination (though not all research is published). Librarians also study their own collections and services to find evidence for making their own decisions.

Agile Librarians inform their own decisions with evidence both from published research and from their own local research and evaluations. They also provide research evidence to decision makers, evidence intended to strengthen such stakeholders' understanding of and support for library services. This dissemination can include internal research, benchmarking, publications of relevant research, and various combinations of kinds of research evidence.

Evidence is the result of using appropriate methods to analyze appropriate data to answer a question. In other words, quality and value may be measured or described, or both. Quantitative data and analysis have long been preferred in the basic sciences, whereas qualitative data and analysis methods were refined by work in the social sciences. In *What's Good? Describing Your Public Library's Effectiveness,* Childers and Van House (1993) write the following: "Qualitative evidence is more subjective . . . But it is no less valid—for example, a visual assessment of the cleanliness of facilities or the overall helpfulness of the staff." They differentiate between systematically collected evidence for questions that require data gathered from a large sample and idiosyncratic evidence that applies to only one situation. Thus, the answer to the question, "Do clients in general believe that our staff is friendly?" requires different evidence to answer than asking, "Do particular new clients or administrators believe our staff is friendly?" The cleanliness of the facility can be evaluated in descriptive qualitative terms such as, "There is a dark stain on the carpet" or quantitative terms such as, "We vacuum the carpet five days a week."

Some people trust measurement more than qualitative evidence and assert that, "If you can't measure it, it doesn't exist," whereas others may distrust statistical analysis and agree with "Not everything that counts can be counted and not everything that can be counted counts," (often attributed to Albert Einstein, but probably not from him) (Einstein and Calaprice, 2000 p. 318). Education and library and information science (and most other disciplines today) use whichever data and analysis methods are most relevant to the question. Questions beginning with "Why" more often need qualitative answers than questions beginning with "How much," "How many," or "How often," which may need quantitative answers.

Librarians and other researchers may have more personal experience with one kind of data gathering and should resist the temptation to attempt to apply one set of research methods to all questions. The truly Agile Librarian can use quantitative, qualitative, and mixed methods—depending on the kind of evidence needed to accurately answer the question.

Librarians' Research Education

How do librarians learn research methods? To be effective consumers of research as well as contributors and disseminators, librarians have to know the basics. McKnight and Hagy (2009) found that almost all ALA-accredited MLIS programs offer courses in research methods, and about half of them require such courses. Nevertheless, elective courses may be offered less often than required courses, and graduates of such schools may not have the opportunity to take a research methods course. McKnight and Hagy also found that the content of the research courses in MLIS programs varies widely.

To be effective consumers, contributors and disseminators of LIS research, professionals must continue their research education through self-study and continuing education classes. Many current and commonly used texts for MLIS research courses are useful for self-study. The most commonly used texts in such courses include Powell and Connaway's *Basic Research Methods for Librarians,* 4th ed. (2004),

Babbie's *The Practice of Social Research*, 11th ed. (2007), Cresswell's *Research Design: Qualitative, Quantitative and Mixed Methods Approaches*, 3rd ed. (2009), and Leedy and Ormrod's *Practical Research: Planning and Design* (2005). Dudden's *Using Benchmarking, Needs Assessment, Quality Improvement, Outcome Measurement, and Library Standards* (2007) describes some specific measurement and evaluation techniques. Professional associations offer workshops and classes. Some promote research activities and use of the results of research more than others.

Research and Professional Associations

Some associations have active research sections or interest groups; others are not so active. For the American Society for Information Science and Technology (ASIS&T), all contributed papers presented (most are reports on research) at the annual meeting are rigorously peer reviewed. All such papers are published in their entirety before presentation in the several hundred pages of *Proceeding of the American Society for Information Science and Technology*. The society produces a peer-reviewed research journal monthly, *JASIST*, which has a Thomson-ISI impact factor of 1.436, ranking number 13 in Information Science and Library Science (Thomson Reuters, 2007). Members of this association are mostly in academic institutions, and it is a relatively small association.

At its annual meeting, the Medical Library Association (MLA) features peer-reviewed papers, and many of these papers present research results (the abstracts are published online). The quarterly *Journal of the Medical Library Association*, also a respected and peer-reviewed journal, has a Thomson-ISI impact factor of 1.392 and a ranking of 14 in Information Science and Library Science (Thomson Reuters, 2007). MLA recently adopted a new policy, *The Research Imperative* (2007) and members work in a variety of institutions, including universities, hospitals, and corporations.

Though larger than ASIS&T and MLA, the Special Libraries Association (SLA) does not promote presentation of research at its annual meeting. A small special interest group presents one session on current research. The quarterly journal, *Special Libraries*, which featured full length articles, ceased publication in 1996. The association now publishes only brief practical articles in its *Information Outlook*.

The largest, the American Library Association (ALA), has an Office for Research and Statistics that advises and supports various research endeavors carried out by units of ALA and government agencies. Specifically it carries out studies of the ALA membership, and assists several roundtables and committees. Some of the divisions of ALA, including The American Association of School Librarians (AASL), The Association for Library Service to Children (ALSC), The Library Information and Technology Association (LITA), and The Reference and User Services Association (RUSA) have their own research and publication programs. Most notable are the ACRL's *College & Research Libraries*, LITA's *Information Technology and Libraries*, and RUSA's *RUSQ* with impact factors of .820, .326, and .175, respectively (Thomson Reuters, 2007). In addition to publishing a peer-reviewed quarterly, *Journal of Education for Library and Information Science*, The Association for Library and Information Science Education maintains a database of research interests of LIS faculty.

Evidence Based Librarianship

Evidence based practice is a term first used in medicine. It means using reliable published research to inform practice whenever possible, rather than relying only on personal experience and tradition. It is an active communication between theoretical research and practical application. Of course, the body of published research in library and information science is much smaller than that of medicine, but, nonetheless, our practice can be informed by using the results of valid, generalizable research. Evidence Based Library and Information Practice is an international movement with biennial conferences in different countries and an online open access journal (Evidence Based Library and Information Practice, 2009).

Evidence based librarianship (EBL) uses a process similar to that of the reference service—marketing and quality and value assessment—illustrated in Table 1 in Chapter 8. The first step in EBL, as in research itself, begins with the formulation of an answerable question. For instance, a university librarian might ask, "Why don't our undergraduates use our online virtual reference services?"

Although professional opinion can be useful, EBL requires consulting evidence from research. So, the second step is to, "Search the published and unpublished literature, plus any other authoritative resources for the best-available evidence with relevance to the posed question" (Eldredge, 2000, p. 291). This is how EBL differs from browsing professional journals: it has a specific purpose. Librarians are skilled at using bibliographic databases and can use *Library and Information Science Abstracts*, *Library and Information Science and Technology Abstracts*, *Library Literature and Information Full Text*, *ERIC*, or other appropriate databases to identify articles related to the question. Although such subject searches will retrieve citations to a variety of interesting articles on the subject, for real EBL, one needs those which are reports of scientific research on the subject, not just personal opinion.

The third step further reduces the pool of relevant articles: "Evaluate the validity . . . and relevance of the evidence" (Eldredge, 2000, p. 291). Not everything that is published as research is good reliable research. So the Agile Librarian uses knowledge of research methods and skills in source evaluation to decide which of the retrieved articles present the best evidence. The conclusions the article writers claim are useless if the research was poorly planned and executed. An example of a research report relevant to our sample question would be Naylor, Stoffel, and Van Der Laan's "Why isn't our chat reference used more? Finding of Focus Group Discussions with Undergraduate Students" (2008).

The fourth step is to make an action plan for local practice, based on the evidence from published studies. In our virtual reference example, EBL may merge with the marketing process at this point and develop a plan to gather local evidence from the library's target population.

The fifth step is, of course, to execute the plan for change, and the sixth step is to use valid and reliable research methods to evaluate how well it worked. The EBL process includes testing results locally—perhaps replicating a study locally—to inform local decisions.

Assessment and Measurement of Quality and Value

Assessment is not necessarily the same thing as measurement because not every assessment needs to be expressed as a numerical value. *Quality* and *value* are not synonyms. Quality is "a degree of excellence" or "superiority in kind" and value may be monetary worth, "relative worth, utility or importance," or general desirability of something (*Merriam-Webster's Collegiate Dictionary*, 2003).

Librarians, clients, and administrators have different role-based perceptions of quality and value. Different individuals and organizations may define quality and value differently. Both are judgments very much "in the eye of the beholder." Thus, one administrator may not value a high quality service enough to support it and another may value it highly even if its quality is only mediocre. Therefore, librarians may provide high-quality services that clients don't value.

Perceptions of quality and value often overlap, and many decisions affect all three groups of people, but there are ways of gathering evidence specific to the interests of one group. For instance, librarians have generally been more interested in collection size and circulation numbers than have their clients and administrators, and non-librarian administrators may be more concerned with costs than with client satisfaction.

In the "Public Library Effectiveness Study," Thomas Childers and Nancy Van House (1993) surveyed seven groups of public library stakeholders for their opinions of what performance measures demonstrated library effectiveness. Community leaders, local officials, trustees, friends, users, library managers, and service librarians generally valued different measures, and different groups prioritized those measures on which they agreed in different orders. In addition to publishing a report of the study, these authors published a book for practitioners including a form that librarians can use as a template for their own data gathering (Childers and Van House, 1993). Abels, Cogdill, and Zach (2004) reported major variations in values held by library administrators and institutional administrators in the health sciences. Because values vary so much by role perspectives, the assessment and evaluation methods in the rest of this chapter are grouped roughly by role perspective: librarians, clients, and top administrators.

Librarians' Standards and Benchmarking

Librarians, particularly under the auspices of associations or agencies, have made many attempts to establish standards for particular kinds of libraries, standards which define what they believe library services and collections ought to be. So have government agencies and accreditation bodies. Benchmarking is different from setting standards in that it emphasizes what is currently true by gathering data from many libraries so that individual libraries may be compared to others. Some believe that benchmarking data provides evidence of best practices, although it really measures the *status quo* rather than what could be. Thus, benchmarking is more descriptive and standards are more prescriptive. In both cases, the emphasis is on evaluating libraries based on the values held by other librarians or stakeholders and not necessarily values of clients.

Standards

Standards can influence librarians' decisions or help define questions to ask about a given library's service. Standards reflect the philosophies, biases, expertise, and opinions of those who write them. These standards may express minimum requirements or goals for optimum performance. Usually written by librarians for librarians, standards may be qualitative or quantitative and include collections, buildings and furnishings, staffing, staff education, and services. In any case, standards are "a tool to be used in the service of patrons, not an ultimate goal to which patron service is a secondary concern" (Anderson, 2007, p. 192).

Standards have been used as goals or minimums for a very long time (Lynch, 1982). The American Library Association and its affiliate organizations have a number of different standards, as do other librarians' associations (American Library Association, 2008; Association of College and Research Libraries, 2008). State or national libraries may issue standards for particular kinds of libraries. Professional associations for certain types of libraries have standards for those libraries and geographically based library associations will have standards for their constituencies.

Educational accreditation bodies and government agencies also set standards for librarians or libraries—as do organizations that support their own libraries. Although these standards are issued by non-librarians, they usually are developed with input from librarians. Although standards set by regulatory or accreditation organizations are technically enforceable, often they are not enforced. Such standards, like codes of ethics, are usually written by committees and subject to some debate. Even standards for very carefully described kinds of libraries may not be appropriate for some particular library that fits that description.

Baker and Lancaster (1991, pp. 321–322) categorize standards as either technical or performance, and Dudden (2007, p. 183) adds a third category, accreditation, which includes some of both.

Materials-centered approaches to collection evaluation often relate to meeting standards, and use-centered approaches usually relate to retrospective measurements of what materials and services have actually been used. Like many librarians' approaches to assessment of quality and value of services, such evaluative methods present more evidence of past activity than of future needs. Baker and Lancaster (1991) doubt that unenforceable guidelines have had much effect on improving services, although they may be "useful in providing evidence for budget requests" (pp. 321–331). Because they were written by librarians for librarians and are rarely evidence based, they may not have much influence on non-librarian decision makers.

Benchmarking

Given librarians' penchant for gathering numerical data about their own libraries, it comes as no surprise that they would embrace benchmarking, a comparison of data from many libraries. "There is a considerable history of benchmarking in libraries" (Brophy, 2006, p. 153). Matthews (2002) describes it as "an organized process for measuring products, services and practices against external partners" (p. 49). It is "concerned with developing systematic and structured approaches to finding and implementing best practice" (Brophy, 2006) based on the idea that best practice can be measured and compared (p. 149). Benchmarking data may include relatively static figures such as collection size, floor space, or number of employees. It can also include quantitative measurements of processes and services. Todd-Smith (2002) uses the example that, if a librarian discovers that a benchmarking partner's interlibrary loan process takes less time and costs less than her own, then she might explore that partner's process to discover improvements she could make in her own library.

At its very simplest, it can be a one-on-one, but it is more meaningful to compare data from many libraries. Associations and consortia may sponsor benchmarking projects for their members. However many organizations participate, there are ethical issues to consider, including legality, confidentiality, misuse of information, disclosure to other parties, etc. (Dudden, 2007, 134–135). One difficulty is that benchmarking is always "limited by the compatibility of the data which are gathered" (Brophy, 2006) and another is that benchmarking may not take into consideration differing needs of different client populations (p. 157).

Librarians usually like to count things. Most have elaborate systems for gathering numeric data (Baker and Lancaster, 1991; Brophy, 2006; Dudden, 2007; Matthews, 2002, 2004, 2007, 2008, and others). Although many librarians often refer to this data as *statistics*, simply reporting numerical data is not the same as (or as useful as) statistical analysis of such data. For instance, "We checked out 5,000 books last year" is only data. "We have checked out an average of 5,000 books a year in the last five years" or "We checked out 10% more books this year than we did last year" are useful statistics. The numbers alone don't reveal any evidence librarians or administrators need for making decisions unless they are analyzed in context. One way of analyzing such data in context is to compare data from one library with data from others, or even compare data from different periods or time or different library branches.

Some kinds of activities can be directly measured—for instance, the number of books checked out—whereas others may be described with indicators that, presumably, are affected by less measurable activities such as students' frustration looking for term paper material. The weakness of such data for planning purposes is that "[T]he vast majority of performance measures and statistics collected by public libraries reflect past performance, often called 'lagging indicators'" (Matthews, 2004), but they are still a large part of the evidence that is used for planning budgets (p. 5).

Statistics from librarians' benchmarking among themselves can be counterproductive when presented to non-librarian decision makers. As Pratt and Altman (1977) write, "[Public] [l]ibrarians, by and large, think that high per capita spending on libraries is a good thing. City officials with budgetary woes do not necessarily share that view" (p. 49). This should be fairly obvious unless you can convince your city administrators that being the Joneses is better than trying to keep up with the Joneses.

Another problem may occur with matching salaries. Turner (2003) describes how non-librarian administrators can misuse market rate salary comparisons to justify low staff compensation. To counter this, one must point out that higher salaries attract better qualified staff, and it is important to get the best possible staff to serve your clientele. When benchmarking indicates that a library is doing well, you must work to make sure that non-librarian decision makers do not interpret this to mean that there is no reason to increase the budget; or, if a library service is shown to be less sought after, you must help them understand why that service is essential.

Evidence of Client Satisfaction

Formal *continuous quality improvement* (CQI) activities are useful for assessing and increasing client satisfaction. Quality improvement (QI) is a consummately client-oriented management technique to gather data and make changes to improve processes. It has philosophical roots in the mid-20th century industrial business philosophies of Deming's post World War II work in Japan, and the later of philosophies of Crosby, Juran, and Feigenbaum (Brophy, 2006, p. 36). The most obvious deviation from previous business management practices is its emphasis on improving processes to promote client satisfaction, rather than inspecting products or services for errors and blaming or punishing workers for those problems. Originally called Total Quality Management (TQM), other variations of the approach appear as quality assurance (QA) and performance improvement (PI) (Dudden, 2007, pp. 105–129). The beauty of this approach (working for client satisfaction), is that it also promotes worker and stakeholder satisfaction. The title of Laughlin and Wilson's 2008 book, *The Quality Library: A Guide to Staff Driven Improvements, Better Efficiency, and Happier Customers* pretty much sums it up.

Central to CQI is valid evidence of client satisfaction. For successful QI, there has to be organizational commitment, process focus, staff and client involvement, and careful gathering and analysis of numeric data (Mein, 2000). If the library staff is big enough, a team of some staff members carries out the CQI activities for the service process; in a smaller library, the entire staff is the team. They begin with careful study of the current process and level of client satisfaction. They devise an activity that might improve the process, implement the change, then check on process improvement and client satisfaction after the change. If it has improved, it's time to move on to another process; if it hasn't, then it's time to try something else. In any case the process of improving service quality is continuous, not occasional. Good sources for instruction in how to do CQI are in Brophy (2006), Dudden (2007), Holst and Phillips (2000), and Laughlin and Wilson (2008).

Evaluations can be small but frequent. In fact, Charles P. Friedman makes the strong case that studying the effect of community-based information interventions may be better understood with multiple "smallball" evaluations over the course of a project than with fewer "powerball" larger assessments. Smallball evaluations can

> ensure that information resources address real community needs during deployment, they ensure that the systems are suited to the capabilities of the users and to community constraints' and, after deployment, they enable as much as possible to be learned about the effects of the intervention in environments where randomized studies are usually impossible. (Friedman, 2005, p. 543)

The actual data gathering methods are often the same as those used for marketing studies or information needs assessment. Often marketing and quality improvement activities address the same questions and need the same before-and-after data gathering and analysis.

No one data gathering and analysis method is intrinsically better than all others. The goal is to produce evidence to answer the question. Be very wary of the practice of picking a data gathering and analysis method first and a question later! Depending upon the question, good evidence may come from data gathered by direct observation or from that reported through interviews, focus groups, surveys, or questionnaires. Processes may be described with flow charts, cause and effect diagrams, etc.

Surveys, especially surveys of client opinions of quality, are popular with librarians (Adams, 1994; Holst and Phillips, 2000; Shinn, 1997). Some librarians design their own surveys for their own specific clients, others borrow such tools freely available from colleagues or relevant literature, and others purchase specific tools designed for general use. Like surveys, focus groups and interviews work well for gathering evidence of clients' current perceptions and opinions. Data from retrospective self-report may be less reliable than data from direct observation.

LibQUAL+ is an expensive and extensive survey instrument for academic libraries based on an earlier tool, SERVQUAL developed for use in for-profit businesses. Researchers at Texas A&M University developed the original LIBQUAL for the Association of Research Libraries (ARL) through a grant from the U.S. Department of Education Fund for the Improvement of Post-Secondary Education (FIPSE). Although ARL claims that over 1,000 libraries are using this tool, it can be costly for libraries with small budgets. Basic registration for the program in 2009 was $3,900. Its assumptions are wholeheartedly embraced by some and castigated by others. (Association for Research Libraries, 2008; Brophy, 2006, pp. 44–48; Edgar, 2006).

Numeric data may come from universal counting or, following good data gathering protocols, from sampling. When carrying out an experiment with a treatment group and a control group it is necessary to use truly random sampling and not just a convenience sample.

In other cases, particularly those meant to gather qualitative data, a representative sample including representatives of all relevant organizational departments or demographic groups may be more useful. In any case there has to be a direct relationship not just between the question and the results, but between the data gathering and data analysis methods. For instance, if numeric data is gathered from a convenience sample—whatever is handy, rather than a random sample—then analysis using statistical methods designed for random samples will produce useless evidence.

Value Evidence for Top Administrative Decision Makers

The third, and at times most influential, perspective on the value of library services is that of top non-librarian decision makers. Librarians must gather and present evidence that fits the decision makers' current concepts of assessment of services to organizational values. Evidence of the decision makers' current concepts comes not only from their statements and documents, but also from skillful conversations much like the traditional reference interview. Sometimes administrators' value assessment tools include a particularly complex system that involves defining, measuring, and evaluating inputs such as various resources, processes, outputs as utilization of collections and services, and impacts on individuals and the community (Matthews,

2004, pp. 73–154; Phillips, 1990), for example "balanced scorecard" (Dudden, 2007, pp. 280–281; Matthews, 2004, pp. 169–177; Matthews, 2008). Agile Librarians have to become very familiar with value measures or descriptive evaluations currently in vogue with their administrators. Fortunately, Agile Librarians can use their professional expertise at finding information to educate themselves. Usually, they can find ways to use and analyze data gathered from librarians' and clients' perspectives into forms valued by administrators.

When an organization pays for library collections and services, that organization's administrators must use good business practices and have bottom line concerns librarians cannot ignore. The true Agile Librarian finds ways to express the value of library services in terms of administrators' values, even though it is very difficult to express social values in economic terms.

Scott Plutchak describes in an editorial librarians' deeply held belief that the value of their services transcends economic considerations, and how some even take umbrage at the very idea that the administrators who authorize library expenses in the budget want to measure the value of library services in financially measurable terms. As a director of a large academic library, he has to worry constantly about having enough money to do everything he thinks his library needs to do (even though he knows he never can do it all). Yet when he compares his struggles to those of newer units in the institution, he is grateful for the earlier growth of the library before the days of such detailed cost accounting. On the other hand, he sees the value and fairness of good cost analysis and modern business practice. Regardless of the funding formulas and mechanisms of the larger organization, it is very important that every administrative unit (e. g., department or college) gets its money's worth for the funds that go to the library instead of the administrative units. It all comes down to figuring out what keeps "the people in charge awake at night and then figure out how the services you are providing could help them sleep better," because those people will fund their top priorities and what they perceive as critical needs first. As Plutchak explains, "They may feel that the library is worthwhile; they may say all of the right words about information being the heart of the enterprise. But in the competition for funding and priority and attention, they are going to focus on what they feel is most critical to moving the organization forward." He concludes "The belief in our hearts that we are doing a 'good thing' may be what gets us back in the trenches every day, but the coolly calculated work of our brains, making the case for the bottom line, will help to get us the resources to keep doing that work" (Plutchak, 2002, p. 274–275).

Expressing the financial effectiveness of library services *in administrators' terms* is not optional. You can't just brush them off as bean counters' games; you have to take the time to learn them well so you can use them effectively. It may appear as deceptively simple as cost accounting in which you count all possible library transactions (make it a *big* number) and then divide by the total library budget to arrive at a cost-per-transaction (Finkler, Ward, and Baker, 2007). It may be one of many methods of expressing the organization's return on investment (ROI).

And don't be surprised if just about the time you've got one business management method learned, they come up with another. Administrators change jobs, and the new person may be into a newer, or even older business approach that you have to learn quickly. This is another area where we can use our own superior levels of information literacy to find literature to help us learn what's behind the new business buzz word!

Summary

Anyone can make decisions based on beliefs and feelings. We all do it frequently. But for important decisions we need facts and evidence of facts. Agile Librarians use both local evaluation and generalizable published research to guide professional decisions. Occasionally they use rigorous formal research methods to answer questions with valid and reliable evidence. In any case, you have to have good evidence to improve the quality of information services and resources, for real marketing, and to practice evidence based librarianship. When appropriate, you can use such evidence to support your communication with clients, administrators, and other stakeholders.

The nature of the question determines what research methods are best to gather and analyze data. Good evidence is the result of good research. The research methods used to gather and analyze data to create evidence are determined by the nature of the question, not the preferences of the researcher. Education in valid research methods begins in an MLIS program and continues throughout a professional career. Some professional associations promote the presentation and publication of research as well as provide continuing education for practitioners. Evidence based librarianship is the practice of seeking, evaluating, and applying published research to improve local collections and services.

Quality and value are different concepts and different groups or individuals will have different opinions of what constitutes quality and what constitutes value. Assessments and measurements of quality and value can and should come from answers to a variety of questions. Many librarians use standards defined by professional associations and other appropriate agencies as guides for assessing the quality of their services and resources. They may use benchmarking (compiled quantitative measures) to compare their services and resources with those of others.

Client satisfaction, discussed in Chapter 2, can be assessed and increased through continuous quality improvement activities, often in coordination with the marketing process. Administrators' perspectives, discussed in Chapters 4 and 5 are naturally different from those of librarians and clients. They are more likely to be concerned with value, especially in relation to organizational spending for library services. Agile Librarians gather, use, and often disseminate good evidence of service and resource quality and value from different perspectives to support their own decision making as well as that of their clients and stakeholders.

References

Abels, Eileen G., Keith W. Cogdill, and Lisl Zach. 2004. Identifying and Communicating the Contributions of Library and Information Services in Hospitals and Academic Health Sciences Centers. *Journal of the Medical Library Association* 92:46–55.

Adams, Deborah L., Nancy Bulgarelli, Karen Tubolino, and Gayle A. Williams. 1994. Hospital Customer Survey: A Needs Assessment Tool. *National Network* 19(2):4, 24–27.

American Library Association. 2008. *Guidelines and Standards.* http://www.ala.org/ala/professionalresources/guidelines/index.cfm. Accessed November 6, 2008.

Anderson, Rick. 2007. It's Not About the Workflow: Patron-Centered Practices for 21st–Century Serialists. *Serials Librarian* 51:189–199.

Association of College and Research Libraries. 2008. *Standards and Guidelines.* http://www.ala.org/ala/mgrps/divs/acrl/standards/standardsguidelines.cfm. Accessed November 13, 2008.

Association of Research Libraries. 2008. *LibQUAL+.* http://www.libqual.org/. Accessed November 28, 2008.

Babbie, Earl R. 2007. *The practice of social research.* 11th ed. Belmont, CA: Thomson Wadsworth.

Baker, Sharon L. and F. Wilfrid Lancaster. 1991. *The Measurement and Evaluation of Library Services.* 2nd ed. Arlington, VA: Information Resources Press.

Brophy, Peter. 2006. *Measuring Library Performance: Principles and Techniques.* London: Facet.

Childers, Thomas and Nancy A. Van House. 1993. *The Public Library Effectiveness Study: The Complete Report.* Chicago: American Library Association.

———. 1993. *What's Good? Describing Your Public Library's Effectiveness.* Chicago: American Library Association.

Creswell, John W. 2009. *Research Design: Qualitative, Quantitative and Mixed Methods Approaches.* 3rd ed. Thousand Oaks, CA: Sage.

Dudden, Rosalind Farnam. 2007. *Using Benchmarking, Needs Assessment, Quality Improvement, Outcome Measurement, and Library Standards.* A How-to-Do-It Manual. A Medical Library Association Guide. New York: Neal-Schuman.

Edgar, William B. 2006. Questioning LibQUAL+™: Expanding its Assessment of Academic Library Effectiveness. *Libraries and the Academy* 6:445–465.

Einstein, Albert. 2000. *The Expanded Quotable Einstein.* Alice Calaprice (Ed.). Princeton, NJ: Princeton University Press.

Eldredge, Jonathan D. 2000. Evidence Based Librarianship: An Overview. *Bulletin of the Medical Library Association* 88:289–302.

Evidence Based Library and Information Practice. http://ejournals.library.ualberta.ca/index.php/EBLIP/index. Accessed September 11, 2009.

Finkler, Steven A, David M. Ward, and Judith J. Baker. 2007. *Essentials of Cost Accounting for Health Care Organizations.* 3rd ed. Sudbury, MA: Jones and Bartlett.

Friedman, Charles. 2005. "Smallball" Evaluation: A Prescription for Studying Community-Based Information Interventions. *Journal of the Medical Library Association* 93 (supplement): S43–S48.

Holst, Ruth and Sharon A. Phillips. 2000. *The Medical Library Association Guide to Managing Health Care Libraries.* New York: Neal-Schuman.

Laughlin, Sarah and Ray W. Wilson. 2008. *The Quality Library: A Guide to Staff Driven Improvements, Better Efficiency and Happier Customers.* Chicago: ALA Editions.

Leedy, Paul D. and Jeanne E. Ormrod. 2005. *Practical Research: Planning and Design.* Upper Saddle River, NJ: Prentice-Hall.

Lynch, Beverly P. 1982. University Library Standards. *Library Trends* 31:33–47.

Matthews, Joseph R. 2002. *The Bottom Line: Determining and Communicating the Value of the Special Library.* Westport, CT: Libraries Unlimited.

———. 2004. *Measuring for Results: The Dimensions of Public Library Effectiveness.* Westport, CT: Libraries Unlimited.

———. 2007. *The Evaluation and Measurement of Library Services.* Westport, CT: Libraries Unlimited.

———. 2007. *Library Assessment in Higher Education.* Westport, CT: Libraries Unlimited.

———. 2008. *Scorecards for Results: A Guide for Developing a Library Balanced Scorecard.* Westport CT: Libraries Unlimited.

McKnight, Michelynn and Carol Rain Hagy. 2009. The Research Imperative: MLA Policy and the Curricula of Schools of Library and Information Science. *Journal of the Medical Library Association* 97:134–136.

Medical Library Association. 2007. *The Research Imperative: The Research Policy Statement of the Medical Library Association.* Chicago, IL: The Association. http://mlanet.org/research/policy/policy-07.html. Accessed July 5, 2008.

Mein, Nardina Nameth. 2000 "Quality Improvement" in Holst, Ruth and Sharon A. Phillips eds. *The Medical Library Association Guide to Managing Health Care Libraies.* New York: Neal-Schuman, 55–73.

Merriam-Webster's Collegiate Dictionary. 11th ed. 2003. Springfield, MA: Merriam-Webster, Inc.

Naylor, Sharon, Bruce Stoffel, and Sharon Van Der Laan. 2008. Why isn't Our Chat Reference Used More? Finding of Focus Group Discussions with Undergraduate Students. *Reference & User Services Quarterly* 47:342–354.

Plutchak, T. Scott. 2002. Determining Value. *Journal of the Medical Library Association* 90:273–275.

Powell, Ronald R. and Lynn Silipigni Connaway. 2004. *Basic research methods for librarians.* 4th ed. Westport, CT: Libraries Unlimited.

Pratt, Allan D. and Ellen Altman. 1997. Live By the Numbers, Die By the Numbers. *Library Journal* 122:48–49.

Shin, Kyungja. 1997. Library Customer Survey at the Ottawa Civic Hospital: An Importance vs. Satisfaction Gap Analysis. *Bibliotheca Medica Canadiana* 19:15–17.

Thomson Reuters. 2007. ISI Web of Knowledge: Journal Citation Reports. JCR Social Sciences Edition. *Information Science and Library Science* Journal Summary List sorted by impact factor. Searched July 7, 2008.

Todd-Smith, Bernie. 2002. The Value of Hospital Library Benchmarking: An Overview with Annotated References. *Medical Reference Services Quarterly* 21:85–95.

Turner, Anne M. 2003. Your Money's Worth: Market Rates Can Sell You Short. *Library Journal* 128(15):41.

Chapter 10

Behaving Ethically

Providing the best possible services is the foundation of librarians' professional ethics. Information services require not only knowledge and expertise, but also respect for the profession, the clients, and society. That respect is expressed in the consistent ethical use of that knowledge and expertise. Codes of ethics are goals and standards of practice for any profession, including librarianship.

Mention ethics to a group of librarians and the conversation quickly focuses on complex ethical dilemmas. Everyone has a story or a "What if?" scenario about a situation in which the professional is faced with a difficult action choice. People like to discuss dramatic stories. Whether they are completely hypothetical or somewhat based on real life situations, the teller can manipulate the hypothetical details to increase the significance of the conflicting choices.

In response to challenges to her pacifism, Joan Baez wrote "Someone once said 'if you have a choice between a real evil and a hypothetical evil, always take the hypothetical one'" (Baez, 1969, p. 159). Most of these puzzle anecdotes make for more interesting conversation than the common, everyday ethical demands of professional practice. The more common evil in professional librarianship is not the rare dilemma based on obvious conflicts between various ethical principles or the tough choice between the lesser of two evils or the greater of two goods, but rather it is the habitual lapses based on convenience rather than professional principles. For instance, toward the end of the day, we may take shortcuts that result is less than our best service, service that isn't as good as what we provide earlier in the day.

The Agile Librarian has moved beyond regarding ethics as a set of externally imposed rules and has integrated them into personal professional habits at the level of virtues. Paul Woodruff describes virtue ethics as so ingrained in our behavior that we are motivated by literally feeling better about behaving ethically than not. That capacity is not developed just by reason and learning rules, but from constant practice. "A virtue is a capacity, cultivated by experience and training, to have emotions that make you feel like doing good things. . . . Virtue is about cultivating feelings that will lead you in the right way whether you know the rule in a given case or not" (Woodruff, 2001, p. 61–62).

It isn't always easy to feel like doing the right thing, but, like anything else, it gets easier with consistent practice. Of course, so does unethical behavior. Occasionally, we all make the mistake of acting out of less-than-professional feelings, but the Agile Librarian

Web sites for Association Codes of Ethics and Ethical Guidelines

American Association of Law Libraries *Ethical Principles:* http://www.aallnet.org/about/policy_ethics.asp

American Library Association *Code of Ethics:* http://www.ala.org/ala/aboutala/offices/oif/statementspols/codeofethics/codeethics.cfm

American Library Association *Library Bill of Rights:* http://www.ala.org/ala/aboutala/offices/oif/statementspols/statementsif/librarybillrights.cfm

American Society for Information Science and Technology *Professional Guidelines:* http://www.asis.org/AboutASIS/professional-guidelines.html

Association of Independent Information Professionals *Code of Ethical Business Practice:* http://aiip.org/Default.aspx?pageId=88881

Medical Library Association *Code of Ethics for Health Sciences Librarianship:* http://www.mlanet.org/about/ethics.html

Reference and User Services Association *Guidelines for Information Services:* http://www.ala.org/ala/mgrps/divs/rusa/archive/protools/referenceguide/guidelinesinformation.cfm

Society of American Archivists *Code of Ethics for Archivists:* http://www.archivists.org/governance/handbook/app_ethics.asp

Society of Competitive Intelligence Professionals *Code of Ethics for CI Professionals:* http://www.scip.org/About/content.cfm?ItemNumber=578

All accessed March 10, 2009

The Special Libraries Association (SLA) does not currently have its own document, but instead refers its members to the ethical codes of the American Library Association (ALA), the Association of Independent Information Professionals (AIIP), and the Society of Competitive Intelligence Professionals (SCIP), as well as the Professional Guidelines of the American Society for Information Science & Technology (ASIS&T) and the ALA Library Bill of Rights (Special Libraries Association, 2006).

strives to make that kind of behavior as rare as possible. Unethical behavior creates conflicts for colleagues, clients, employers, and employees, real conflicts that are much more difficult to resolve than hypothetical ones. The first part of this chapter describes the most basic ethics of the profession, then it moves on to dealing with ethical conflicts.

Basic Professional Ethics in the Codes of Ethics

One of the marks of a profession described in Chapter 1 is the existence of an accepted, expected, and practiced body of ethical standards usually described or codified in one or more professional associations' formal codes of ethics. Dictionaries can be descriptive, how words are actually used, or prescriptive, how words should be used. Professional codes of ethics may be considered both descriptive of what a real practitioner of this profession does and also prescriptive, what a real practitioner of this profession ought to do. Some professions have formal methods of enforcing these standards and punishing those who do not uphold them. Librarians' associations do not have formal enforcement procedures, but librarians' employers often do.

Formal codes of various professional associations for librarians vary in style, scope, and format. Such documents may also be called statements of ethical principles or professional guidelines. (See box above for URLS for some librarians' association codes.) Careful study of these codes reveals common themes of necessary, everyday ethical practices. The codes agree on the importance of (1) responsibility for the provision of the best possible information service; (2) respect for others, protection of privacy, and preservation of confidentiality; (3) promotion of equitable information access while respecting intellectual property rights and the institutional mission; (4) professional development of the self and others; and (5) advocacy for library services and information access in society beyond the institution. The dramatic ethical scenarios mentioned at the beginning of this chapter tend to center on (2) and (3), but day to day professional practice demands an equal or greater awareness of (1), (4), and even (5)!

Responsibility for the Provision of the Best Possible Information Service

Each of the above addresses stress the provision of the best possible information service:

> From the *Code of Ethics of the American Library Association (ALA):*
> We provide the highest level of service to all library users . . . and accurate, unbiased, and courteous responses to all requests. (ALA, 1995)
> From the *American Society for Information Science & Technology* (ASIS&T) *Professional Guidelines:*
> . . . providing the most reliable and accurate information . . . (ASIS&T, 1992)
> From the Medical Library Association (MLA) *Code of Ethics for Health Sciences Librarianship:*
> The health sciences librarian ensures that the best available information is provided to the client. (MLA 1994)
> From the Association of Independent Information Professionals (AIIP) *Code of Ethical Business Practice:*
> Give clients the most current and accurate information possible. . . (AIIP, 2005)
> From the American Association of Law Libraries' (AALL) *Ethical Principles:*
> We provide zealous service using the most appropriate resources. . . . (AALL, 1999)

Professional service is the connection between the clients' needs or expressed desires for information and the best possible sources of that information. The ethical librarian is responsible for carefully discovering and understanding those needs, identifying the best possible source of information to meet those needs, and completing the transaction by ensuring that there is a successful and satisfying delivery of that information to the client or population. Many experienced but untrained lay people can find *an* answer for many information requests. The professional must ensure the delivery of the answer that is *the best possible* information for the client, not just sometimes, but always. It's an everyday responsibility.

Professional ethics require that even if librarians believe they know the answer to a particular question, they may not offer it without citation to an authoritative and reliable source. That means that even if asked how to spell "cat," they must give a dictionary reference for the spelling of the word, even though it is part of their personal general knowledge. Librarians are not professional know-it-alls, but, more importantly, the professional know-how-to-find-it-alls. Librarians can and do share with their clients their own professional opinions about how best to evaluate and to use sources of information. That is an important part of professional service; however, librarians do not provide personal opinions or advice outside of their professional role. For instance, a professional librarian may help a client find unbiased reviews of different makes and models of cars, but the librarian may not advise the client as to which car the client should buy. Likewise, the librarian may provide clients with a wide variety of health and legal information, but may not make any diagnosis or give a personal opinion on what action individual clients should take. They can and do, of course, refer clients to the appropriate professionals for such personal advice.

Ethical professional librarians search for published information or reference sources for the client, even if they are uncomfortable with the information or find the opinions of the client personally distasteful. Professional teachers set educational goals and decide what information a learner should have. Librarians' clients set their own goals, and it is the librarian's responsibility to facilitate their clients' pursuit of those goals with the best possible information sources, whatever those goals may be.

Respect for Others, Protection of Privacy, and Preservation of Confidentiality

The principles of respect, privacy, and confidentiality are also central to the practice of professional librarianship. All of the professional codes and guidelines comment on the importance of this ethic.

Respect

The true professional understands that excellent service requires a high level of respect for clients, colleagues, and others, as well as confident self-respect. Courtesy is the mutually understood cultural ritual that expresses that respect. The librarian has a responsibility to know, understand, and practice those rituals at all times.

The practice of courtesy is self regulated and not just a reaction to others' actions. Librarians cannot control how others act, but they can, and must, control how they react to any behavior of others that makes them uncomfortable. Sometimes that requires some acting or behaving in ways at odds with current personal feelings, but that is professional practice. Agile Librarians know how to separate professional business from personal emotions. The Agile Librarian sometimes has to play a role and follow a script while working. Thus, the librarian has the ethical obligation to treat clients and coworkers with dignity and respect, even if the clients or coworkers are not exhibiting the same kind of behavior.

Behaviors that are considered courteous vary geographically and culturally, and it is the librarian's responsibility to understand not only the individual clients, but also the culture in which their interactions take place. For instance, in some parts of the United States, if the librarian wants a secretary to make an appointment with an administrator, the librarian shows respect by minimizing the time that it takes to ask for the appointment. In other areas, it would be considered more polite to chat with the secretary for a while about several subjects, perhaps the local sports team, the weather, or the secretary's family, before introducing the request for an appointment. Neither ritual is better than the other, but using the wrong one for a particular culture could appear to be very rude.

Two important professional behaviors based on respect are the protection of both the client's privacy and the confidentiality of any information that the client reveals to the professional. Privacy and confidentiality are not the same thing. Here are some definitions that illustrate the difference:

> *Privacy.* The condition or state of being free from public attention to intrusion into or interference with one's acts or decisions.
>
> *Informational privacy.* A private person's right to choose to determine whether, how, and to what extent information about oneself is communicated to others, esp. sensitive and confidential information (Garner, 1999, p. 1253).
>
> *Confidentiality,* 1. Secrecy; the state of having the dissemination of certain information restricted (Garner, 1999, p. 318).

Professional codes of ethics include specific principles of privacy and confidentiality in information services.

Privacy

> From the *Code of Ethics of ALA:*
>
> We protect each library user's right to privacy and confidentiality with respect to information sought or received and resources consulted, borrowed, acquired or transmitted. (ALA, 1995)
>
> From the *ASIS&T Professional Guidelines:*
>
> To uphold each user's, provider's or employer's right to privacy and confidentiality. (ASIS&T, 1992)
>
> From the MLA *Code of Ethics for Health Sciences Librarianship:*
>
> The health sciences librarian respects the privacy of clients and protects the confidentiality of the client relationship. (MLA, 1994)
>
> From the Society of American Archivists' *Code of Ethics for Archivists:*
>
> Archivists protect the privacy rights of donors and individuals or groups who are the subject of records. They respect all users' right to privacy by maintaining the confidentiality of their research and protecting any personal information collected about them in accordance with the institution's security procedures. . . . Archivists may place restrictions on access for the protection of privacy or confidentiality of information in the records. (SAA, 2005)
>
> From the AALL *Ethical Principles:*
>
> We uphold a duty to our clientele to develop service polices that respect confidentiality and privacy. (AALL, 1999)
>
> From the AIIP *Code of Ethical Business Practice:*
>
> Respect client confidentiality. (AIIP, 2005)

In the context of library services, anyone should be able to ask questions and use information sources without making any commitment to a particular idea or leaving any traceable trail of that inquiry. Indeed, there are few places, outside one's own mind, where one has that kind of privacy. The individual client has the right not to reveal to a librarian the substance, purpose, or context of the client's query.

Confidentiality

The professional has a responsibility not to reveal any information confided or revealed by a client in the course of library service. Thus, privacy is the client's right and confidentiality is the professional's responsibility. The professional also has a responsibility to respect confidential information about donors, colleagues, employees, or others involved in the provision of library services.

In the United States, most states and the District of Columbia have statutes protecting the privacy of library clients and requiring that information about what they seek, use, borrow, or acquire, including online sources, be kept strictly confidential. In a few cases there are legal exceptions for school children. Librarians should post such laws on library Web sites or walls and refer to them in brochures or even e-mail signatures.

Such ethics and laws are not commonly understood by the general public, so it is the Agile Librarian's responsibility to graciously describe them in appropriate contexts. For instance, if a client seems reticent about asking a question, the librarian may reassure the person that librarians have a responsibility to keep confidential whatever the client wants to know. In cases when someone asks a librarian to do something against the law or against the librarian's ethics, the librarian can offer the that person a more ethical option and provide references (in a sign, brochure, Web link or other method) to ethical codes. When done well, this practice helps to clarify the fact that the librarian is not being obstructive, confrontational, or manipulative, but is working for the good of all, including protecting the confidence of any clients involved.

Sometimes different clients involved in similar or the same activities may ask for similar material. For instance, in a public library, clients supporting opposing political stances on a particular issue may ask for material on that subject. Likewise, teachers in a school considering a new kind of curriculum may want research about that curriculum for different reasons, and in a hospital different caregivers may want material about a given patient's condition. Obviously, it is advantageous for politically active people, teachers, and caregivers to be informed. The ethical librarian cannot, however, reveal to one client what another has requested. A client may ask about another's request for information relating to the same issue, and even ask about what someone else with whom they may or may not agree has requested. Even though the request itself may be well meaning and should not be offensive to the librarian, it cannot be granted directly. One solution is to answer with "Tell me what you would like to know and I'll make a special search for you," completely avoiding the "What did you give so-and-so?" question. Another response could be "Ethically I can't reveal anyone's library information requests, but you could ask that person directly yourself." If there is a library confidentiality statute in effect, it may be necessary to point out that such a revelation would be illegal.

Librarians, of course, know a reader's use of particular information sources does not imply that the reader agrees with the material, accepts the author's advice, or intends any particular action based upon the material. A librarian projecting personal assumptions can do a lot of harm by making such conjectures. For instance, the librarian cannot assume that the sniffing, tearful person asking for information about how to commit suicide has the intention of doing so. The person may be dealing with the suicide of a friend or relative, or may be writing something about suicide while suffering from a cold or seasonal allergy. Librarians cannot and should not try to be the thought police, but certainly can offer additional sources of information relative to the subjects requested. For instance, in all three possibilities for this scenario, it would be perfectly ethical for a librarian to offer the client contact information about local agencies associated with suicide prevention and survivor support.

A favorite hypothetical ethical dilemma is whether or not a librarian should allow a seemingly distraught person to see the book *Final Exit* (Humphry, 2002). Too often, the individuals involved in the discussion have not read the book. Although it does include descriptions of effective methods of suicide, all of which take a good deal of time, money, and effort to arrange, it constantly reiterates reasons for not committing suicide, including serious consideration of the legal and physical mess left behind. In addition, it describes the severely impaired state that an individual may suffer after unsuccessfully attempting suicide by some popular methods. The simple fact that suicide is the subject of the book does not, in and of itself, make reading the book dangerous.

Restricting information services based on presumed potential future actions can be severely counterproductive to ethical information service. Some non-librarians may find it hard to understand or accept this principle; sadly, that ignorance has lead to many a library witch hunt. Everyone in the world is a potential criminal; everyone in the world has the potential to abuse themselves or others. People are responsible for their own real actions, not their potential actions or those of someone else. A good analogy of this principle is that just because a person knows how to drive a car and could use it to kill themselves or someone else does not mean that they *will* do so. An adolescent asking directly for information about the illegal use of drugs is not necessarily going to use them illegally. The young person may be looking for information to refute or support what they have heard from parents or peers, or could just be trying to understand something in a movie or television show. Offering a balanced variety of information sources encourages a client to think about alternatives.

During the reference interview, in order to provide the best possible information for the client's use, it may be necessary for the librarian to try to find out why the client wants the information. The client's right to privacy includes the right not to tell anyone the purpose behind the request. Some go so far as to say that the librarian should never ask why the client wants the information. Others maintain that if the librarian needs to know why in order to provide the most relevant information, the librarian must explain to the client not only the reason for the librarian's question, but also that the librarian will not reveal to any other party the information shared by the client in this context. In any case, the librarian may not withhold information services (a) because the client has not divulged the reason, (b) because of the reason that the client gives the librarian, or (c) because of the librarian's suspicion of an unacceptable reason for the request. That principle leads to some of the most common discussions of hypothetical ethical dilemmas and some of the most disturbing real life ethical dilemmas.

Our professional goal of free and open access to information is contradicted by librarians who take it upon themselves to become censoring thought police. Free and open access is more often legitimately limited by legal property rights and by the specific mission of the particular library and its parent organization.

Promotion of Equitable Information Access while Respecting Intellectual Property Rights and the Institutional Mission

From the *Code of Ethics of ALA:*
We provide the highest levels of service to all library users through . . . equitable service policies; equitable access . . . (ALA, 1995)
From the ALA *Library Bill of Rights:*
A person's right to use a library should not be denied or abridged because of origin, age, background or views. (ALA, 1996)
From the MLA *Code of Ethics for Health Sciences Librarianship:*
The health sciences librarian works without prejudice to meet the client's information needs. (MLA, 1994)
From the *ASIS&T Professional Guidelines:*
To treat all persons fairly (ASIS&T, 1992)
From the AALL *Ethical Principles:*
. . . [P]rofessionals committed to the belief that serving these information needs is a noble calling and that fostering the equal participation of diverse people in library services underscores one of our basic tenets, open access to information for all individuals. (AALL, 1999)
From the SAA *Code of Ethics for Archivists:*
Archivists strive to promote open and equitable access to their services and the records in their care without discrimination or preferential treatment, and in accordance with legal requirements, cultural sensitivities, and institutional policies. (SAA, 2005)

Ethical dilemmas may arise from conflicting information access needs, for instance, the logistical conflict between the need of a person who has a particular print resource checked out and the need of another person who wants to use it. Service policies exist to maximize rather than to restrict client access to information. Professionals write and follow such policies so that quality of service is not unduly influenced by the status of the client in the community.

This is not to say that all librarians in all institutions have to provide exactly the same services to all people. The mission of the institution and the library may require the librarians to restrict services to particular client groups to fulfill that mission. For instance, even though an academic library is in a government supported institution and open to the public, checking out material may be limited to that institution's students, faculty, and staff. It is also common for faculty to have longer loan periods than students. Though some members of the community may believe that all tax-supported libraries should provide services for all residents of the tax district, that isn't necessarily true. For instance, tax-supported public school libraries usually restrict service to the students, faculty, and staff of the particular school.

When faced with too many requests at the same time, the Agile Librarian sometimes has to prioritize responses with respect to the institutional mission or the importance of the request to human health and safety, and not just the order in which the requests were received. The librarian may triage the requests so that those with the most significant impact are completed first. The term "triage" comes from the practice in battlefield medicine of dividing patients into three groups: those who can safely wait for treatment, those who are most likely to die with or without treatment, and those who should be treated first, the ones who will live with immediate treatment but will die without it. That does not mean that patients in the first two groups are denied treatment, they just may not be the first patients treated. The librarian's triage may mean that some requests are handled immediately, some are delayed, and some are delegated or referred to other services.

In the case of librarians' services, no one should be denied service just because the librarian is busy, but it does mean that there are occasions when the complete response may be ethically delayed while the librarian is providing a more institution-crucial service. For instance, the school librarian may not respond to a teacher's personal request for a recipe until after she has provided another teacher with the material he needs for a class that is meeting in a few minutes. The academic librarian may give attention first to the professor developing a large grant proposal with a submission deadline, next to the professor collaborating for a class research project, and ask the third professor to wait for a short time for help finding a missing citation for a manuscript. Hospital librarians always give information needed for clinical emergences or immediate patient care precedence over information needed for administrative emergencies, and, in turn, administrative emergencies take precedence over more routine services. The public librarian may give precedence to the mayor who needs information before the council meeting over finding a quotation for a library volunteer. None of these requests are denied, but they may have to be delayed because of the mission of the librarians in the organizations.

Administrative emergencies are, of course, quite different from the student's emergency. Many students postpone working on an assignment until it has become a crisis for the student, and sometimes for the parent who comes in for the information. An example of an administrative emergency might be when an institutional spokesperson is about to be interviewed by a reporter and needs quick, short, and accurate facts to quote.

In any case, the ethical librarian does not punish or delay service for someone who wants it yesterday. Everyone has a right to ask for service, even chronic procrastinators. Every librarian has a responsibility not only to take all requests seriously, but also to prioritize responses to those requests relative to the immediacy of the request in relation to why that information is needed, for what, and the potential consequences of not having the information. Even a truly lazy client has the right to respectful professional service!

Professional ethics also require respect for legal rights and ownership, and that includes intellectual property rights. The Agile Librarian often encounters conflicts between clients' desires for information and the practices of owners of copyrighted information. More and more we have to deal not only with the U.S. Copyright Law and Guidelines, but also with legally binding licensing agreements and the complexities of intellectual property rights in many media.

Intellectual Property Rights

> From the *Code of Ethics of the ALA:*
> We recognize and respect intellectual property rights. (ALA, 1995)
> From the ASIS&T *Professional Guidelines:*
> . . . Freely reporting, publishing or disseminating information subject to legal and proprietary restraints of producers, vendors and employers . . . (ASIS&T, 1992)
> From the AIIP *Code of Ethical Business Practice:*
> Recognize intellectual property rights. Respect licensing agreements and other contracts. Explain to clients what their obligations might be with regard to intellectual property rights and licensing agreements. (AIIP, 2005)

Librarians in the United States have a responsibility to understand U.S. Copyright Law and Guidelines and to comply with them. They also must help their clients do the same, without giving their clients legal advice. Librarians have a responsibility for consistent, accurate, and constant citation of sources, for discouragement of plagiarism, and for helping clients find just and equitable ways to meet their information goals. Ethical librarians respect licensing restrictions to which they agree in the acquisition process for print or online sources and services.

Sometimes a client, not realizing the limitation of copyright Fair Use, will ask a librarian to make multiple copies of a journal article to be given to other people. The requestor may mistakenly believe that such copying is legal as long as the copies are not sold, but the librarian knows better and cannot comply directly. So, the Agile Librarian will suggest other solutions appropriate to the situation. Unlike most articles, bibliographic citations are not covered by copyright. In some cases, the librarian can make an annotated bibliography of citations to relevant material and include library contact information. The client is free to distribute these to others who then can consult the original or request a copy for their own immediate personal use. The application of copyright law and guidelines to library practice is complicated. At the end of this chapter are some suggested readings that explain the issues in much more detail than is possible here.

Rights of the Institution

> From the *ASIS&T Professional Guidelines:*
> To act faithfully for their employers or clients in professional matters. . . . Information professionals shall engage in principled conduct whether on their own behalf or at the request of employers, colleagues, clients, agencies or the profession. (ASIS&T, 1992)
> From the MLA *Code of Ethics for Health Sciences Librarianship:*
> The health sciences librarian provides leadership and expertise in the design, development, and ethical management of knowledge-based information systems that meet the information needs and obligations of the institution. (MLA, 1994)

Every library exists for a particular institution or organization, and every librarian has an ethical responsibility to support the parent institution's mission with the most appropriate information services. No library can be the universal information source for all possible clients. The Agile Librarian not only knows the parent institution's general mission and specific goals, but uses professional information expertise to design and provide services that promote them. This often precludes the provision of services offered by other libraries with different missions. It may make it imperative for the librarian to offer services not generally found in other libraries.

We get into trouble with our colleagues when we assume that our type of library, whether public, academic, school, or special, is the true prototype for all good libraries everywhere. Even three commonly accepted values of librarianship, access to information in the public good, promotion of literacy and information literacy, and ensuring preservation of the accumulated wisdom of the past (Groen, 2007), are not all equally integral to the mission of every library. For instance, hospital librarians may keep nothing in their collections more than 10 years old because outdated clinical information can be dangerous. Librarians with a strong archival mission to preserve historical documents may have to severely restrict current access to material in order to enhance future access to it. Librarians working for government agencies may have legal restraints on the release of certain kinds of information. Librarians in schools do more literacy promotion than some other libraries. Librarians working for corporations may have to protect information considered part of the company's trade secrets. Librarians in public libraries provide information access to a much wider demographic mix of people than do school librarians. Some librarians promote literary fiction and some collect none at all.

Librarians in all types of libraries need to make sure they both maintain their skills and they add to their body of professional knowledge so they can continue to offer the best service available. They work on their own professional development and they encourage the professional development of others.

Professional Development of the Self and Others

From the *Code of Ethics of ALA:*
We strive for excellence in the profession by maintaining and enhancing our own knowledge and skills, by encouraging the professional development of co-workers, and by fostering the aspirations of potential members of the profession. (ALA, 1995)

From the *ASIS&T Professional Guidelines:*
Pursuing ongoing professional development and encouraging and assisting colleagues to do the same. . . . (ASIS&T, 1992)

From the AALL *Ethical Principles:*
We strive for excellence in the profession by maintaining and enhancing our own knowledge and skills, by encouraging the professional development of co-workers, and by fostering the aspirations of potential members of the profession (AALL, 1999)

From the MLA *Code of Ethics for Health Sciences Librarianship:*

The health sciences librarian advocates and advances the knowledge and standards of the profession.

The health sciences librarian assumes personal responsibility for developing and maintaining professional excellence. (MLA, 1994)

Ethical practitioners always stay green and growing, and encourage their colleagues and potential colleagues to do the same. Professional librarianship is not a trade that can be learned only by apprenticeship and experience. It is a profession that requires not only formal graduate study, but also continuing education throughout one's career.

Self-Development

The joys of our profession are often a well-kept secret, and few choose this profession during their undergraduate education unless they are in a teacher education program that includes school library certification. We come to graduate library and information school with valuable experiences from a variety of other fields of study and work histories, none of which is wasted. Some of us come directly from an undergraduate degree right after high school; many are changing careers in their middle or even later adult life. Some have been paraprofessionals in libraries. Many have had no previous experience working in libraries.

During the pursuit of a Master of Library and Information Science degree from a program that is accredited by the American Library Association, the budding professional learns basic principles that will guide practice no matter what changes come to society, media, and technology. The student also begins to study current professional practice and research, a process that must be continued throughout the professional career. What a librarian learns in the short period in school is certainly not enough to sustain an entire professional career. Those whose education stops with graduation are very unethical; they do their clients and society a great disservice.

A few may continue their education by returning to an LIS school for an additional course or earning an additional certificate or degree, but most continue their education with professional association offerings, mentors, and self-study. All of the professional associations provide a wide variety of educational opportunities. Some librarians improve their understanding of their clients' needs by seeking classes outside of the curriculum of library and information science, learning additional management skills or attaining more expertise in a subject area. What is important is that you continue to learn, rather than repeat over and over what you have been doing. The constantly developing librarian can work in a professional position and really grow with five years of experience instead of just one year of experience repeated five times.

One of the benefits of having high levels of information literacy and information seeking skills is the fact that librarians can and do identify sources of information for their own self-study. The Agile Librarian becomes well informed about the business of the parent institution or organization. That knowledge contributes directly to the Agile Librarian's capability of understanding the clients' information needs.

Indeed, some school librarians once were teachers, some law librarians may have practiced law. Some specialized medical librarians are rumored to have taken and passed specialty board certification exams, even though they had little or no previous medical education. In any case, we are curious people who learn from our own collections and services.

Not only will you continue your own professional development, but you also have an ethical responsibility to help others continue theirs. You and your colleagues can and should encourage each other to continue learning.

Fostering the Development of Others in Your Organization and Beyond

Professional growth thrives in a spirit of cooperation more than in a spirit of isolation or competition, and the Agile Librarian is a good mentor. The common model for professional mentoring is that of a more experienced professional guiding someone newer to the profession, but in reality the information give-and-take can run both ways. The more experienced librarian may learn from insights that the newer librarian has coming to the profession with fresh eyes, while the newer librarian can learn from the experienced librarian who has been green and growing for many years. Even the solo librarian seeks such interaction.

Indeed, the ethical professional not only attends meetings, reads, and takes classes, but also serves professional associations in various ways, writes, and perhaps teaches classes or takes part in original research that will benefit the profession. You also encourage colleagues, coworkers, and employees to do the same. You actively recruit promising future professionals and encourage their education and development.

The Agile Librarian actively promotes access to information. This becomes difficult when a segment of the community chooses to question what should be available through libraries, or even the very existence of libraries.

Advocacy for Library Services and Information Access in Society

From the *Code of Ethics of ALA:*
We uphold the principles of intellectual freedom and resist all efforts to censor library resources. (ALA, 1995)
From the *ASIS&T Professional Guidelines:*
To promote open and equal access to information, within the scope permitted by their organizations or work, and to resist procedures that promote unlawful discriminatory practices in access to and provision of information by . . . seeking to extend public awareness and appreciation of information availability and provision as well as the role of information professionals in providing such information. (ASIS&T, 1992)
From the MLA *Code of Ethics for Health Sciences Librarianship:*
The health sciences librarian promotes access to health information for all and creates and maintains conditions of freedom of inquiry, thought and expression that facilitate informed health care decisions. (MLA, 1994)

Library professionals think outside the job, not only in relationship to their own profession, but in relationship to information access for all. They may not only read, but also write publications promoting access. Society values knowledge services, and in many cases librarians are the only people who can promote, preserve, and expand information services for all.

The various librarians' associations publicly promote the access rights of their constituencies. In some situations involving government and commercial interests, they may be the only organized advocates for such constituencies. Librarians have participated for generations in the development of copyright and other intellectual property issues, in the preservation of documentation that might otherwise be lost to future generations, in promoting citizen access to government documents, and in resisting efforts to violate readers' privacy. Public librarians are often involved in literacy initiatives, and librarians serving scholars are active in the rapidly developing new models of electronic document access, including various open access models.

Individual Agile Librarians are aware wherever they are communicating with someone: on a plane, at a party, at work, or somewhere else. They are, at that moment, the very embodiment of the profession to everyone around who knows they are a librarian. They have the ethical responsibility to carry that awareness with confidence.

Real-Life Ethics

Many ethical dilemmas arise in the context of competing principles and rights. The client's need for access to information may come into conflict with intellectual property rights, licensing, or cost of access. Reserve and circulation policies are designed to balance the access rights of multiple users of the same printed documents. Collection development policies must consider diversity of opinion and freedom of expression on one hand, and selection based on the authority of the source and institutional mission on the other.

The most dramatic dilemmas are, of course, clients' access and confidentiality rights in situations that may involve serious harm to the client or to the community. Complaints often consist of clients wanting more library services and resources, not less. The librarian's budget choices often raise ethical dilemmas directly related to that principle issue.

Authorities or other persons in any institution may ask librarians to do something that would obviously violate professional ethics. When this happens, Agile Librarians recognize the opportunity rather than escalating it into an open conflict. They know that the situation is probably based on the authorities ignorance of librarians' professional ethics.

Consider the issue of client confidentiality. Many non-librarians do not know that such an ethical imperative exists and may believe that the librarian can report which students have checked out particular reserve readings. Students may believe that their library use is reported to faculty; faculty may believe that they can get such reports from the librarian. If faculty members ask for such reports, it is not only the librarian's responsibility to uphold the ethical principle of confidentiality, but also to help them understand these principles and find other ways to meet their legitimate information goals.

Thus, a faculty member believing that circulation records will reveal which students have read reserve material may ask for this confidential information. The

Agile Librarian can point out that students who checked it out may not have read it, some students may have read it when it was checked out to another student, and some students may have obtained the material from another library or source. A better way to determine which students have read and understood is to quiz the students.

All professionals will make mistakes during their careers, but with conscious, conscientious practice of ethical principles, Agile Librarians develop virtue ethics for the benefit of all.

Summary

The practice of professional ethics is as important to the value of the service to the client as the education of the professional and the excellence of the information sources. Behaving ethically includes persistent "know," "show," and "tell." Administrators and decision makers need to experience and see how ethical professional librarians contribute to the success of the organization.

The various associations' codes of ethics and professional practice guidelines are both descriptive and prescriptive. They describe the ethical behavior of the profession and prescribe goals and standards for practitioners. Agile Librarians have internalized these principles so well that applying them to their daily practice actually feels good. They can practice what Paul Woodruff calls "virtue ethics." Rigid Librarians may get stuck in seeing them as rules to be stretched, bent, or punitively enforced.

An analysis of various codes reveals that they all agree on the professional's responsibility for the provision of the best possible information service for clients. They all agree on the importance of respect for clients, colleagues, and stakeholders, especially in the protection of the clients' right to privacy and in the staff responsibility for keeping information services confidential. In any case, the professional has the ethical responsibility to provide equitable information access in the context of intellectual property rights and the institutional mission. Continuing professional development for all practitioners is not an optional frill, but a central ethical responsibility and privilege. Finally, the codes and guidelines emphasize professional advocacy beyond the immediate job or institution and into society at large. The ethical professional can easily think outside the job.

References

American Association of Law Libraries. 1999. *Ethical Principles.* http://www.aallnet.org/about/policy_ethics.asp. Accessed March 10, 2009.

American Library Association. 1995. *Code of Ethics of the American Library Association* http://www.ala.org/ala/aboutala/offices/oif/statementspols/codeofethics/codeethics.cfm. Accessed March 10, 2009.

———. 1996. Library Bill of Rights. http://www.ala.org/ala/aboutala/offices/oif/statementspols/statementsif/librarybillrights.cfm. Accessed March 10, 2009.

American Society for Information Science and Technology. 1992. *ASIS&T Professional Guidelines.* http://www.asis.org/AboutASIS/professional-guidelines.html. Accessed March 10, 2009.

Association of Independent Information Professionals. 2005. *Code of Ethical Business Practice.* http://aiip.org/Default.aspx?pageId=88881. Accessed March 10, 2009.

Baez, Joan. 1969. *Daybreak*. New York: Avon Books.

Garner, Bryan A. (Ed.). 1999. *Black's Law Dictionary*. 8th ed. St. Paul, MN: West Group.

Groen, Frances K. 2007. *Access to Medical Knowledge: Libraries, Digitization, and the Public Good*. Lanham, MD: Scarecrow Press.

Humphry, Derek. 2002. *Final Exit*, 3rd ed. New York: Delta.

Medical Library Association. 1994. *Code of Ethics for Health Sciences Librarianship*. http://www.mlanet.org/about/ethics.html. Accessed March 10, 2008.

Reference and User Services Association. Guidelines for Information Services. http://www.ala.org/ala/mgrps/divs/rusa/archive/protools/referenceguide/guidelinesinformation.cfm. Accessed March 10, 2009.

Society of American Archivists. 2005. *Code of Ethics for Archivists*. http://www.archivists.org/governance/handbook/app_ethics.asp. Accessed March 10, 2009.

Society of Competitive Intelligence Professionals. *Code of Ethics for CI Professionals*. http://www.scip.org/About/content.cfm?ItemNumber=578. Accessed March 10, 2009.

Special Libraries Association. 2006. *General Industry FAQ's*. http://www.sla.org/content/membership/Genfaq.cfm. Accessed October 17, 2007.

Woodruff, Paul. 2001. *Reverence: Renewing a Forgotten Virtue*. New York: Oxford University Press.

Additional Suggested Reading

Aoki, Keith. 2006. *Bound by Law? (Tales from the Public Domain)*. Durham, NC: Center for the Study of the Public Domain. http://www.law.duke.edu/cspd/comics/zoomcomic.html. Accessed March 10, 2009. Also distributed in print by New York: Soft Skull. [graphic format.]

Crews, Kenneth D. 2005. *Copyright Law for Librarians and Educators: Creative Strategies and Practical Solutions*. Chicago: American Library Association. [This is somewhat based on and updated from the earlier ALA title *Copyright Essentials*.]

Gasaway, Laura N. 1997. *Growing Pains: Adapting Copyright for Libraries Education and Society*. Littleton, CO: Fred B. Rothman & Company. [A classic.]

Lathrop, Ann and Kathleen Foss. 2005. *Guiding Students from Cheating and Plagiarism to Honesty and Integrity*. Westport, CT: Libraries Unlimited.

Lipinski, Thomas A. 2006. *The Complete Copyright Liability Handbook for Librarians and Educators*. New York: Neal-Schuman.

McClure, Lucretia, et al. c. 2007 [last update of page] *Medical Library Association Guidelines for Selecting Copyright Management Options*. Medical Library Association. http://mlanet.org/government/positions/copyright_mgmt2.html. Accessed March 10, 2009. [Includes useful links.]

Russell, Carrie. 2004. *Complete Copyright: An Everyday Guide for Librarians*. Chicago: American Library Association. [Eight hypothetical case studies]

Simpson, Carol. 2005. *Copyright for Schools: a Practical Guide*. 4th ed. Worthington, OH: Linworth Books.

Chapter 11

Sustaining Your Green and Growing Career

The key to enjoying a fulfilling career over many years is staying green and growing. Even the most energetic Agile Librarian will lose enthusiasm without nourishing professional growth and refreshing reflection. Opportunities for learning or innovation may come from clients, stakeholders, and colleagues, but professionals take responsibility for their own development.

The first 10 chapters of this book may seem overwhelming. All the things the Agile Librarian should be doing may seem very challenging; however, you can be proud of what you are doing already. For the thoughtful person, no experience is ever wasted. Now you also have some new goals. Where do you start?

Your Own Professional Mission

In order to become the best possible professional, you must be able to manage not just others, but your own work, your own career, and your own life. We can use the same tools and skills for managing others to manage ourselves. Most business management books include principles that can be translated into personal planning and organization. Both kinds of management take advantage of reflection, vision, planning, execution, and evaluation.

Mission statements, goals, and objectives are helpful not just for your library, but also for the management of your career. Reflecting on and writing out your own concept of your professional mission and goals is great, but periodically reviewing, revising, and developing such plans is even better. That makes the difference between a mindful professional practice and just drifting mindlessly through the years. Coaches and mentors may help, but only you can see your career in the context of your other missions in life, as well as your own talents and interests. You need more than an answer to the standard interview question, "Where do you see yourself five years from now?" Your professional mission includes not only your job, but all the rest of your personal professional growth. As such, it is only one part of your personal spiritual, physical, social, and emotional missions and goals in life.

Reality Check

Simple Algebra: Institution Z needs service Y, which Librarian X provides and promotes, so Librarian X is happy and fulfilled.
It's not that simple.

Librarian wants A.
Boss wants B.
Librarian's family wants C.
Organizational cousins want D.
Library stakeholders want E.
Venders and publishers want F.
Community wants G.
Clients want H to Z and beyond.

Any of the above may be shared or in direct conflict, depending upon who owns them. How is an Agile Librarian to cope with all?

A good source of self-discovery questions and exercises for your career is Richard Bolles's perennial best-seller *What Color is Your Parachute?* (2009). It's not just about getting a job. Ten Speed Press publishes a new edition every year with enough changes that it's worth it to seek the most recent edition. There's also a workbook (Bolles, 2005), a special edition for teens (Bolles, 2006), and even one for retirement (Bolles, 2007). I've worked through the exercises quite a few times over the last 30 years and my conclusions have been different at different points in my own career journey.

Setting Priorities

Often the problem isn't so much setting goals as it is the myriad of possible tasks and activities it takes to meet those goals, some of which may be in some kind of conflict with each other. There are ways to make good choices among them.

What lies behind the old proverb "If you want something done, ask a busy person" is the assumption that the busy person has learned how to set priorities and will not say yes to a request unless it really can be done. It has to fit into the busy person's higher priorities or else it's a no. The proverb assumes that the busy person has to be organized enough not to let promises and obligations drift from wishful thinking and procrastination to completely forgotten. That person will plan and complete accepted tasks efficiently and effectively, and have the wisdom to say no to others.

It's easy to make out a very long "to-do" list. Anybody can do that. Everyone should do it from time to time. The trick is for it to be a useful tool and not a hopeless exercise. In *How to Get Control of Your Time and Your Life,* Alan Lakein wrote, "All the items on the list are not of equal value. Once you have made a list, set priorities based on what is important to you now. In my opinion, no list is complete until it shows priorities" (Lakein, 1973, p. 28).

The most useful lists are carefully prioritized so that the most important things are at the top and get done first; it's just fine if the least important things farther down the list don't get done at all. The point is not necessarily to finish everything the list, but to make sure that you start with what's most important.

Which things on the list are most important? That depends on your decisions based on your mission and values. No one else can tell you what they should be, but the best advisors help you ask yourself good questions about putting your values to work.

The first three of Stephen Covey's *Seven Habits of Highly Effective People* (1989) are "proactivity," "begin with the end in mind," and "putting first things first." They directly address your very private decisions about values, priorities, and actions. He calls them "private victories" of self mastery. The habit of proactivity includes taking responsibility for your own decisions and actions. It's the opposite of living reactively, with your self-esteem, values, and even your happiness being blown around by whatever is in your environment (Covey, 1989, p. 66–94).

Psychologist Martin E. P. Seligman (1990) describes moving from self-destructive extreme reactivity or "learned helplessness" to the productive "learned optimism" of a better habitual explanatory style for both good and bad experiences. It turns on considering positive or negative events as permanent or temporary, pervasive or specific, and internal or external. Optimists can consider positive events as permanent, pervasive, and internal and negative events as temporary, specific, and external. As in Reinhold Niebuhr's "Serenity Prayer," it takes wisdom to know the difference between what can be changed and what cannot (Sifton, 2003, p. 277). You can proactively make changes in important ways.

The second Covey habit is to "begin with the end in mind." It includes understanding and identifying the principles most important in your thinking, seeing your mission in life clearly enough to write a personal mission statement, and knowing what meeting your most important goals looks like (Covey, 1989, p. 95–144; Bolles, 2009). Some people keep journals of their work with their mission, goals, and progress, keeping them alive and visible. Covey's third habit, putting "first things first" is personal self management. It involves actively fulfilling your mission and doing the most important things first (Covey, 1989, p. 146–182). One of my favorite New Year wishes for my friends is "May you have enough time for everything that's important and none left over for what isn't."

Of course, important things come in many shapes and sizes, and whether or not they get done is influenced by their urgency and their cost in your available time and mental effort. They also come in different colors depending upon your different mission roles. In any case, you are constantly making choices about what to do right now. How do you choose well?

Urgency and Importance

Urgency can skew our values. Some of the most important things in life and your career may not seem to be urgent on any given day, but it's easy to get caught up in the tyranny of the urgent to the extent that you never get around to what's important. Covey (1989, p. 151) presents a matrix (later appearing in Siess, 2002, p. 163) of two variables for activities: importance and urgency. The matrix has four quadrants to which one can assign activities as (1) important and urgent, (2) important but not urgent, (3) urgent but not important, and (4) not important and not urgent.

Most would agree that spending time on things which are neither important nor urgent is a waste of time. Most would also agree that what is both important and urgent, often a crisis, has to be a first priority. It can be less obvious to us how much time we waste on things that are urgent but not important, and how attending to things that are important but not urgent can lessen the stress of too many things becoming crises (both important and urgent) that did not have to become crises.

Covey's first quadrant examples are "crises, pressing problems and deadline-driven projects" (Covey, 1989, p. 151). For the Agile Librarian the first quadrant might include:

> a budget deadline
> a public program
> being too stressed-out to function
> times when a combination of staff vacation and staff illness makes the library understaffed
> a car breaks down on the way to work
> times when the library is understaffed because an open position hasn't been filled
> running out of essential supplies
> an administrator calls angry about a client complaint
> a community-wide disaster, such as a storm, or a local emergency, such as a power outage or broken pipe at the library

Covey's second quadrant of important but not urgent activities include production capability building activities, preventive activities, and " relationship building, recognizing new opportunities, planning, recreation" (Covey, 1989, p. 151). For the Agile Librarian, these would include all of the major themes of this book. It would include maintenance to prevent the copy machine from breaking down; collection development for future information needs; continuing education for improved service; building relationships with clients, administrators, and stakeholders; grasping great new opportunities; planning; play; and regular relaxation.

Second quadrant activities may take less time to do than the first quadrant crises caused by their neglect. For instance, establishing a place to keep an important tool and regularly returning it to that spot after using it can prevent a time consuming crisis looking all over for it! Building good habits of positive communication with clients, staff, and stakeholders is always a quadrant two activity that can greatly reduce quadrant one crises with the same people.

Covey's third quadrant includes urgent but not important activities "interruptions, some calls, some mail, some reports, some meetings, pressing matters and popular activities" (Covey, 1989, p. 151). For the Agile Librarian, these include many seductive time wasters such doing tasks that don't need to be done or even diversion activities that are not recreation. If we were not all so susceptible to this temptation of the urgent, the retail sales pitch "Only until tomorrow night!" would not be so successful in luring us to buy what we would not buy without the urgency. Some meetings with unimportant content may be valuable from a quadrant two relationships-building perspective, or they may not. Many third quadrant situations pop up because someone asks us to do something, and we are not sure whether it is important or not. We get drawn into doing favors and carrying on long conversations that eat up our time for more important things. The thing is, we can't recognize whether an urgent activity is important or not if we have not done our planning and prioritizing in quadrant two.

Covey's fourth quadrant of activities that are neither urgent nor important are the worst for wasting our time and energy. He lists examples such as "trivia, busy work, some mail, some phone calls, time wasters and pleasant activities" (Covey, 1989, p. 151). For the Agile Librarian these would include idle chit-chat beyond relationship building, doing something very well that doesn't need to be done at all, and a whole raft of procrastination and avoidance strategies. It can include doing things too often that need only be done occasionally, like cleaning out your desk drawer for the third time this week. Quadrant two recreation could include watching a television show or socializing online in such a way that you feel better afterwards. Spending several hours watching whatever happens to be on or drifting around blog and Web sites could be quadrant four activities that leave you feeling just as tired when you finish as you did when you started.

C. S. Lewis famously wrote to his godchild, Lucy Barfield, "Remember that there are only three kinds of things anyone need ever do: (1) things we ought to do, (2) things we've got to do and (3) things we like doing. I say this because some people seem to spend so much of their time doing things for none of these reasons" (Lewis, 1949, in Dorset and Mead, 1985, p. 27). Quadrant four is the home of all those other things we don't need to do. We all can probably think of several things we have done recently and wish we hadn't that belong in quadrant four.

Mission Roles and Balance

Personal professional management includes the maturity to integrate all of your personal roles, not just your career role, into your second quadrant self-management. That includes taking care of your physical, emotional, spiritual, social, and family roles; general maintenance such as paying the bills and doing the dishes; and the different professional roles that you have identified for yourself. If you neglect quadrant two activities for any important role, you *will* face too many crises in the first quadrant. One reason that busy people get so much done and still have time to play is that they include real recreation and personal, quiet time in their planning. According to Csikszentmihaly (1996, p. 160–162) and others, a certain amount of real down time is a necessary prerequisite for creative thinking and problem solving.

Perfect or Good Enough

The Agile Librarian can be proud of what is excellent and what is definitely good enough while continuously growing and improving. Busy people pay attention enough to know which activities must be done very well, which can be good enough, and which can be ignored altogether. They can accept some conflict, balance, and even ambiguity in their lives. Too much perfection in everything can be a form of procrastination if it delays too long the completion of a task, or even prevents the accomplishment of another, more important one. One of Rick Anderson's mantras includes "You can't eliminate error—you can only prioritize it" and "Not everything is worth doing well (let alone perfectly)" (2007, p. 192). Those statements echo one of Voltaire's (1772) most popular maxims, which can be roughly translated as a warning for us not to let the best be the enemy of the good.

Cost in Time

As with many things in life, sometimes the most important cost the least. The most important activity on today's to-do list may take the least amount of time, and your worst procrastinating, time-wasting activity may cost you much more.

The worst thing about wasting too much time in unimportant quadrants three and four is that they can be directly responsible for a crisis in quadrant one. Also, anyone who consistently neglects quadrant two, the important but not urgent activities, is going to be a habitually ineffective crisis manager. Many library managers who have avoided quadrant two activities too long will suffer political and financial losses.

Crises in quadrant one can eat up your time and energy. Although not all crises are avoidable, concentrating on the important but not urgent activities will reduce them to a minimum. For instance, exercising and eating right when it does not seem urgent will prevent many serious health crises. Taking time to listen and pay attention to your boss and employees when it isn't urgent can keep you out of crises when it's too late to repair relationships.

Of course, telling yourself to stop wasting time does as much good as telling yourself to stop thinking about green elephants. It diverts your attention. Instead of telling yourself to stop, just *start* something important, even if it is as little as getting out the tools to do it. Better yet, keep your tools handy. Keep what's most important to do on your desktop, real or virtual. Put your time wasting temptations out of sight.

Priority Management Tools

People perform best when they concentrate on one thing at a time. Multitasking is an illusion, because it really is just moving attention from one thing to another in rapid succession and losing thought continuity in the spaces between. Given that one can do only one thing well at a time, and that there is never time enough to accomplish all possible things, one has to prioritize even important activities. It's not too difficult to make priority choices about 2 or 3 tasks, but it is difficult to order more than 10 activities. Barry Schwartz addresses the problem in his book *The Paradox of Choice: Why More is Less*. He writes, "We would be better off if we embraced certain voluntary constraints on our freedom of choice instead of rebelling against them" (Schwartz, 2004, p. 5). Voluntary constraints, of course, require us to make some decisions for ourselves, to set our own priorities. Waiting for someone else to decide what's important for us or leaving our activities up to the chance whim of the moment may temporarily feel good, but it won't work in the long run. We have to "drift, drown or decide" (Lakein, 1973, p. 18–24).

For most purposes, the professional does not need a large automated decision support system. It's okay to accept that not all decisions will be the best possible ones and that few decisions are permanent and nonreversible (Schwartz, 2004, p. 5). The professional only needs a few basic conceptual tools. The prioritization tools that follow are based on the fact that it is easier to choose between two or three options than many options. Each tool could appear to be very simple or very complicated and time consuming. In practice each one may really take as much time as any other. The cost of time spent prioritizing is less than the cost of time spent procrastinating or doing what really doesn't need to be done. You *do* have time to plan.

Lakein's Classic As, Bs, and Cs

Whether you are planning what to do in the next two hours, in the next month, or on your next vacation, you have choices. You'll get more out of the time if you have some idea of what's most valuable. After creating a list, perhaps from brain storming or from items on a different list, go through it quickly, assigning an "A" to those things that are most important to you to do, a "C" to those that it doesn't really matter whether or not you do them, and a "B" to those in the middle. As, Bs, and Cs are relative depending on your point of view and on what else is on your list. In any case, you do the deciding (Lakein, 1973, p. 27–29). It doesn't take long to assign one of these three priorities to everything on the list. One way is to go through and mark the obvious As and Cs first, then go back and mark the rest in relationship to the priorities you have already assigned. If the list is made with a word processor or spreadsheet program, it's easy to do a paragraph sort to put them in order.

Most people will still have a fairly long list of As. So you clarify your priorities by going through the As and marking them all either A-1, that is, I really have to, want to, or ought to do this in this period of time or else I will feel bad, or A-2. Likewise, one may divide the Bs into B-1s and B-2s, just in case one finishes all the A-2s. To use your software to sort them, you have to type it as 1A, 2A, 1B, 2B. Don't bother prioritizing the Cs until you are actually ready to do them. You may never get that far.

The Paired Number System

Obviously, using the ABC system still requires you to make decisions as you go along, decisions like "Which of these A-1s should I do next?" The paired number system uses easy choices between two things to produce a clearly ordered list with each task ranked precisely.

Step 1. You start, just as before, with a mixed list in no particular order, and you assign each item a number corresponding to where it happens to be on this list. The first is number 1, the second number 2, and so forth. At this point the numbers are just identifiers for the items.

Step 2. Then you make or copy, if you have a template made up, a matrix of all the possible combinations of 2 numbers representing items on the list. Thus, if there were 6 items on your list, you will have 15 possible pairs, and your matrix would look like this:

1/2	1/3	1/4	1/5	1/6
2/3	2/4	2/5	2/6	
3/4	3/5	3/6		
4/5	4/6			
5/6				

If there are twelve items, it would look like this:

1/2	1/3	1/4	1/5	1/6	1/7	1/8	1/9	1/10	1/11	1/12
2/3	2/4	2/5	2/6	2/7	2/8	2/9	2/10	2/11	2/12	
3/4	3/5	3/6	3/7	3/8	3/9	3/10	3/11	3/12		
4/5	4/6	4/7	4/8	4/9	4/10	4/11	4/12			
5/6	5/7	5/8	5/9	5/10	5/11	5/12				
6/7	6/8	6/9	6/10	6/11	6/12					
7/8	7/9	7/10	7/11	7/12						
8/9	8/10	8/11	8/12							
9/10	9/11	9/12								
10/11	10/12									
11/12										

If you use this system often, it's good to have the grid template on paper, or as a spreadsheet or word processing template on your computer. Richard Bolles has a particularly handy version in his *What Color is Your Parachute?* (2009, p. 203) and its workbook (Bolles, 2005). Beverly Ryle has an easy to use Web-based version attributed to Bolles at www.groundofyourownchoosing.com/grid.htm (Ryle, n.d.). Other versions are available on other sites (Bosquet, n.d., Picture it Solved, 2007).

Step 3. Look at the two items represented by the two numbers in the box in the upper left corner. Circle the number for the item that is most important. Then do the same for the pair of numbers in the box below it. When you finish a column, go on to the top of the next column. Each column will be shorter than the last. Don't take a lot of time to make each decision; go with your first instinct. You can mark the pairs in any order you choose, just so one of each pair is circled when you finish Step 3.

Step 4. Count the number of times that you circled each number. At this point, don't every think about the tasks they represent. Just count and record something like this:

1. 3 circles
2. 0 circles
3. 4 circles
4. 6 circles
5. 1 circles
6. 2 circles

If you had 6 items, you should have a total of 15 circles. If you had had 12 items, there would have been 68 circles. You can do it of any number of items; the matrix must include every possible pair. If you make a template for, say, 30 items, you can use it for a shorter list; just don't use any of the pairs with a number higher than the number of items on your list.

Step 5. Put your list in order. With the results in our example, number 4 had six circles, so it becomes the first item on your to do list. Number 3 would be second, number

1 would be third, and so on. Should two numbers be tied for the same number of circles, just look at the one place where those two numbers were compared and put the circled one first. In the end, you have an ordered list that accurately reflects your priorities.

It's interesting that this process also works for group decisions. Let's say you're on a nominating committee for a professional association, and you need an ordered list of people to ask to run for president. You can't ask them all at once; you have to prioritize whom you are going to ask first. After you ask one or two people, you have to wait for each person to say yes, in which case you are finished, or no, in which case you ask the next person on the list. What usually happens in the committee meeting is that either the most influential or persuasive committee member pushes everyone else into supporting his or her choice, or you go through several rounds of balloting and run-offs. It takes less time to just make up a numbered list of possibilities (Step 1) and hand out copies of matrices with the appropriate number of number pairs (Step 2). For Step 3, the committee members turn in their matrices, or even just their totals for each number, as anonymous ballots, and someone not on the committee who doesn't know the names that go with the numbers adds up the totals for each number. The final totals clearly rank the names of people to ask. The beauty of this method is that it fairly takes into account how strong people's preferences are. The numbers from the person who rates a possible candidate very high will be balanced out in the middle by the numbers from someone who ranks the same candidate very low, and the result is a middle rank. Candidates who generally fall in the middle but have a few high votes will have a higher rank than those who generally fall in the middle but have a few low votes. The same process can work for a department planning a party or a family planning a vacation.

Long and Short

Anyone who's ever worked from a to-do list knows the temptation to do first what takes the least time. The reward is seeing a lot of things crossed of the list. The down side is that one can use the items that take less time to postpone doing the larger items. There are several ways to compensate for this bias.

One option is to break up things that will take a lot of time into smaller, more or less equal pieces. Large, time-expensive projects, just like big purchases, can be broken down into small regular payments. It's certainly easier to complete that project well in small, quadrant two doses than to crash into a quadrant one crisis without the time to do it! One way is to break it up into discrete tasks to accomplish toward finishing it, and another is to simply break up your work on it into set periods of time. This is what Lakein (1973) calls the "Swiss Cheese Method." The idea is that you take a bite out of the whole project here, then another bite there, and eventually, after taking out enough bites, you're left with the remaining work being like a piece of Swiss cheese with a lot of holes in it and very little left to swallow. He explains that we often put off doing a big project we know will take a lot of time because we are wishing for a large enough block of uninterrupted time to do all of it at once. Of course, that means putting off starting the project while we wishfully wait for that block of time. When that happens, we either never get around to the project, or we force it into a quadrant one crisis when we have to binge to get it done and in the process don't do it very well. He writes, "The key to getting an Overwhelming A-1 under control is to get started on it as soon as you've identified it as an A-1 task." He recommends starting with an "instant task" that "requires five minutes or less of your time and makes some sort of hole in your Overwhelming A-1" (Lakein, 1973, p. 103–104).

Some of the instant tasks will lead to longer periods of involvement. Some won't. "Don't try to bite the same hole twice." In any case, biting out enough holes can make the entire process seem easier to accomplish than it seemed at first (Lakein, 1973, p. 96–108). When you are driving at night, your headlights reveal only a few feet of pavement in front of you, but it's enough for you to complete the entire journey.

Many prolific writers do not have large blocks of time for writing. According to psychologist Robert Boice (1990, 1994) "writer's block" is often manifested by procrastination. Writers may be waiting for inspiration or large blocks of time, neither of which appear to be forthcoming. Most successful writers, even those few blessed with large amounts of time, write on a strict daily schedule of a set period of time or a set number of pages, neither of which is very large. Regularity is what makes it work. Boice strenuously recommends brief daily sessions, which he calls "bds," of as little as 15 to 30 minutes. Interestingly enough, because of how our minds work in the background while we sleep or do other tasks, these daily sessions can generate surprising inspirations that seem to pop up out of nowhere in the shower or on the drive to work. Successful musicians, athletes, writers, and students understand not only the value of daily practice, but also that what Boice calls "binging," not working for a while and then working for a long time, even to the point of exhaustion, is counterproductive. Built into the practice of "bds" are three important points: the time to start, the time to stop, and leaving a note, a sentence or a thread, as in needlework, hanging where one can pick up the work the next session.

One way to combat the tendency to do the smaller A-1s first and reap the satisfaction of seeing things crossed off the list is to break the longer tasks up into shorter ones. Another way is to stick strictly to the prioritized order established through the paired numbers method. Both are easier said than done. A third option is to group tasks by how much time we estimate that they will take. My own lists are actually tables with columns for A-1s, A-2s, B-1s, and B-2s, with no Cs, and rows for tasks that would take more than an hour, 15–60 minutes, and less than 15 minutes. It helps me keep things in perspective.

Scheduling

"The key is not to prioritize what's on your schedule but to schedule your priorities" (Covey, 1989, p. 161).

Physical first; pay attention to your own natural daily biorhythms. Although sleep and exercise are necessary for good health, most people can't go for a long run, then hop into bed and immediately fall asleep. When are you your most mentally alert? It's probably not right after a big lunch. Right after lunch may be a good time to do something not too difficult that includes some moderate moving around, like running an errand or straightening your desk or office. Some people naturally do better solo creative work in the morning; others at night. Find a daily rhythm that works for you and use it to your advantage.

Make Appointments with Others . . . and Also with Yourself

If something is important enough to be an A-1 plan for you, it's important enough to set a specific time to do it. If visiting teachers in your school, individual members of your board, or your managerial cousins are a high priority for you, you have to schedule time to do it. The same goes for reoccurring maintenance and for parts of larger projects you need to do. "I am going to exercise more" or "I am going to spend more time doing X" won't work unless you schedule the time to do it. Just wishing that someday you'll have the time won't work. Of course, you also have to schedule time to review and revise your plans and lists.

One List Is Never Enough

Calendars are a good start, but they aren't enough. Be sure to schedule time for yourself to review your goals, evaluate your tasks, and rearrange your priorities. Keep a running to do planning list of prioritized one-time tasks in several areas of your life, or keep separate lists.

Recurring tasks are easier to keep track of in a spreadsheet than a list. Some things need to be done daily, some weekly, monthly, quarterly, or annually, so you can have different spread sheet pages or sections for each time period. Just enter the date every time you do one of those tasks. As time goes on, you will discover that you can afford to move things you thought had to be done weekly to monthly, and so forth. Occasionally, you'll discover you need to do some repetitive task more often than you thought.

Of course, you can't work from all of these lists and spreadsheets every day. Pick a period of time for your ultimate current list; it could be for today, for the next two days, or for the next week, but don't try to make a list for more than a week. Consult your big lists and spreadsheets to choose what to put on the current real list. That creates the voluntary constraints to make it all work for you. For more detailed suggestions for librarians, see Judith A. Siess's *Time Management, Planning and Prioritization for Librarians* (2002).

Risk Taking and Reward

When you were a toddler, you didn't learn to walk by waiting until you could be sure that you would not fall down. You did fall down, but then you got up and tried again because you really wanted to get somewhere! Staying green and growing means being willing to see and seize new opportunities. It means being mature enough to understand that even failures can be learning opportunities.

Marketing, innovating new service, writing a grant proposal, or doing research are all risks that require investment of thought and time. "But we've never done that before!" never should be the sole reason for not trying something new.

Dare to Be Proactive

"People frequently think they are doing good marketing when they *react* to what their customers want, however, the most effective service marketers *anticipate* customer demands and satisfy them before competitors do. When Fred Smith came up with the idea of overnight delivery of packages, freight workers rejected the idea because no one had asked for it. Yet Federal Express became a successful company by anticipating customer needs and proactively creating the services to address them. Coming up with new service products requires creativity and a certain level of risk. (Gorchels, 1995, p. 503).

When in doubt, DO something. When I used to teach music lessons, my students sometimes found it difficult to play in tune. They were aware that something wasn't quite right about a note, yet they sustained the note exactly the same to the point of annoying themselves and everyone else. When asked, the student said, "I knew something wasn't right, but I didn't know whether it was flat or sharp, so I didn't change it." The simple reply is "Change it anyway. You've got a 50/50 chance of going the right direction immediately and if it gets worse, you'll know which direction to go to fix it."

When bored, discouraged, delighted, excited, or curious, try something! Observe users, ask clients, pay attention not just to other libraries, but to other services that welcome clients. What attracts you? Can you adapt that idea for your library?

Thomas Watson, the founder of IBM, reportedly said, "If you want to succeed, double your failure rate" (Brown, n.d.). Harry Beckwith reminds people marketing services that "To Err is opportunity . . . big mistakes are big opportunities. . . . Write an ad for your service. If after a week your best ad is weak, stop working on the ad and start working on your service" (Beckwith, 1997, p. 12). Try out new ideas with the understanding that if they fail, they are a learning experience you would have missed had you not tried.

Risk spending some time on continuing education courses;

Drive-Up Service

Mary Cosper LeBoeuf put in a drive-up window with a call button at the Terrebonne Parish Library in Houma, Louisiana, because she liked being able to drive up to get her dry cleaning and fast food. She was careful to place the drive-up window near the desk of someone doing interruptible technical work in a staff area. Requested and returned material were on nearby shelving and the person providing the window service was not providing other public services. Once the service was running, LeBoeuf discovered that it was very popular with mobility challenged clients. These were clients who found it difficult to walk all the way from a parking space into the large, impressive (and ADA-compliant) building and through the stacks. They could shop for library materials online, call the library, and then just drive by for pick up and return. Other clients used it, like she used the business drive-ups, just because it saved their time.

Libraries have had drive-up drop boxes for decades. Why not drive up pick-up windows? What message does having one without the other present? Does it say that it's more important to return library materials than to get them to use? How much less useful would ATMs be if bank customers could use them only for deposits and not for withdrawals?

use your best information retrieval skills to find out what you want to know. Librarians may publish "How I done it good" articles, but they rarely publish accounts and analyses of innovations they tried that failed. Talk to colleagues who tried things that did fail and figure out why they failed in that circumstance. You don't have to "reinvent the wheel," you can learn from both your failures and those of others if you can figure out why the projects didn't work. Practice Winter's second mark of a professional, lifelong learning, even if you have to risk some of your own off-work time and personal funds (Winter, 1983, p. 10). You have to invest in yourself to stay green and growing.

The Agile Librarian has the thoughtful knowledge and experience to grab an opportunity quickly, literally in the blink of an eye. Malcom Gladwell describes such good, quick, intuitive decisions as a result of expertise and study (Gladwell, 2005). A century and a half ago, Louis Pasteur wrote that chance only favors prepared minds (Pasteur, 1854), and the Agile Librarian is, by definition, prepared for opportunity. Even in times of downsizing, cutback, and even school or organizational closures, the Agile Librarian *can* finds opportunities for new ways to delight clients, please bosses, and impress decision makers in the organization, even if it means taking the risk of leaving one organization and going to another institution.

Summary: We Just Keep Starting Again

"We must accept finite disappointment, but we must never lose infinite hope. Only in this way shall we live without the fatigue of bitterness and the drain of resentment" (Martin Luther King, Jr., 1963, p. 93).

To be vibrantly green and growing, we plan, we act, and we risk disappointment. Innovative risk taking means that some things will fail. Then we just start again. Even if we succeed, we have to get up the next morning and start again. Even if we exercised and ate well yesterday, we have to start over again today. Even if we delighted all of our clients and stakeholders yesterday, we have to start again today. Even if we've taken a lot of classes, read a lot of professional journals, and talked to a lot of colleagues in the past, we get up and start again today to stay green and growing. Even though we know that the boss, the clients, and the decision maker once got the message that we could make life easier and better for them, we still have to know, show, and tell again.

Staying "green and growing" is a matter of continuously starting again. If something is important, it's important enough to start again and again and again. That's how we stay green and growing.

We're agile professional librarians—doing better what we've always done well.

References

Anderson, Rick. 2007. It's Not About the Workflow: Patron-Centered Practices for 21st–Century Serialists. *Serials Librarian* 51:189–199.

Beckwith, Harry. 1997. *Selling the Invisible: A Field Guide to Modern Marketing.* New York: Warner Books.

Boice, Robert. 1990. *Professors as Writers: A Self-Help Guide to Productive Writing.* Stillwater, OK: New Forums.

———. 1994. *How Writers Journey to Comfort and Fluency: A Psychological Adventure.* Westport, CT: Praeger.

Bolles, Richard Nelson. 2005. *What Color is Your Parachute Workbook: How to Create Picture of Your Ideal Job or Next Career.* Berkeley, CA: Ten Speed Press.

———. 2009. *What Color is Your Parachute? A Practical Manual for Job Hunters and Career Changers.* [Annual.] Berkeley, CA: Ten Speed Press.

Bolles, Richard Nelson, Carol Christen, and Jean M. Blomquist. 2006. *What Color is Your Parachute for Teens: Discovering Yourself, Defining Your Future.* Berkeley, CA: Ten Speed Press.

Bolles, Richard Nelson and John E. Nelson. 2007. *What Color is Your Parachute for Retirement: Planning Now for the Live You Want.* Berkeley, CA: Ten Speed Press.

Bousquet, Joie. n.d. *The Prioritizing Grid.* http://www.joiedelor.com/siteperso/qualitytools/PriritizingGrid.htm. Accessed December 27, 3008.

Brown, John Seely. n.d. John Seely Brown. http://www.johnseelybrown.com/. Accessed January 1, 2009.

Covey, Stephen R. 1989. *The 7 Habits of Highly Effective People.* New York: Simon & Schuster.

Csikszentmihalyi, Mihaly. 1996. *Creativity: Flow and the Psychology of Discovery and Invention.* New York: Harper Collins.

Gladwell, Malcolm. 2005. *Blink: The Power of Thinking without Thinking.* New York: Little, Brown and Co.

Gorchels, Linda M. 1995. Trends in Marketing Serivces. *Library Trends* 43:494–509.

King, Martin Luther, Jr. 1963. *Strength to Love.* Reprinted. Philadelphia: Fortress Press, 1981.

Lakein, Alan. 1973. *How to get control of your time and your life.* New York: Signet.

Lewis, C. S. 1949. Letter to Sarah Neylan. 3 April 1949. In C.S. Dorset, Lyle W., and Margaret Lamp Mead. (Eds.). *C. S. Lewis Letters to Children.* New York: Macmillan, 1985.

Pasteur, Louis. 1854. Le hazard ne favorise que les esprits préparés. *Lecture.* University of Lille. Quoted in Eves, H. *Return to Mathematical Circles.* Boston: Prindle, Wever and Schmidt, 273.

Picture It Solved 2007. Prioritizing Grid for 10 options. http://www.pictureitsolved.com/resources/prioritizinggrid.cfm. Accessed December 27, 2008.

Ryle, Beverly. n.d. Richard Bolles' Prioritizing Grid. *Ground of Your Own Choosing.* http://www.groundofyourownchoosing.com/grid.htm. Accessed December 27, 2008.

Schwartz, Barry. 2004. *The Paradox of Choice: Why More is Less.* New York: Harper Collins.

Seligman, Martin E. P. 1990. *Learned Optimism: How to Change Your Mind and Your Life.* New York: Pocket.

Siess, Judith A. 2002. *Time Management, Planning and Prioritization for Librarians.* Lanham, MD: Scarecrow Press.

Sifton, Elizabeth. 2003. *The Serenity Prayer: Faith and Politics in Times of Peace and War,* New York: W. W. Norton.

Voltaire. 1772. *Contes.* Quoted in Envision Software. 2005. Voltaire quote: The Perfect is the Enemy of the Good. *Famous Quotes.* http://www.famous-quotes.net/Quote.aspx?The_perfect_is_the_enemy_of_the_good. Accessed December 9, 2008.

Winter, Michael F. 1983. The Professionalization of Librarianship. *Occasional Papers,* no. 160:1–46. Champaign, IL: University of Illinois Graduate School of Library and Information Science.

Index

About the Author

MICHELYNN MCKNIGHT is an Assistant Professor in the School of Library and Information Science at Louisiana State University in Baton Rouge. For more than two decades she was the director of the Norman Regional Hospital Health Sciences Library in Norman, Oklahoma. She has also worked in the reference departments of a public library and an academic library, as well as in a school library and a music library. She has served on the Medical Library Association Board of Directors and the Biomedical Library and Informatics Review Committee of the National Library of Medicine. Her publications include *Mathematics Education Research: A Guide for the Research Mathematician* (with McKnight, Magid, and Murphy), chapters in four books, and more than sixty-five articles in professional journals.